Asia-Pacific Transitions

Asia-Pacific Transitions

Edited by

David E. Andersson
Visiting Research Fellow
Institute of Economics
Academia Sinica
Taiwan

and

Jessie P. H. Poon
Associate Professor
Department of Geography
University at Buffalo – SUNY
USA

palgrave

First published 2001 by
PALGRAVE
Houndmills, Basingstoke, Hampshire RG21 6XS and
175 Fifth Avenue, New York, N. Y. 10010
Companies and representatives throughout the world

PALGRAVE is the new global academic imprint of St. Martin's Press LLC Scholarly and Reference Division and Palgrave Publishers Ltd (formerly Macmillan Press Ltd).

ISBN 0–333–80301–9

This book is printed on paper suitable for recycling and made from fully managed and sustained forest sources.

A catalogue record for this book is available from the British Library.

Library of Congress Cataloging-in-Publication Data
Asia Pacific transitions / edited by David E. Andersson, Jessie P. H. Poon.
p. cm.
Includes bibliographical references and index.
ISBN 0–333–80301–9
1. Asia—Economic conditions. 2. Pacific Area—Economic conditions. I. Andersson, David E., 1966– II. Poon, Jessie P. H., 1963–

HC462 .A85 2000
338.95—dc21

00–031112

10 9 8 7 6 5 4 3 2 1
10 09 08 07 06 05 04 03 02 01

Printed and bound in Great Britain by
Antony Rowe Ltd, Chippenham, Wiltshire

Contents

List of Figures and Tables

Figures

Tables

List of Contributors

Åke E. Andersson
Professor, Department of Infrastructure and Planning, Royal Institute of Technology, Stockholm and former director of the Swedish Institute for Futures Studies.

David E. Andersson
Economist with the World Economics Institute in Taipei. He holds a Ph.D. in Regional Planning from the Royal Institute of Technology, Stockholm.

Mukul G. Asher
Associate Professor, Department of Economics, National University of Singapore.

Pontus Åberg
Consultant, Temaplan Sweden.

David F. Batten
Professor, Temaplan Australia.

Martin Beckmann
Professor, Department of Economics, Brown University and Department of Economics, University of Munich.

Hua Chang-i
Professor, Graduate Institute of Building and Planning, National Taiwan University.

Jan Engberg
Associate Professor, Director of the Center for Interdisciplinary Studies, Umeå University.

Niklas Eklund
Lecturer, Department of Political Science, Umeå University.

Finn R. Førsund
Professor, Department of Economics, University of Oslo.

Janerik Gidlund
Professor, Department of Political Science, Umeå University.

Kiyoshi Kobayashi
Professor, Graduate School of Civil Engineering, Kyoto University.

Lawrence R. Klein
Benjamin Franklin Professor of Economics, University of Pennsylvannia. He was the recipient of the 1980 Nobel Memorial Prize in Economic Sciences.

Kurt Lundgren
Professor, National Institute for Working Life, Sweden.

Jessie P.H. Poon
Assistant Professor, Department of Geography and Canada–US Trade Center, University of Buffalo–SUNY.

Edmund R. Thompson
Assistant Professor, School of Business, University of Hong Kong.

Zhang Wei-bin
Professor, Department of Economics, National University of Singapore.

1
Overview

David E. Andersson and Jessie P.H. Poon

In the last two decades, a number of books has emerged in the academic market, explaining, theorizing and even speculating on the rapid growth of the economies in the Asia Pacific.[1] Expositions on the region's 'miracle' countries are now commonplace, with some economists attaching the region's remarkable growth rates to free market policies and prudent macroeconomic management (Corbo, Kruger and Ossa 1985; Kasper 1994). On the other side of the coin, we find state-centered explanations, namely 'development states' being offered by political sociologists (Wade, 1990), buttressed by observations of extensive state intervention and strong government–business cooperation. A third and final academic thrust focused on the cultural values of Asian societies, best embodied in the 'Asian Values' debate (Emmerson, 1995), which originated from the argument that first-tier Asian newly industrializing countries were heavily Confucian in social organization.[2]

The economic development of the Asia-Pacific countries has attracted widespread attention, mainly because of their curious abilities to maintain high growth rates of over 6 per cent annually for more than thirty years, thereby contradicting normative assertions of worldwide convergence in the history of economic growth (Ito and Krueger, 1995). But as scholars debated over this anomaly, past high growth rates in many countries plummeted in 1997 as financial instability spread throughout the region.

Notwithstanding the convulsions released by monetary disequilibia, as early as 1994, Krugman (1994) had already begun to question the sustainability of the region's high growth rates. In fact, the oft-proclaimed Asia-Pacific century has ignored the geography of the region, juxtaposing dissimilar economic and political systems rather uncritically. Further, while industrial diffusion has clearly occurred, it is far from obvious that the evolving economic and political character of the countries has converged.

On the one hand, many countries in the region remain committed to economic development. Hence China, the Philippines, South Korea, Taiwan and Vietnam are all moving towards freer trade and a greater amenabililty to foreign direct investment (FDI), albeit from very different starting points. Meanwhile, popular demands are mounting for public-sector provision of costly retirement pensions and health-care systems in low-tax economies such as Hong Kong, Taiwan and the countries of Southeast Asia. There are even indications in some countries that the much-vaunted saving rates are starting to fall. On the other hand, it is becoming increasingly evident that there are two divergent political trends in the the Asia-Pacific region. One trend comprises authoritarian (or illiberal) entrenchment, as seen in the increasingly assertive nationalisms of the governments of China, Malaysia and Singapore. The other conflicting trend is that of growing pluralism and democratization, as exhibited by Japan, South Korea, the Philippines, Taiwan, and Thailand.

This book aims to shed light on the salient features of various transitions taking place in the Asia Pacific. The essays arose from a series of workshops on Asia-Pacific development initiated by the Stockholm-based Institute for Futures Studies. They should be viewed as being concerned with the background to current trends and potential *future* outcomes. We highlight the *interdependence* of economic, political and institutional forces which are likely to reproduce non-uniform responses among the countries; hence the book's emphasis on transitions. Moreover, the interplay of all three realms may well result in conflicting aims while, at other times, acting in concert. In the economic realm, one force is made up of the actions of individual economic actors, resulting in, among other things, entrepreneurship, spontaneous network formation, and cross-border investments. But there is also the effort of governments to spur growth through, for example, development plans, regional cooperation, and industrial parks. It is not automatic that the financial crisis will lead to a diminished level of state intervention uniformly because, in countries such as Singapore, the state continues to play an active role in its industrial and social policies. For this reason, a country's social capabilities (Rowen 1997) are argued to be just as important in assessing the countries' transitions here.

According to North (1994), institutions may be external (rules with formal sanctions, laws, constitutions) or internal (norms of behavior, conventions, self-imposed codes of conduct). Institutions influence economic and political outcomes because of their impacts on incentives, transformation costs and governance structures. The interdependence of institutions and economic development is perhaps best summarized as the tendency of economic development and industrialization to affect the balance of competing value systems and, additionally, as the effect of institutional systems on economic behavior. But because institutions are not necessarily always socially efficient, we find that transaction costs exist in both Western-style democratic regimes (the Philippines, Thailand, Taiwan and increasingly South Korea) alongside communitarian and authoritarian systems that are heavily influenced by Confucianism (China, Singapore, and to some extent Japan) and Islam (Indonesia, Malaysia). From this vantage point, transitions associated with economic development should be seen as a series of incremental, though not necessarily linear, changes. Each phase of the development process may require new or modified rules of contract and control as older institutions encounter contraints or reach their limits in enforcing political and market agreements.

The book begins with a broad comparison of the region against the economic history of the OECD countries. In Chapter 2, Åke Andersson shows that the high growth rates of East and Southeast Asia should have been expected because the countries are part of the 'fourth-wave' of industrializers in the history of world economic development. Extrapolating from the trends first observed in Europe, he shows that Italy has had a higher long-term growth rate than France, while France, in its turn, has had a higher long-term growth rate than Britain. Similarly, South Korea and Taiwan both have higher growth rates than any European country in the last 30 years, indicating economic advantages in being industrial latecomers.

However, the advantages of being latecomers may have run its course, especially for the most developed countries, in view of the wave of economic and industrial restructuring now taking place in Asia. The rest of the book, which is divided into three parts, examines the form and nature of transitions that Asian countries are likely to experience as they attempt to join the 'Third Industrial Revolution' where previous performances based on producer over consumer interests, cheap and disciplined labor, and paternalistic social and political governance, no longer provide the necessary or sufficient conditions for long-run sustainable growth in the context of increased global interdependencies. Part I, 'Institutional Frameworks', discusses some of the underlying institutional arrangements as well as institutional changes in selected Asia-Pacific countries. Part II, 'Environmental and Economic Constraints', examines the environmental and economic constraints on government policies in the face of changing demographic and economic structures.

Finally in Part III, 'Cross-Border Networks', deals with the various facets of increasing interactions between countries as well as actors in the Asia Pacific.

Institutional frameworks

To the extent that institutions are constructed to help manage, if not overcome, uncertainties and assymetrical information, they provide a structure for which human interactions can take place whether in the context of a firm, a political organization, or an economic market. Certainly a striking observation of East and Southeast Asia is the existence of implicit contractual agreements between the governments and their citizenries. In Chapter 3, Kurt Lundgren notes that, although lacking the alleged prerequisites for economic growth, China nevertheless has been able to progress rapidly in the last twenty years, underscoring the significance of China's emerging institutions, especially after 1979. China may lack the external institutions that form the cornerstone of Western capitalist systems, designed to achieve reasonable levels of economic efficiency, but its social organization nevertheless provides sufficient incentives for a certain degree of competitive and rational economic behavior. This may be seen, for example, in the development of township and village enterprises, which have been able to introduce some market incentives while being part of the larger state-driven infrastructure.

We could argue that China's top-down social structure may be attributed to the influence of Confucianism historically – where paternalism is encouraged – an explanation that has featured strongly in the socio-political organization of Chinese-dominated societies elsewhere in East Asia. The fourth chapter, 'On Lao-Tzu' by Zhang Wei-bin, however, suggests that East Asian societies do not necessarily have less cultural affinity for individualism than Western societies. Taoism embraces a multiplicity of wisdom that precludes one that is championed by a single authority. This contrasts with Confucianism which provides a framework for social order through its emphasis on familism. Lao-Tzu taught that organizations and external institutions interfered with the responsibility of each indivual to herself. Zhang concludes that Lao Tzu's teachings are in fact compatible with the economic system of *laissez faire*.

The influence of non-economic institutions in Asian development is further explored by Martin Beckmann in Chapter 5. Beckmann notes that Western systems of scientific cooperation favor the creation of technological innovations and scientific achievements because the principal aim in Western scholarship is the production of knowledge where competition for recognition, 'priority' status, and research funds reign. In contrast, traditional Confucian ideals emphasize the consumption of knowledge and a disinterested search for the truth, attainable through the immersion in a canonized body of knowledge. Differences in academic philosophy have resulted in a more productive community of scholars in the West (see also Chapter 19).

Moreover, despite the wave of Western liberal prescriptions for economic recovery in the aftermath of the financial and economic crisis, pluralism is expected to continue to characterize the region. There is no guarantee that all of the countries in the region will travel the same path as Western Europe and North America in their modernization crusade. In Chapter 6, Jan Engberg observes that Communist one-party states, full-fledged democracies, and different authoritarian systems exist side by side in the Asia Pacific. The fact that economic success in Singapore and Malaysia has not led to the flourishing of civil society and pluralism challenges the conventional view that political democratization necessarily accompanies economic development. Hence, despite the fact that governments in the two countries rule on a foundation of public consent, democratic development is argued to be 'illiberal' where the 'rule by law' rather the 'rule of law' reigns.

The rise of political illiberalism alongside sizable economic freedoms in Malaysia, Singapore and possibly China is not only likely to continue to contribute towards regional divergence, but also provides support for distinctive sub-Asian models of development. As Niklas Eklund argues in Chapter 7, the proliferation of growth triangles in Southeast Asia reflects a contradiction between technological and systemic legitimization. Transnational capital flows have been important in the countries of Malaysia and Singapore and, to a lesser extent, in Indonesia. Combining the need of foreign investors for greater efficiency against nascent nation-states' guardedness in sovereignty has led to countries such as Malaysia and Indonesia integrating part of their territories (Johor and Riau Islands) with Singapore in order to realize and enhance subregional divisions of labor. To the extent that such cross-border subnational developments are distinct from supranational developments best seen in the case of the European Union, growth triangles in Southeast Asia constitute an important example of political divergence from the West despite similar desires for greater factor mobility.

The shape of political transitions is therefore unclear in spite of incipient political reforms in Indonesia, South Korea, the Philippines and Thailand. In fact, political transitions are likely to continue to cause diverging development paths. This is reinforced in David Andersson's comparisons of Taiwan's and Singapore's approaches to land-use controls (Chapter 8). He argues that conventional constructions of economic freedom indices ignore the effect of land-use regulations on opportunities for entrepreneurship, and raises the problem of distortions that such regulations cause to the decentralized market process of continuously evolving land-use patterns. In comparing the two countries, he shows how differences in urban development, which is left to individual economic actors in the case of Taiwan, and to the state in Singapore, can lead to different levels of economic freedom in the market for land, despite similar initial conditions.

Economic and environmental constraints

Institutions exist to reduce transaction costs and their construction entails a learning process (North 1994). Asia-Pacific countries may have benefited from the mistakes of their predecessors as latecomers to the industrialization process, but they are not immune to new mistakes or constraints. Perhaps the most serious potential limits affecting their transitions relate to environmental, economic and social sustainability. In Chapter 9, by extending neoclassical economic theory on natural resource depletion based on Hicks's distinction between flows and stocks, and where the enviroment is regarded as being a capital stock analogous to man-made capital stock, Finn Førsund shows that, while it may be conceptually possible to derive sustainable development policies from ecological economic models, lack of knowledge about future prices and preferences make them impossible to operationalize for practical purposes. Thus, Førsund suggests using an international standards approach for cross-border environmental problems, which should primarily be concerned with not exceeding 'critical loads'.

Hua Chang-i, in Chapter 10, examines the interrelationships between demographic, ecological and pollution transitions. Based on carbon dioxide emission levels in the countries of India, China, South Korea, and Japan, he shows how pollution increases (decreases) are largely explained by *per capita* incomes, and, to a lesser extent, by the effect of the demographic transition. Perhaps the most important finding of Chang's study is that, in addition to the well-established correlations between demographic, ecological, and pollution factors, emission levels in the four Asian countries are not expected to decrease unless what Chang has called the 'output quality transition' has also occurred.

Undoubtedly, environmental constraints are exacerbated by the lack of coherent regional cooperation in Asia. The Association of Southeast Asian Nations (ASEAN), for instance, had seemed paralyzed by the financial economic problems in Southeast Asia. Similarly, the countries were unable to structure a unified response to serious haze pollution that had plagued the region at the same time. Instead, ASEAN members looked to countries outside of the region for help and money in containing the haze. Clearly, previous emphasis on economic growth has neglected other dimensions of societal development. This is reinforced in Chapter 11 by Mukul Asher who highlights the tendency among Asian policy-makers to ignore social equity issues. In examining social security incomes, he observes that Southeast Asia has, until recently, relied much more on informal support from extended families and local communities than on government programs to finance social security. However, as demographic transition runs its course over the next few decades, and, as these countries undergo rapid urbanization and industrialization, informal channels of social welfare and security may become increasingly less important. Pension funds constitute one of the few important alternative sources of social safety nets for Asian countries, yet Asher's study of the five countries of Indonesia, Malaysia, the Philippines, Singapore and Thailand indicates that these funds have been suffering from low revenue productivity since the 1980s. Asher argues for urgent reforms as these countries move towards publicly mandated provident systems that would enhance their sustainability.

Other potential constraints are further analyzed by Lawrence Klein in Chapter 12. Klein shows how China's open door policy, as well as favorable demographics and macroeconomic policies, have contributed to the country's high growth rates since 1979. At the same time, he also notes problems of sustainability related to wide regional disparities between the coastal and inland areas, and the non-competitiveness of large and inefficient state-owned enterprises. While informal institutions may have contributed to successful economic performance in the past, as Chapter 3 demonstrates, formal institution-building that brings about greater economic transparency is likely to play a more important role in the future.

Cross-border networks

While the first two Parts focus on themes related to institutional settings and economic–environmental constraints, Part III looks at the emergence of network economies that are shaping capital as well as industrial organization in the region. We view the creation of industrial, as well as knowledge and electronic communication networks, as major forces that will influence Asia Pacific's transitions. One implication of this for the region is that the ability of the countries to position themselves within relevant global or regional networks, or, to create network links between and within themselves, will likely shape economic sustainability in the long run.

In Chapter 13, David Batten begins by illuminating the processes that underlie the formation of human and economic networks in cities. He suggests that the development of an urban economy is difficult to predict: periods of relative stability are interrupted by sudden, and often unexpected, changes. Batten argues that the future development of a city often is contingent on seemingly minor events in the past, which implies that long-term determinism or predictability is unattainable. Such intrinsic unpredictability implies that planning based on optimization is impossible. Cities are theorized to be akin to living organisms whose patterns of development have the character of complex dynamic systems. Moreover, cities co-evolve with other cities. This co-evolution is self-organizing and may produce unexpected outcomes or 'emergent behavior.' Batten concludes that an understanding of self-organizing networks and emergent behavior is necessary if we are to grasp the evolution of urban networks in Asia.

In a sense, Batten's contribution suggests that network formation by individual actors, firms or governments reflects the organization of apparent disorderliness; a means to structure complexities associated with economic performance through their impact on transaction costs and exchanges. Network-building, for instance, is increasingly used by countries in the Asia Pacific to establish rules of cooperative behavior, as seen in the case of the Association of Southeast Asian Nations (ASEAN) which has created numerous dialogue channels within the region such as China, and, outside of the region, with Europe and the United States. In Chapter 14, Poon and Thompson's comparison of trade patterns between Asia and Europe shows how the Asian countries have been adept at maintaining both intra and extra-regional trade links through 'open' regionalism. There is no doubt that countries within the Asia Pacific are becoming more integrated through trade but, even more surprising, is that 'bloc-like' Europe also shares Asia's characteristics of extra-regionalism. Both regions' trade interactions are also found to center around regional nodes, indicating the nodal strength of particular regions which helps them capture the intersecting synergies of multiple economic and industrial networks.

Similarly, by examining the relationship between Japanese foreign direct investment (FDI) and trade in the Asia Pacific, Chapter 15 looks at the impact of increased regional networking between Japanese and other Asian firms, and how these networks have facilitated trade and capital flows in the region. In modeling the determinants of Japanese FDI in the Asia Pacific, Pontus Åberg found the countries of East Asia to be Japan's most 'productive' export markets. Particularly interesting as well is his finding that Australia and New Zealand were able to capture a disproportionate share of outward Japanese FDI between 1990 and 1994.

In addition to macroeconomic trade and investment analyses, Chapters 16 and 17 provide case studies of transition issues in the context of network development in the the more developed economies of Hong Kong and Singapore. Both economies are similar in that they are small city-states and are faced with limited factor and market endowments. However, Hong Kong's economic limitation is offset by its proximity and production integration with China, while Singapore has embarked on a deliberate policy of establishing transnational linkages that help extend its hinterland. In the chapter by Edmund Thompson, firm-level evidence of vertical network linkages between garment firms in Hong Kong and their operations in China is provided. Thompson found that traditional factor-costs were much less important explanations for shifting garment production from Hong Kong to Guangdong. Instead, he attributes cross-border firm networks and integration to flexibility, spread, quality control, and avoidance of costly market transactions by Hong Kong's garment firms. In contrast to Hong Kong, where private firms play a more influential role in building cross-border linkages, the state in Singapore has actively cultivated relations with its neighbors that help the country to overcome its size problem. In the face of growing factor scarcity, Janerik Gidlund shows how the Singapore government attempts to reconcile soft authoritarianism with both economic efficiency and the city-state's quest, through industrial parks in Indonesia and China, to be a global business center.

The book begins with Åke Andersson's observation of the important role of transitory variables such as high savings and investment levels in Asia's economic transformation. But, as the title of the book suggests, the region is undergoing transitions and there is no guarantee that traditional factors such as export reliance, business–government cooperation, and paternalistic social policies, will continue to play the roles that they once did in the past. As the world becomes increasingly integrated, the need to create or access technological knowledge becomes important, especially when the social acquisition of knowledge is dynamically irreversible. The final two chapters address this challenge.

Chapter 18 by Kiyoshi Kobayashi suggests that Asia's transitions in the future will be affected by fundamental transformations that are occurring in world logistical networks. As Asian countries become more integrated, development corridors are emerging that will spur the drive for more human contacts. This, in turn, will spawn the construction of communications networks that are likely to enhance the exchange of knowledge within the region. Kobayashi assumes that knowledge is a source of increasing returns, because knowledge generates externalities that enable individuals to be more productive as the aggregate human capital of the environment increases.

Chapter 19 concludes the book with an empirical assessment of the determinants of cross-border knowledge creation and transfers within Asia, and between Asia and the West. South Korea, Taiwan and Thailand appear to have the strongest linkages with the United States, while Hong Kong, Malaysia and Singapore have greater scientific cooperation with English-speaking countries such as the United Kingdom and Australia. Furthermore, cross-border scientific activity is highest in the Asia Pacific when it is conducted with scholars in North America. South Korean scholars, for example, conduct more than three times as much research in science, medicine and engineering with American scholars than they do with scholars from Japan. The level of scientific interactions within Asian countries is relatively low. This is in spite of the fact that gravity-like distance-decay effects are in place, which suggest that the level of scientific interactions between Asia Pacific and the West might have been higher were it not for the barrier of geography.

Together, the authors in the book share a common concern for the structural transformations that the region is likely to face in its imminent economic and political transitions. Two conclusions are noteworthy. First, the region remains sufficiently diverse that processes of convergence and divergence are occurring simultaneously. This is apparent in the chapters on institutional development and approaches to growth, whether in the political or economic arena. Second, while many scholars elsewhere have emphasized a distinctive Asian model of development, certain 'universal' problems, such as those related to environmental sustainability and structural adjustments, are becoming increasingly important, suggesting the need for solutions that are more international in scope, and the establishment of governance systems that reduce the region's institutional weaknesses.

Notes

1. In this book, the economies of Asia Pacifc include only countries in East and Southeast Asia.
2. More recently, Fukuyama (1995) has argued that the Japanese and Chinese versions of Confucianism have fundamentally different impacts on economic behavior. Japanese Confucianism implies a much greater degree of national loyalty and generalized social trust, whereas Chinese Confucianism is to a much greater extent familistic. Fukuyama contends that the generalized trust exhibited by Japan makes it more similar to Protestant Western societies than to Chinese societies, with an inclination toward the formation of large-scale private firms. Chinese Confucianism, on the other hand, with its emphasis on familism and personalism, is particularly conducive to the creation of small family businesses. As a consequence, the Chinese share many more traits regarding their economic behavior with Italians than with the Japanese.

References

Corbo, V., A.O. Krueger and F. Ossa (eds), *Export-Oreinted Development Strategies: the Success of Five Newly Industrializing Countries* (Boulder: Westview Press, 1985).

Emmerson, D.K., 'Singapore and the "Asian values" debate'. *Journal of Democracy*, 6 (1995) 6–100.

Fukuyama, F., *Trust: The Social Virtues and the Creation of Prosperity* (New York: Free Press, 1995).

Ito, T. and A.O. Krueger (eds), *Growth Theories in the Light of the East Asian Experience* (Chicago: University of Chicago Press, 1995).

Kasper, W., *Global Competition, Institutions, and the East-Asian Ascendancy* (San Francisco: ICS Press, 1994).

Krugman, P., 'The Myth of the Asian Miracle', *Foreign Affairs* 73 (1994) 62–78.

North, D.C., 'Economic Performance through Time', *American Economic Review* 84 (1994) 359–68.

Rowen, H.S. (ed.), *Behind the East Asian Growth* (New York: Routledge, 1997).

Wade, R., *Governing the Market: Economic Theory and the Role of Government in East Asian Industrialization* (Princeton: Princeton University Press, 1990).

2

Growth and Development in East Asia and the OECD Countries

Åke E. Andersson

The industrialization of the world has been an extremely prolonged process of economic growth and development. It is a growth process in the sense that real *per capita* incomes have been continuously increasing since the start of industrialization, wherever it has occurred. It has also been a development process in the sense that the structure of production and employment has been changing. Relative shares of agriculture, forestry, fishing, hunting and mining have thus been steadily decreasing throughout the process of industrialization. But the process of industrialization can also be seen as a process with a decreasing relative share of manual labor. In the long time perspective the process of economic growth cannot be divorced from a simultaneously changing economic structure. Growth and development cannot be separated from each other as is often implied by standard growth theory. A change in the composition of industrial activity, and in employment, seems to be inseparable from the growth process itself. The theory of balanced growth with constant sectoral proportions is grossly at variance with the way growth has occurred historically, at least within the context of the history of industrial societies. Macroeconomic models of real income growth thus only capture a small part of the real dynamic process. Most of the dynamics of the growth process remains unexplained. This is, of course, the reason why the 'residual factor' had to become the focus of the empirically oriented growth analysts (Denison 1979).

Industrialization in stages

The history of industrialization is a geographically uneven dynamic process. It was initiated in England and Belgium in the late-eighteenth century. Even within these countries the industrialization process focused only on those regions where the accessibility of raw materials, labor, or markets were at a maximum. It is thus no accident that these countries were located on the east coast of the North Atlantic Basin. It also is no accident that the most accessible regions on the west coast of the basin were soon to become involved in the first wave of industrialization in Europe and North America.

Already the first period of industrial growth and development contains the most important causal ingredients of the patterns of change. First, there is usually an agricultural reform allowing agricultural production to escape being subjected to the peasant principle of production for survival. This principle implies that the number of persons employed on the farm is driven to a point at which average consumption per unit of time corresponds to the average productivity of labor. If a transformation into capitalist farming occurs, employment is quickly adjusted to a level at which the average consumption of the laborers (the real wage) corresponds to the *marginal* productivity of labor. In the standard situation of diminishing returns to labor, this implies that employment will decrease, generating a surplus of production and labor. The surplus of production can then be used for capital accumulation. The structural unemployment due to agricultural reform can be used in manufacturing, as long as such industrial activity is initiated as a consequence of agricultural profits and rents being channeled into industrial capital accumulation.

Second, manufacturing is not necessarily associated with any massive use of material capital. As pointed out long ago by Adam Smith in his *Wealth of Nations*, manufacturing is an organizational principle, of which the most important trait is the division of labor. The division of labor leads to an increase in the benefits of specialization and learning by doing.

Third, a thoroughgoing industrialization has always been accompanied by a deregulation of economic life, allowing for the free entry of entrepreneurs. The importance of deregulation as a precondition for industrialization is today best exemplified by the growth of newly established firms in the countries that have abolished socialist economic planning.

The four stages of industrialization

Although it can be shown that there are certain commonalities in the conditions for industrial economic development to take off, there are also systematic differences.

The most remarkable difference between the various histories of industrialization is the difference in long-term rates of growth of real *per capita* income. The earliest starter of the industrial revolution, Britain, recorded a growth rate of approximately one per cent per year, when measured over the whole history of industrialization. France and Germany, which belong to the second wave of industrialization, expanded their economies at a rate of about 1.8 per cent per year over a whole century of industrial development. Sweden and Japan, belonging to the third wave, could record an even higher average annual growth rate of 2.9 and 3.3 per cent, respectively, over a century of industrialization. Some East and Southeast Asian regions are now involved in the fourth wave of industrialization, recording even higher rates of economic growth. Although it is improbable that rates of growth of more than 7 per cent per year can be sustained over a whole century, it is obvious that many of the Asian countries have experienced growth rates that are higher than in the first three waves of industrialization (Table 2.1).

An important regularity can be noted: the later the wave of industrialization, the higher the long-term sustainable growth rate. There seems to be an economic advantage of being backward.

Some economists have claimed that the lower the level of income at the start of industrialization, the faster the growth rate will be. This does not

Table 2.1 Growth rates of representative economies during the four waves of industrialization

	Period	*Average rates of growth of real income per capita* (%)
First wave		
UK	1785–1967	1.0
USA	1834–1967	1.7
Second wave		
France	1840–1966	1.8
Germany	1860–1967	1.8
Third wave		
Sweden	1870–1967	2.9
Italy	1899–1967	2.3
Japan	1879–1967	3.2
Fourth wave		
South Korea	1950–1992	5.8
Taiwan	1950–1992	6.0

Source: Maddison (1995), Crafts (1996).

seem to be supported by the growth histories of industrialized countries. Sweden and Britain had almost identical levels of average real income when their industrialization started and yet Sweden's growth rate was almost three times higher, if estimated over a full century. Italy had a higher real income *per capita* than France had at the start of the industrialization process, yet Italy exhibited a higher growth rate during its long period of industrialization.

There seems to be a technological and organizational advantage to be reaped if industrialization starts at a later stage. There is, in short, a greater potential for learning from best practice by bench-marking, if a country belongs to a later wave of industrialization. A successful imitation is easier to achieve if there is a large number of successful industrialized countries to imitate. Britain and the United States, being early starters, had very few examples to follow. Conversely, a country embarking on industrialization in the contemporary world can enjoy the advantages of employing state-of-the-art principles of organization and production. They can use modern principles for the division of labor and the use of inexpensive machinery for the production of, for example, textiles, preserved food and other tradable goods, such production being typical of the early stages of industrialization. Greater accessibility to regions with technological knowledge in this way becomes a growth and development advantage.

The role of the growth of capital and labor supply

In the first period following the Second World War, there was an extensive debate on the conditions for balanced growth in a national economy. The common assumption was that the growth of a closed economy (presumed to be a nation) requires that savings must equal investments, for each period. In the simplified macroeconomic production function with only two inputs, labor and capital, it was shown by Robert Solow (1956) that the share of investments and savings in GNP (or national real income) would have only a transitory effect on the rate of growth. Unless there is technological progress, a higher level of savings and investment would never be capable of raising long-term growth rates.

Most analysts of economic growth have assumed that an equilibrium requires investments to be equal to savings and that the output of the economy is a weighted average of some malleable material capital and homogeneous, and equally malleable, labor. Sometimes the amount of labor input is assumed to be strictly proportional to the population, an assumption that simplifies the analysis of real *per capita* income growth. One further conventional simplification is to assume that the production function is of the *geometric average* form, in other words, of a Cobb–Douglas specification. Sometimes the generalized mean value function is used (often termed the CES-production function). With the Cobb–Douglas function as a basis, the rate of growth of production equals a weighted average of the rates of growth of capital and labor supply.

The rate of growth in the supply of labor is thus an important factor in determining the rate of economic growth. However, little attention has been focused on what happens to the rate of growth in the supply of labor in the development process. In most of the long-term economic growth studies, labor is assumed to grow through forces that are exogenous to the economic process itself. This is grossly at variance with what has been empirically observed. The supply of labor *per capita* has been falling at a fairly steady rate in most of the advanced industrial economies. In Sweden, for example, the total employable population declined substantially as a result of emigration in the initial stages of the industrialization process. The same happened in most of the European countries after the industrialization process had gathered some momentum. Thereafter, the work-force that remained as a resource for industrial production began demanding shorter working hours as soon as productivity increases gave rise to higher real wage rates. The average number of hours worked, for the total labor force, declined from approximately 3000 hours *per capita*, in the early stage of Swedish industrialization, to an average of approximately 1500 hours in the late 1980s. This corresponds to a real wage rate elasticity in the supply of labor of approximately –0.25.

Although it is difficult to measure the size of the Swedish labor force at the start of the industrial revolution, a rough estimate implies that the doubling of the labor force from the beginning of the industrial revolution to the early 1990s, was accompanied by a *per capita* reduction in the number of hours worked of approximately fifty per cent. Thus, in the long term the *supply of working hours* in Sweden has been approximately constant. This constancy of labor supply is a reasonable response to the very rapid increase of real income *per capita*, as would be predicted both by microeconomic consumer theory as well as by micro-econometric studies of labor supply. The faster the rate of labor productivity growth and real wage rate growth, the less it should be expected that this growth is explained by an increasing supply of labor (in quantitative terms). The tendency to decreases in labor supply *per capita* is a general phenomenon in the OECD region and is illustrated in the Figure 2.1.

Based on these observations a realistic (i.e. empirically oriented) long-term growth analysis should not require a very careful analysis of the quantitative role of the labor supply and its expansion over time. The

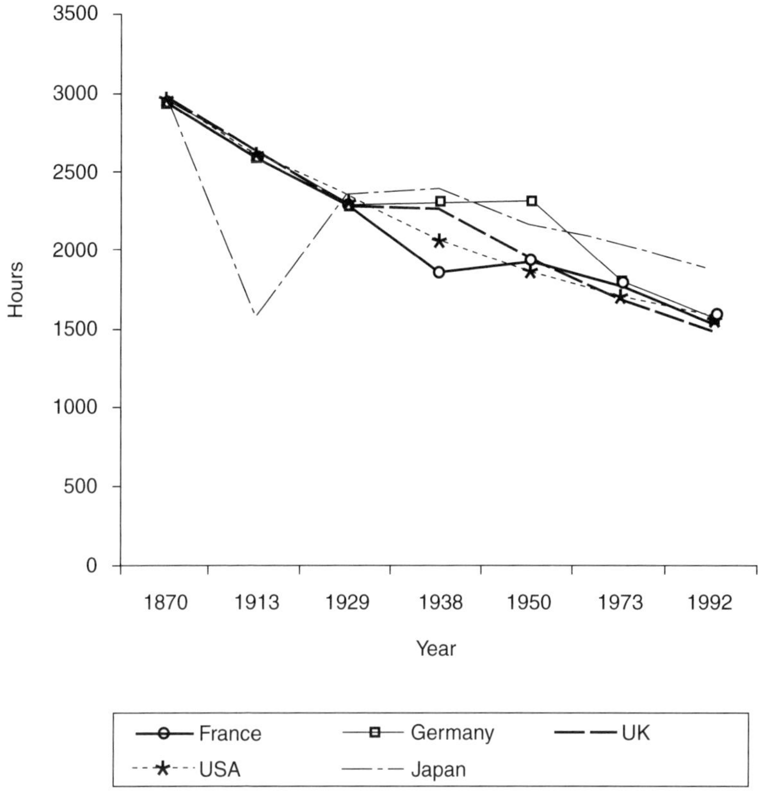

Figure 2.1 Average annual hours worked in selected countries, 1870–1992
Source: Maddison (1995)

focus should instead be on the supply of material capital, as well as on the private educational capital, which is embodied in the labor force, and in the accessibility of public knowledge.

A broad capital concept and its specification ought to be the focus of the long-term economic growth history of the OECD countries and the future of the newly industrialized economies of East Asia.

The supply of educational capital

Industrialization has tended to go hand in hand with increased educational opportunities for the labor force. In the initial stages of industrialization, limited education programs for the prospective industrial workers is a precondition for the establishment of a reliable industrial organization of production. Much of industrial work requires coordination over time and space of a large number of specialized industrial tasks, performed by workers whose activities are assigned according to the principle of division of labor. In order to avoid an excessive number of foremen, each worker must be capable of following simple written instructions and be able to understand the meaning and importance of very exact time measurements. Transforming a person from a farmhand into a manufacturing worker requires some minimum of teaching of time discipline, reading and arithmetic. Data on the education levels of newly industrialized countries indicate that these minimum educational levels require two to three years of formal schooling.

Data from the OECD countries indicate that the countries belonging to the third wave of industrialization seem to have had approximately three years of formal education as an average for the labor force in the initial decades of industrialization and approximately eleven years (on the average) in the late 1970s. This would imply that the rate of growth in educational capital would be approximately 1.5 per cent on a *per capita* basis and 2.5 per cent in terms of total educational capital, measured as man-years of education.

If we measure the amount of material capital per unit of educational capital, the growth of material and human capital seems to have been relatively balanced over the century of industrial development. The long-term rates of growth of output, material capital and educational capital seem to have been roughly equal in a number of OECD countries, at least during the second half of the hundred years of industrial development after 1870. There seems to be a strong case for the conclusion that the increasing quality of labor is a fundamental explanation for the long-term rate of income growth, besides the obvious advantages of complementing the increasing quality of labor with increasing amounts of machinery and other capital equipment. There is, on empirical grounds, much to be said in favor of the broad capital concept advocated by, for example, Rebelo (1991), Mankiw *et al.* (1992), Romer (1993), and Crafts (1996).

Increasing accessibility of public knowledge and information

In the analysis of the history of long-term growth, and its future prospects, there has been a common tendency to equate knowledge in the form of theorems, models, blueprints and recipes for production with the education and skills embodied in the labor force. Such a procedure is conceptually invalid. Education is as individual as a unit of production machinery. Education has to be accumulated over and over again by each new generation of workers and it is used up during the life of the individual worker. If a worker becomes unemployed or dies, his or her skills and educational capital become useless as a factor of production. A theorem or a recipe, on the other hand, is a public good in the sense that, even if it is used by one producer, it can be used again and again by other producers, without exhausting its productive powers. Patents can of course limit the public usefulness of a new recipe for production, but patents and similar constraints on the rights of use are only means of securing positive incentives to engage in creative and innovative activities.

Knowledge is not only *public*; it is also, in principle, *dynamically irreversible*. With proper principles of storage, each generation of knowledge creators add on to the indestructible stock of knowledge, created by earlier generations. As an example, the theorems of Euclid still remain useful, although mathematicians have shown that the Euclidian theorems belong to a special, rather than a general, theory of geometry (or topology). This irreversibility property of knowledge is in stark contrast to educational or embodied knowledge and skills.

One superficially astonishing counter-example is Stradivarius's violin construction. Violin-making reached a qualitative peak in Cremona at the time of Stradivarius. Thereafter, most violin makers have in vain tried to reconstruct the blueprint of the Stradivarius violin. This reconstruction effort has been built on the assumption that a Stradivarius is reproducible by a (possibly very complex) production recipe. But the Stradivarius violin can probably not be seen as something that can be produced by a sophisticated computer, properly driven by the right, sophisticated software. It might not be algorithmic at all, but is rather one of the instances where pure, public knowledge must be complemented with skills, necessarily embodied in possibly uniquely gifted human artisans.

Such examples are however not commonplace. Many, if not most, instances of creative knowledge are algorithmic, dynamically irreversible, and public in scope. Both the irreversibility of creative knowledge and the publicness in the use of such knowledge prohibit the aggregation of this knowledge with education and other forms of humanly embodied capital. Research and development and its accumulation into a growing stock of knowledge must be kept as separate concepts in the analysis of growth and development.

The fact that technological and other applicable knowledge is a public good does not imply that it is of uniform availability across geographical or organizational space. Accessibility to knowledge is not only limited by institutional constraints such as patents, but is also limited by other types of friction. Modeling the impact of public knowledge on production therefore requires an accessibility approach. An accessibility approach could be a representation of the distribution of knowledge in space, where an increase in any of the stocks of knowledge will have a positive impact on production in all regions, *ceteris paribus*. The impact on production is also assumed to decline monotonously with increasing distance between the point in space where knowledge is produced and the point where it is used. While the growth of private capital only influences growth of production locally, the growth of public knowledge can influence the rate of growth of production anywhere. An improvement in the transport and communication system somewhere would consequently lead to an increased rate of growth everywhere, if a given rate of knowledge accumulation is assumed. The steady rate of improved transportation and communication possibilities would therefore have been one of the explanatory factors behind the higher growth rates in the newly industrializing countries (NICs) in East Asia.

More importantly, the consequences of modeling the endogenous growth process require attention. It is often assumed that an augmentation of the capital concept to include human capital in the form of labor force education enables us to model sustained long-term growth. A further assumption is that an increased share of (augmented) investment in GNP would be a means of achieving this increased, sustainable long-term rate of growth. In order to ensure such a conclusion, R&D investments cannot be aggregated with investments in education as suggested by Crafts (1996). Firms, regions and countries separated in space would then, by the public-good effect of research and development, be interdependently related to each other in a mutually reinforcing growth process, even if all private resources were subject to diminishing marginal productivity. This can be demonstrated by the following model:

$$Q_i = K_i^{\alpha}\left[\sum_{j=1}^{n} e^{\beta d_{ij}} R_j^{\gamma}\right]; (i = 1, ...n) \tag{2.1}$$

$$\dot{K} = \sigma_i(1-\tau_i)\cdot K_i^{\alpha}\left[\sum_{k=1}^{n} e^{-\beta d_{ij}} R_j^{\gamma}\right] - \delta K_i \cdot (i = 1, ...n); \tag{2.2}$$

$$\dot{R}_i = \sigma_i \tau_i \rho_i \left[K_i^{\alpha}\left(\sum_{j-1}^{n} e^{-\beta d_{ij}} R_j^{\gamma}\right)\right]; (i = 1, ...n); \tag{2.3}$$

where K_i = augmented capital of region i

R_j = accumulated public knowledge in region j

σ_i = investment-/GNP-ratio in region i with σ.
τ_i = relative share of investment allocated to research and development in region i with $0 \leq \tau \leq 1$
ρ_i = marginal productivity of resources allocated to R&D-investment
α = elasticity of production with respect to augmented capital (material plus educational capital)
γ = public knowledge elasticity
β = distance friction parameter
d_{ij} = measure of distance

In the two equations (2.2) and (2.3), public knowledge is assumed (as before) to be irreversibly accumulating, which means that the amount of new knowledge produced will be positive in every region where τ_i is positive. But the accessibility of knowledge will be growing in *every* region, even if only one of the regions has a positive share of investments in R&D. The system of economies would, under the condition of positive investment (and positive R&D-allocation parameters), converge towards a common growth rate (the eigenvalue) in the very long run, after a history of adaptation towards equilibrium relative proportions of the regions in the total production of the system. Simulation studies with positive and equal parameter values have shown that an integrated economy with a center and a periphery (in terms of differences in accessibility) will tend to have a growth history of higher growth rates initially for the regions, with high accessibility to knowledge up to a critical point in time when the growth rate of the periphery would permanently surpass the growth rate of the center (Andersson and Mantsinen 1980).

Infrastructural investments, growth, and development

In growth model (2.1)–(2.3), public, irreducible knowledge plays an important role in the growth and development process both because knowledge, in this form, is a public good and because it is an irreversibly accumulating resource. Thus, as long as financial resources are allocated to research and development, there will be growth in the economy as a whole. With the extension to a set of economies interrelated by a joint accessibility to knowledge, individual economies will keep growing even if they themselves do not engage in research and development investments. Economic growth will occur as long as there is at least one of the interconnected economies that keeps investing in research and development (provided R&D investments are productive).

Investments in the physical infrastructure are as important for the growth and development process as we have shown public knowledge investments to be. Accessibility measures contain representations of the physical infrastructure. The economic distance between any two regions is primarily influenced by the node and link capacities of the transport and transaction system, which integrates regions and nations into a common economic system. Investing in a new link or improving the flow capacity across the link will ordinarily influence economic conditions in at least two of the regions belonging to the integrated economic system. Two important observations can be made at this stage.

First, material network construction in the form of roads, railroads and terminals, can be empirically shown to be capital-intensive and time-consuming. It is mostly an extremely slow process when compared with investments in private capital.

Second, it has been shown by Stewart Kauffmann (1995) that the general connectivity of a system of regions or nations will undergo a phase transition when the number of links exceeds a critical ratio to the number of nodes. This means that the advantages of trade, and other forms of interaction, will dramatically increase at some point with the marginal addition of a new link to the network.

These two observations are of importance for understanding the nature of growth and development in the global economy, as well as for understanding the development of newly industrialized countries that are currently involved in the creation of new material networks.

The slowness of infrastructural capital accumulation is important for the construction of a complete model of growth and development. It has been convincingly shown by mathematical system theorists that a dynamic system, containing only fast variables interdependently related in a fundamentally non-linear fashion, will be generically chaotic and thus unpredictable and uncontrollable. However, if the dynamic economic system can be subdivided into different parts containing dynamic equations operating on very different time scales, the predictability of the system as a whole can improve radically. If the slowly changing variables are, furthermore, of a collective nature, the possibilities of avoiding chaos may be radically improved (Haken 1980 and Gilmore 1981).

The slowly changing public (infrastructural) variables could be seen as an arena or stage on which the market games are played. The slower the change of the arena, and the more specified and constrained it is, the more predictable the economic market variables will become. With a sufficiently constrained arena of physical and non-material infrastructure, a standard general equilibrium is quite conceivable as a generic solution concept. Even a balanced growth trajectory would be consistent with such a view of the interplay between the arena and the market games. However, although a slow and steady improvement of the infrastructure of a region or a nation is consistent with a sequence of temporary equilibria, sooner or later the slowly evolving sequence of equilibria will be disrupted by a phase transition, occurring when the amount of new infrastructure reaches a critical level at which a new equilibrium level (or growth path) will be structurally stable. Such a new structurally stable solution can only be reached after a period of disequilibrium dynamics.

The current parallel structural transformation process

The world economy is currently in a process of parallel structural transformations of different economies. The former Soviet Union and its satellite states are in a process of structural transformation from heavily controlled, industrialized state capitalism into a market economy based on modern industrial principles. The newly industrialized countries, especially in East Asia, belong to the high-growth-rate fourth wave of industrialization. The already mature industrial countries, such as Japan, the United States, and many European countries, are entering the post-industrial society (sometimes called the C-society), which is based on the exploitation of communication resources as well as cognitive and creative capabilities. It is a transformation which is occurring because of the massive expansion of global infrastructural capital, and the attendant increasing accessibility of public information, knowledge and new ideas. Some regions, notably Hong Kong, the Stockholm region, and the state of Florida, have the advantage of being located as saddle points between regions developing into modern industrial areas and economies undergoing a transformation into post-industrial C-societies.

New networks, new nodes and the industrial dynamics of the future

Networks for land and sea transportation were originally used for the general purpose of conveying goods, people and information between different locations. The twentieth century has seen a fundamental change in this respect. Today there are networks that specialize in the transmission of a specific type of transportables. There are pipeline networks for the transport of oil and gas. There are also networks for the transmission of information and nothing else. Then there are airline networks for transporting people. The air freight network, on the other hand, specializes in transporting high-value-added goods.

At the same time, these newly created systems are based on synergy rather than specialization. They are evolving slowly but steadily into networks of increasing connectivity both between nodes and between networks. Thus, the most important structural change in the last decades of the twentieth century, has been the increasing synergy between different networks. Airline networks are, for example, well connected with each other and these connected airline networks are increasingly dependent upon on-line interaction with the information and communication networks. A well-functioning air network that is independent of spatially extended networks of computers has become an economic as well as a technological impossibility.

In North America, and to some extent Western Europe, trucking corporations are increasingly depending on similar computer assisted telecommunication networks for the proper guidance of their vehicle fleets. Railroad and trucking activities are also increasingly becoming interconnected in the administration of transport and trade flows by the use of computer and telecommunication networks.

The new multi-layered network structure has given rise to new potentials for regional development. Some regions have become centers of fast growth as a consequence of their positioning as *gateway regions* of the world. Among these regions we find Singapore, Hong Kong, Kaohsiung, Chicago and London. In these global gateway regions the capacity and the interactivity of a multitude of different networks has created a globally important position. In Andersson, Anderstig and Hårsman (1990) it has been shown that the interactivity of airport capacity and the research and development potential of the region has become the most important determinant of potential income and, thus, of the long-term development of regions. It is thus of vital importance to post-industrial regions around the world to ensure a strong synergy between modern communications and contact infrastructure with strategies for the development of research, development and higher education.

It goes without saying that multi-layered networks of railroads, roads, air transportation, and telecommunications in synergy with research, development and education that are evolving in self-organizing patterns will carry with them increasing potentials for spatial economic phase transitions. Such a phase transition is not only a question of economic restructuring, but also a network restructuring in terms of the size of clusters of inter-connectivity on the multi-layered networks. Currently such phase transitions are emerging at rather limited spatial scales. But the number of links in relation to the enormous number of production, consumption and logistical nodes are not yet sufficient for a continental or global phase transition in the pattern of trade in goods, or in the transportation of people and knowledge interactions.

We have, however, already witnessed a spatial phase transition of financial services. The next probable phase transition is likely to occur in the retail trade. The transportation networks are already sufficiently developed for such a phase transition to occur. What now remains is a fusion of the efficient networks for transporting goods with the internet and other means of inexpensive global communication. In parallel, there is an obvious need for a new network for the secure transmission of payments from ordinary consumers to the globally operating retail-trading network corporations. When these institutional networking problems have been solved, local and national retail monopolies of the kind that are common in East Asia (as well as in Scandinavia and continental Europe) will be faced with a qualitatively new competitive global situation. Formerly highly protected or monopolized consumer markets will be restructured by a global price equalization leading to the destruction of some of the locally, regionally and nationally oriented distributors of consumer goods. The transformation will be especially rapid in those durable consumer goods with a high price per unit of purchase.

In this phase transition of retail trading there are also opportunities for certain regions, and primarily those regions which have understood that the time has come for a new commercial revolution. In such a new commercial revolution it is of course an absolute necessity to understand the strategies for exploiting and developing the necessary conditions for these new synergies. It is not at all certain that the old trading centers, such as Copenhagen, will seize these new opportunities.

Conclusion

Economic growth and development are inseparable parts of long-term evolution. No long-term growth process has been unaccompanied by a changing structure of production. Economic growth in the industrial age has exhibited a combination of growth of real income *per capita* as well as a changing composition of employment and production.

It also is clear from the economic history of the last 200 years, that countries that industrialized at an early stage have had a slower rate of long-term growth than countries that industrialized at later stages. This is a natural consequence of the irreversible process of organizational and technological knowledge expansion, innovation and diffusion. Learning from more advanced countries becomes increasingly advantageous in the process of economic development.

During the last decade the question of endogenous economic growth and the possibility of influencing the long-term rate growth rate by governments has been hotly disputed. Some analysts have claimed that a high ratio of broadly defined investment to total income (or GNP) can have only transitory growth effects. Others have claimed that augmenting the capital concept so as to include educational and other human capital would lead to sustainable, endogenous long-term growth. However, formulated in this way, the arguments are quite unconvincing. Just adding human capital in terms of an improved level of education of the population adds nothing essential to the growth and development process. Educational capital is essentially private capital in the same way as computers and production machinery constitutes private capital.

The accumulation of available knowledge through investments in research and development is a different matter. The output of research and development investments constitute a public and irreversible capital accumulation. This implies that, even if there are tendencies to stagnation in the accumulation of private material or human capital, there would be no tendencies to a similar stagnation of production. Increasing the share of income allocated to investments in public knowledge (R&D) is thus a factor contributing to sustained long-term rates of growths and a changing composition of production and employment.

Investment in the physical infrastructure has a similar but a spatially more important impact. Improving the possibilities of communicating knowledge between different parts of the world would have a strong impact on the possibilities of long-term sustainable economic growth, even in countries not actively pursuing research and development programs by allocating income to knowledge investment. The accessibility of knowledge is dependent upon network capacity. It can be shown that a slow and steady increase in the number of links in a communication network will sooner or later lead to a phase transition regarding the level of interconnectivity of the global economy and thus to a phase transition also in terms of the accessibility of public knowledge. Such a phase transition, from a low level of accessibility of knowledge to a radically higher level, implies a radical improvement of the prospects for sustained economic growth and development of the world economy and its constituent parts.

References

Andersson, Å.E., C. Anderstig and B. Hårsman, 'Knowledge and Communications Infrastructure and Regional Economic Change', in N.B. Hansen, J. Kenneth and P. Nijkamp (eds), *Regional Policy and Regional Integration* (Elgar Reference Collection. Modern Classics in Regional Science, vol. 6. Cheltenham, UK: Edward Elgar, 1990) 277–94.

Andersson, Å.E., and J. Mantsinen, 'Mobility of resources, accessibility of knowledge and Economic Growth', *Behavioral Science* 25 (1980) 353–66.

Crafts, N., 'Post-neoclassical Endogenous Growth Theory: What are its Policy Implications?', *Oxford Review of Economic Policy* 12 (1996) 30–47.

Denison, E.F., *Accounting for Slowing Economic Growth* (Washington DC: Brookings Institution, 1979).

Gilmore, R., *Catastrophe Theory for Scientists and Engineers* (New York: Wiley-Interscience, 1981).

Haken, H., *Dynamics of Synergetic Systems* (Berlin: Springer-Verlag, 1980).

Kauffmann, S., *At Home in the Universe. The Search for Laws of Complexity* (London: Penguin, 1995).

Maddison, A., *Monitoring the World Economy, 1820–1992* (Paris: OECD, 1995).

Mankiw, N.G. *et al.*, 'A Contribution to the Empirics of Economic Growth', in G.M. Grossman (ed.), *Economic Growth: Theory and Evidence, Volume 2* (Elgar Reference Collection. International Library of Critical Writings in Economics, no. 68, Cheltenham, UK: Edward Elgar, 1992), 3–33.

Rebelo, S., 'Long-run Policy Analysis and Long-run Growth', *Journal of Political Economy* 99 (1991) 500–21.

Romer, P.M., 'Idea Gaps and Object Gaps in Economic Development', *Journal of Monetary Economics* 32 (1993) 543–73.

Solow, R., 'A Contribution to the Theory of Growth', *Quarterly Journal of Economics* 70 (1956) 65–94.

Part I

Institutional Frameworks

3

The Chinese Kaleidoscope: Chinese Economic Development in the Light of the New Institutional Theories

*Kurt Lundgren**

If an economist thirty years ago had been asked to pick out countries that in the immediate future would achieve a high and sustainable economic growth, not many of them would have suggested one of the East Asian countries and still fewer, if any, would have suggested mainland China. The probability of such a prognosis can be taken as an indication of the complexity of the forces connected with economic growth, of the uncertainty in economic prognoses, and of the diversity of factors that can explain why economic growth takes place. For almost two decades China has had an annual economic growth of about 10 per cent on average. How can we explain this impressive development? In the development economics literature, a high rate of economic growth is thought to depend on a quantitative change in factor inputs which could be the result of labour mobility from agriculture to industry. Is this explanation applicable to the Chinese case as well?

It is not difficult to appreciate the magnitude of the impact of labour mobility in China. Let us, for example, study China's allocation of manpower in three sectors: primary industry (agriculture), secondary industry (industry) and tertiary industry (service sector), in 1980 and 1995

* This paper is the result of a study visit to China during autumn 1996 financed by SIDA/Sarec and supported by National Institute for Working Life in Sweden. For advice and support I wish to thank Professor Fang Fukang, Profesor Yu-Yun Wang and the other participants in the conference on 'Sustainable Economic Growth in East Asia' organized by Normal University in Beijing; Professor Chao Gangling and his colleagues at Shanghai University of Finance and Economics; Professor Keyong Dong at Renmin University; Dr Zhang Gang at Stockholm School of Economics; and an anonymous referee, not to mention all persons in different positions in 'countrysides' and state-owned enterprises around the Shanghai area.

Table 3.1 Production and share of employment

	Share of total production 1980	*Share of employment 1980*	*Share of employment 1995*
Agriculture	30.09	68.74	52.92
Industry	48.53	18.26	22.95
Service	21.36	13.00	24.13

Source: China's Statistical Yearbook 1995.

respectively. Let us then make use of the allocation of 1990, but keep the values of productivity at the level of 1980. We assume that the productivity in each sector is independent of the number of workers (Table 3.1). In this case, the increase in GDP *per capita* would be 23.8 per cent. This should be compared with the real increase which for this period was 243.6 per cent. Thus the reallocation of the working force between the three sectors represents less than one-tenth of the total increase. This example should, of course, only be seen as a very rough proxy. But, even if we were to double the share achieved by the reallocation, we would still get similar results. Hence, a large part of growth remains unexplained.

Institutional theory and China's development

During the Cultural Revolution, Deng Xiaoping had argued for a new policy as well as new attitudes, stating that the Chinese should not care 'whether a cat is black or white as long as it catches mice.' This was an argument for institutional reforms, and frequent references to this statement indicate that institutional changes have been understood as crucial for the Chinese development over the last few decades: a change that has been neglected, for example, by Krugman in his famous paper on the Asian 'miracle' (Krugman, 1994). Deng did not hire more red cats to catch more rats, he bought new cats of a quite different colour.

In considering long-term economic development, we need to direct our attention to more fundamental properties of the society rather than merely dealing with current political and business events. Hence it is appropriate to discuss China's development from the perspective of the new institutional economics (NIE) as developed by Ronald Coase, Oliver Williamson, Douglass North and others. The basic assumption in these theories is that long-term economic performance is intimately tied to the institutional framework of enterprises and nations. Such an approach, however, is not simple or straightforward. Institutionally-oriented economists researching Chinese development have been surprised because 'conditions thought to be necessary for growth ... were absent' (Blanchard and Fischer, 1993). Rawlin (1994), for instance, has observed that China's industrial sector has recorded big gains in output, employment, and exports in the *absence* of privatization, effective bankruptcy legislation, and other policy innovations that are widely seen as prerequisites for successful reform. Thus, in spite of the lack of 'necessary requisites for economic growth', China has achieved an economic growth that is unprecedented historically.

This chapter analyses China's economic development over the last two decades using institutional theory, or, more correctly, the ensemble of institutional theories. Fitting modern Chinese development into an economic institutional framework is not an easy task: there are many potential pitfalls. First, the new institutional theories have not been integrated in development economics (North, 1987). Second, our knowledge of China's economy and institutions remains inadequate. For this reason, the content of the present chapter must be understood more as a contribution to a discussion, and suggestions for future research, than a final statement about the relationship between China's economic development and institutional theory.

Institutional theory – a summary

Ronald H. Coase (1937) raised the question why, given the alleged superiority of the invisible hand to allocate resources efficiently, institutions like firms should exist. Coase's explanation is that there are costs, namely *transaction costs,* in running the economic system. Some transactions are most efficiently transacted over the market, and others were more efficiently handled in a hierarchy. The introduction of uncertainty into economic development analysis distinguishes the new institutional theories from the traditional institutionalists such as Thorstein Veblen, John R. Commons and others. These ideas have been developed further especially by Oliver Williamson (1975, 1985), who, in a number of works, analyzed how efficient government structures are related to different characteristics of the transactions involved. According to the new institutionalists, the institutional system would not matter in a world without uncertainty and transaction costs. In a world of uncertainty, it does.

According to North (1987), the key features of the institutional structure of a modern society are: (i) contracting that permits continuous production and distribution, and (ii) the enforcement of contracts over long periods of time. Such a set of economic institutions must encompass a structure of political–judicial institutions that provide for the stability of property rights. This stability implies that there would be no radical changes in the price level and that property rights are embedded in a structure of law far removed from arbitrary confiscation. Finally, there must exist a legal system which gives the parties confidence that contracts will be enforced. In his later works, North adopted a broader definition of institutions. He defines institutions as 'restrictions on our behaviour' which can be of three kinds: formal, informal and self-imposed constraints (North, 1990). He also raises questions which go beyond the scope of the transaction costs theories. What determines the divergent patterns of societies, politics, or economies over time? What accounts for the survival of societies and economies that are characterized by persistently poor performance? Institutions are in many respects connected with increasing returns which make them change incrementally. This makes the development of institutions and economies *path-dependent*. It cannot be taken for granted that efficient institutions will develop. The increasing returns connected with an initial set of institutions will create organizations and interest groups with a stake in the existing constraints.

Rosenberg and Birdzell (1986) carried out a historically-based institutional analysis where they tried to disentangle the main institutional factors that help explain the industrial breakthrough that took place in Western Europe as opposed to Asia. The key elements of their explanation are that a wide diffusion of authority and resources is necessary for experimentation and innovations. This is accompanied by an absence of political and religious restrictions on innovative activities. Finally, there should be incentives which combine rewards with success that carry a risk of penalties for failure in an experiment.

Within the paradigm of the new institutional economics, many researchers have focused their attention on property right theories. As emphasized by Weitzman and Xu (1993), there is no single universally accepted property right theory. A common element in these theories is that, without well-defined private ownership, the firms will tend to operate badly. In particular, the literature on economic transition (i.e. the transformation from 'socialist' to market economies) have argued that the absence of private ownership tends to provide some ground for 'soft budget constraints' (Kornai, 1980; 1992).

Institutional economics and economic growth

In modern theories of economic growth, the basic inputs of economic growth are identified as labor, capital and technology. If only the first two factors are considered, they could account for a quarter or up to a third of countries' economic growth. The part of the growth which cannot be derived from changes in the other factors of production is referred to as 'the Solow residual'. In a recently published summary of economists' research on factors behind economic growth, Landau *et al.* (1996) concluded that 'no single vantage point, or level of aggregation, can encompass the full range of important influences on economic growth'. Instead there seems to be a range of different factors which, taken together, establish the capacity for economic growth, hence the description 'mosaic of economic growth'. The fact that such a large part of total growth remains unexplained is probably an important reason for economists' interest in institutional economics. The risk with this approach, however, is that the concept of institution is left to represent all environmental factors outside the firm which affect its performance. Thus, there is a need to discriminate between these factors.

Institutions, broadly speaking, refer to factors other than the legal system and the latter's capacity for providing incentives. One way to approach institutions is to think about the stock of technological knowledge which enters the production function as potentially available to all producers, but that the ability to absorb, interpret and implement this knowledge differs between different firms and nations. Abramovitz (1989) refers to this ability as a country's 'social capability' in which, not only 'political' and social institutions, but also *cognitive* factors are included. An approach similar to Abramovitz's 'social capability' is the concept of 'absorptive capacity' introduced by Cohen and Levinthal (1990). A reasonable interpretation of existing research is that the absorptive capacity and social capability are built upon different conditions and on nations' different comparative advantages. As a result, the combination of factors that establish the 'mosaic of economic growth' differs between nations and regions.

Bruland (1989) noted that institutional factors, 'however important they might be, might be necessary conditions at best, and by no means sufficient ones ... prerequisites is all they are.' Economic growth is the result of a '*time-consuming and expensive process of learning*' (Nelson, cited in Rosenberg and Frischtak, 1985). Important skills and knowledge diffuse not only, and not even primarily, through literature or transactions of licences. Participation in 'user–producer' interactions can be a decisive source of innovation and development of products. Access to a foreign sales company with experience of the modern and demanding market can also initiate product and process improvements. Contacts with new markets mean meeting with new competitors from which it is also possible to learn. Managerial and manufacturing skills diffuse by engagement in joint ventures, and so on. The purchase of industrial capital equipment often means that the seller instructs the staff in its handling, etc. (for an application of this approach to the Swedish industrial development, see Lundgren, 1995).

North (1990) holds that current economic analyses in institutional theory tend only to explore the most efficient governance structure and organization *within* the given institutional constraints (p. 79). The heritage of comparative institutional analysis in which the outcome of two or more given institutional settings are compared, is still very strong. Nevertheless, North has to some extent, dealt with institutional change. He holds that changing relative prices can induce one party to a renegotiation of the contract. Often, the preferred result of the renegotiation is not possible without restructuring a higher set of rules and agreements. Sometimes, the party with the improved bargaining power can take the costs of changing these higher level rules. In other cases, rules erode over time; they are changed, ignored or not enforced (North, 1990, p. 86). The empirical work on institutional change has primarily focused on the development of institutions in the West. It is poorly developed in the field of economics. Yet, according to North (1995), studying institutional changes can help provide the basis for deriving a dynamic theory of social change.

Chinese firms and their institutions

This section analyses the Chinese experience from the perspective of the institutional theory framework presented above. Special attention is paid to the direction of those institutional changes in China that affect the conditions and behaviour of the units in the economy on which the country's welfare depends, namely the firms.

The 'Countrysides'

The institution that may be seen as the basis of Chinese development is the 'household responsibility system' which was introduced in 1979. This reform abolished the communes' property rights to land, and made each family or household responsible for its output. First, the land was 'lent' to the farmers, then leased for a period of fifteen years or more. The contract may be transferred to other members of the household and it is also possible for the contractor to sell or lease the land. The share of crops that must be handed over to the state has been reduced over time, and the government has also reduced the areas over which it determines prices.

This reform has proved to be a great success. In six years, farmers' real incomes multiplied almost two and a half times. Furthermore, human resources could be released for other work, for example, subcontracting for an industry in a neighbouring city, or, buying components for pumps, putting them together and selling the products in the local market. To a large extent, China's economic success seems to be related to the development of the 'township and village enterprises' (TVEs), that is, small enterprises established in the old communes by county, township, or village authorities more or less in cooperation with an entrepreneur who is also appointed manager of the enterprise in question. In 1980, 1.5 million 'commune and brigade companies' employed less than 30 million people and produced about 10 per cent of industrial output. In 1992, 20 million TVEs employed 100 million people and produced 47 per cent of industrial output. During the first fifteen years of reforms, these companies grew by 30 per cent on average and, by the early 1990s, they accounted for a quarter of China's exports.

TVEs had already existed during the Cultural Revolution. But many urban plants did not work, market shortages became worse and some rural communities increasingly preferred to set up their own firms (Byrd and Lin, 1990). Often, these companies take a form that the Chinese have termed 'collective'. China can be said to have six levels of governments. The top levels are the national and provincial government. Firms owned by these governments are defined as state-owned. The majority of the 'collectives' are, however, under the control of lower-level governments. Some TVEs have been leased to individual managers or are privately owned. Others are joint ventures with other collective firms or with urban or foreign companies. Only a few of them are 'employer owned' in the Western sense of the term (Byrd and Lin, 1990; Naughton, 1994).

The state-owned enterprises

In contrast to the successful development of TVEs, state-owned enterprises have fared rather badly. On the whole, their productivity development has been very slow or even negative, and, the state sector as a whole in 1995, suffered a loss of about RMB 60 billion. Their problems may be attributed to the following reasons (Fang, 1996):

1. Ambiguous ownership. The government and their representatives intervene in the enterprises with their political power but do not hold financial responsibility.
2. Lack of legal status among the enterprises.
3. Lack of profit maximizing objectives among enterprises as they are not controlled by hard financial targets.

Furthermore, the enterprises are burdened with heavy debts. This is a problem that is typically solved by printing new money. In the 1980s, it led to inflation and macroeconomic instability. State enterprises are largely over-staffed. The share of redundant staff has been estimated at 30 per cent. Their employment has been guaranteed by the enterprise and their pensions, health care, etc., are dependent on the company. In many places outside of the big cities, the welfare of whole communities is dependent on the state firms. State-owned companies have also become the victims of a brain drain of talented people to the private sector or to joint ventures. This situation has allowed the management to act against the state with their staff as hostage. However, it appears as well that the management has maximized the earnings of the employees, and the monopoly of their position has facilitated such behaviour.

While the agricultural reform has resulted in a uniform structure (namely the household responsibility system), industrial reforms which began in 1984 have resulted in a property rights structure that varies greatly. Ingredients of marketization as well as privatization can be found for each step in different combinations. Although some kind of decentralization of property rights can be distinguished in the early reforms, it is quite evident that the major ingredient is that of marketization; that is, the major goal has been to make the market work perfectly, rather than to privatize the state sector.

An interesting institutional innovation is to auction off top managerial positions. Candidates can study the firms' accounts and are expected to provide a bid on business plans, strategies, expected investments, profits and so on (Rohwer, 1995; Groves *et al.*, 1995). Other examples of institutional changes are the bankruptcy law passed in 1986, part-privatization of some companies by flotations on the Chinese stock markets, and the separation of directors and managers from governmental bureaucrats. The state-owned companies were allowed to keep a share of their profits, managers were given monetary rewards based on the firm's performance and workers were paid more in bonuses (Groves *et al.*, 1994). Thus, actions were taken to improve incentives as well as selection of managers.

Industrial learning processes in China

Since 1978, Deng's 'open door policy' of courting foreign companies to form joint ventures with a Chinese partner has been rather successful in the following ways:

1 Managers as well as white and blue collar workers are being trained, thereby engendering the transfer of skills.
2 Managerial and organizational patterns are spread throughout many channels, for example, through domestic partners who are engaged in other companies so that experiences gained in joint ventures can be applied.

Joint ventures make high demands on domestic subcontractors, which encourage learning. The products of joint ventures raise consumers' demands on product quality and force domestic producers to improve on both costs and quality.

In many respects, a learning process appears to have gained momentum. In contrast to countries in Western Europe, which over a hundred years ago had tried to catch up with Britain's industrial progress, the Chinese have many more options. They can learn not only from their American, European or Japanese counterparts, but also from their neighbours like Taiwan, Hong Kong and Singapore. Not least important is the access to overseas Chinese who not only possess knowledge about modern technology and administrative procedures, but also meet only a small cultural obstacle to transfer this knowledge to China.

The TVEs appear to be not only a solution that is well adapted to the Chinese institutional conditions, but also to existing skill levels. The countryside possesses latent entrepreneurial and administrative skills that could now be utilized. The small enterprises are close to their markets and agriculture, and can adjust their products to local demands. In other words, under prevailing conditions, the process of 'learning by doing' seems to have worked rather well. Many TVEs also established themselves as subcontractors to more technically advanced state companies located in the urban areas and, perhaps most important of all, the TVEs have brought jobs, incomes and different skills to the countryside where the huge majority of the Chinese population reside.

Chinese TVEs and new private enterprises in the countryside may represent the positive side of the Chinese economy, but it is evident that this sector is moving to another level which demands new institutional solutions for sustained economic development. This can be seen if we study how the number of TVEs has changed over time. The number of TVEs reached its peak in 1993 and has since fallen by 30 per cent. This does not mean that their shares of total production and employees have declined but that, instead, the companies have entered a period of stability, the size of 'countrysides' having stabilized at around 300–500 employees. Furthermore, a new type of 'countryside' is emerging which finances, owns and educates its managers.

Reforms are also underway with respect to state-owned enterprises. Five hundred central 'industrial groups' are being reorganized. Such reorganization is likely to affect about 70 per cent of those employed in the state sector. The reforms mean that the state would be establishing its control and ownership via 'control stock companies', in which it would be a major shareholder thereby allowing it to control the individual companies. These companies are allowed to establish new companies under their ownership. Furthermore, there is no geographical restriction on investments: companies may even invest in foreign countries. The individual companies (both private and state) can also borrow money from banks. All banks are state owned but, on the other hand, there is a fairly large number of banks which are relatively autonomous with respect to credit allocation, and which make independent decisions.

Substitution of formal institutions

What the discussion has shown so far is that there are many *substitutes* for the lack of formal institutions. Weitzman and Xu (1993) have argued that a culturally-based preference for, and the anticipation of cooperative behaviour among, the contractual partners in the countryside enterprises, eliminate the need for formal and detailed description of property rights. Indeed, such a formalization may even work against the cooperative culture and raise transaction costs. Despite a lack of efficient enforcement, transactions can rely on long-term networks of relatives, long-term friendship, party membership, and so on. In small, rural communities particularly, labour mobility is low and people are engaged in long-term relationships which can help develop cooperative strategies within companies. Even if there is some mobility within the community, reputation effects are at work which provide incentives for hard work (Zhang, 1997).

It is also possible that Western economists have underestimated at least some capabilities and institutions in the Chinese economy. Certain transaction costs connected with enforcement can be very high because of the lack of well defined property rights. On the other hand, it cannot be said that the existing property rights are especially unclear, such as those that define the rights between the individual firm and external agents. The banking system, for instance, may be poorly developed in China. Yet high individual savings combined with family networks and rural informal financial institutions, as well as 'rural co-operative funds' (Chen, 1993), supply countryside enterprises with capital. Relatives, within and across communities, regions and even nations, borrow capital for small projects run by people they know, and whose projects are small and possible to monitor. This, together with the connection between TVEs and township and village government, which reduces the risks for external financiers, can be one very important institutional condition for rural development. China's strength in informal institutions may be of important value and should interest other developing countries.

Institutions in their contexts

In a more complex economy in which future outcomes are difficult to predict, the informal way of solving problems through *guanxi* (based on personal trust) can be at least as good as to take an *ex ante* contract to a court. The Chinese *guanxi*-system opens up renegotiation of a contract, something which may reduce the commitment to the contract agreed upon by the partners. On the other hand, the possibility of *ex post* renegotiation provides the parties with an option to write a new Pareto-improving contract, something which can be of great importance in an environment of asymmetric information (Bolton, 1990). Depending on the context, *guanxi* can obstruct a development and provide space for corruption but can, in another environment, be an efficient way of screening and interpreting information.

The efficiency of an element in the institutional framework must be seen in its context and not in relation to what is said in textbooks describing Western institutions. The absence of well defined property rights might be a severe disadvantage if the enterprises in question also possess monopoly power but may not necessarily be the case in a competitive environment. The 'collective' structure of ownership can be an efficient adjustment to specific Chinese conditions, particularly for products in reasonable working markets even though the markets may be underdeveloped for labour and capital (Naughton, 1994). Thus institutions, which are bad in one context, can be good in another. It is possible that meritocratic traditions that were previously an obstacle to the development of a traditional 'old-fashioned' capitalism can, to some extent, be useful in a more modern phase of industrial development.

Institutional learning in China

China is surrounded by countries which have experienced very good economic performances for a number of years. The Chinese household responsibility, in a way, may be said to have been inspired by the reforms in the other East Asian countries. The land reform in Japan after the

Second World War was imposed by the Americans who had feared that Japanese farmers might become communists, as in mainland China. In this way, we can view institutional change as institutional competition. In the 1960s, Kuomintang faced and crushed a riot among the native Taiwanese population who resisted the Kuomintang government. To regain legitimacy, Kuomintang had to carry out a land reform, and the Taiwanese learnt quite a lot from the Japanese reform (Wu, 1994). When the Chinese Communist Party tried to regain legitimacy among the population after the Cultural Revolution, the elites attempted to achieve this by raising the standard of living as had been experienced by its neighbours. Thus dissatisfaction with the present state of performance, in all cases, played an important role for policy change.

Institutional learning has many similarities with 'technological learning' and 'policy learning'. Such a parallel introduces the concept of 'prior related knowledge'. In other words, there must be some kind of relevance of the idea of institutional change to one's own situation. Furthermore, the channels of information must also be present. Is it by chance that so many of China's closest neighbours, Japan, South Korea, Taiwan, Hong Kong and Singapore, at least for a period, had all enjoyed relatively steady economic development when the Chinese reform program was initiated?

Some institutional changes in East Asia have also been consistent with the attitudes prevailing in China. 'Social' channels of information have been most highly developed with its neighbours. Chinese institutions are affected by Taiwan, Hong Kong and not least, by Singapore. The solutions must be adapted to a national setting. In this respect, China had access to a very important resource: overseas Chinese who not only have knowledge about markets and institutions in other countries, but who are also familiar with Chinese culture. The Chinese network therefore constitutes an important source of information.

It is also interesting to note that a process of mutual institutional interdependencies have taken place between China, Japan and other Southeast Asian countries. The countries around the region have adopted a strategy of 'shared growth' (Campos and Root, 1996). An implicit contract appears to be in place between the governments and populace, such that the business sector is courted to build up a dynamic industrial base while the populace has access to long-term economic benefits. Such a contract has become urgent for the political elites because of the geopolitical environment in the 1960s with risks of insurrections, ideologically backed up by Maoist China. Two decades later, China had lost its attraction while its immediate eastern neighbours have become examples to emulate, at least until the recent monetary crisis.

However, access to information channels and good examples is not enough. It is possible that necessary adjustments to national, local or historic peculiarities will not be made. Often, institutions that are fashioned after foreign models fail to attract the individual's loyalty and feelings of ownership (Dia, 1993). Problems are thus not easily solved through mere imitation. But neither is it a solution for developing countries to keep their traditional systems: the two systems must meet to create something new. Research on the mechanisms behind China's institutional learning remains an area for further research.

Conclusion

We return to the question raised in the introduction: does the Chinese case support institutional theories? Even if we cannot consider the Chinese property rights system as satisfactory by Western standards, there is no doubt that *Chinese institutions have changed in the direction proposed by institutional theories*. Markets have been deregulated: entry is not totally free in all markets but a tremendous change has taken place. The economic sector has become much more autonomous in relation to the political sector than it was before the reforms. On the other hand, we can say that the Chinese development *challenges* institutional theory in that one-sided and cursory approaches very quickly come to light when we are confronted with the Chinese reality (see Chow, 1997). There are two lessons to be learned from the Chinese experience.

First, different elements of the institutional framework should not be seen separately but in their context; that is, how they together shape the institutional mosaic for economic growth. Such 'system oriented' institutional approaches can be found in Aoki (1994) and Williamson (1991). Economists are often disinclined to study institutions. For this reason, they can neglect informal institutions and the interaction between formal and informal institutions. Moreover, institutions must be seen in a dynamic perspective: they are path-dependent and must be placed in a historical context. In most economic theories, institutions often change only over a long period time. This assumption oversimplifies the problem since it is not the case for China.

Second, China's ability to grow rapidly despite a lack of traditional prerequisites can be attributed to the kaleidoscopic nature of China's economic experience. Three factors, in particular, may be highlighted:

1 At the beginning of the reform period, the most important driving force behind the institutional change was the high level of discontent

among the population after the Cultural Revolution, and this made a renegotiation of the contract between the leaders and the population possible.
2 Chinese development took place in spite of the lack of strong formal institutions. On the other hand, China possessed many social capabilities and informal institutions. This means that the country, in some areas, had the characteristics of 'impoverished sophistication'; abilities which, however, could not be fully utilized during the Maoist period, especially during the period of rural industrial development.
3 Industrial and institutional learning has been facilitated because of the access to many different channels of information together with 'good examples' in the geographic and cultural neighbourhood.

The Chinese experience has shown that existing social capabilities can be used in a successful process of transformation. But the question remains if China can continue to rely on its informal institutions in the future. If the Chinese institutional framework is to be seen as an interdependent system, it is necessary that the political institutions be reformed far more extensively than is currently the case. It is an open question as to whether China's problems will grow faster than the speed of development of the institutions that are necessary for dealing with them. The current problems in the financial sectors in many East Asian countries highlight the importance of well-functioning and transparent institutions in this sector. Modern institutional theories have much to say about problems which seem to be highly relevant to China. Of greater importance, however, is the potential that China continues to realize from 'the pedagogics of good examples'; that is, not merely to imitate, but also to implement and adapt the experiences of others to its own conditions.

References

Abramowitz, M., *Thinking About Growth* (Cambridge: Cambridge University Press, 1989).

Aoki, M., 'The Japanese Firm as a System of Attributes: A Survey and Research Agenda', in Aoki, M. and R. Dore (eds), *The Japanese Firm. The Sources of Competitive Strength* (Oxford: Oxford University Press, 1994).

Blanchard, O.J. and S. Fischer, *NBER Macroeconomics Annual* (Cambridge, MA: MIT Press, 1993).

Bolton, P., 'Renegotiation and the Dynamics of Contract Design', *European Economic Review*, 34 (1990, May).

Bruland, K., *British Technology and European Industrialization. The Norwegian Textile Industry in the Mid Nineteenth Century* (Cambridge: Cambridge University Press, 1989).

Byrd, W.A., and Lin Q., *China's Rural Industry* (World Bank: Oxford University Press, 1990).

Campos J.R. and H.L. Root, *The Key to The Asian Miracle* (Washington, DC: Brookings Institution, 1996).

Chen, X., 'Several Recent New Developments in Rural Economies', *Journal of Comparative Economic and Social Systems*, 2 (1993).

Chow, G.C., 'Challenges of China's Economic System for Economic Theory', *American Economic Review: Papers and Proceedings* (May 1997).

Coase, R.H., 'The Nature of the Firm', *Economica* (1937) 386–405.

Cohen, W.M., and D.A. Levinthal, 'Absorptive Capacity: A New Perspective on Learning and Innovation', *Administrative Science Quarterly*, 35 (1990).

Dia, M., 'A Governance Approach to Civil Service Reform in Sub-Saharan Africa', *World Bank Technical Paper No. 225* (World Bank: Washington, DC, 1993).

Fang F., 'The Evolution of China's Economy and Its Modelling', unpublished manuscript (Beijing: Beijing Normal University, 1996).

Groves, T., Y. Hong, J. McMillan and B. Naughton, 'Autonomy and Incentives in Chinese State Enterprises', *The Quarterly Journal of Economics,* 109 (1995).

Groves, T, Y. Hong, J. McMillan and B. Naughton, 'China's Evolving Labor Market', *Journal of Political Economy,* 103 (1994).

Kornai, J., *The Economics of Shortage* (Amsterdam: North Holland, 1980).

Kornai, J., *The Socialist System* (Princeton: Princeton University Press, 1992).

Krugman, P., 'The Myth of Asia's Miracle', *Foreign Affairs* (November/December 1994).

Landau, R., T. Taylor and G. Wright, *The Mosaic of Economic Growth* (Stanford: Stanford University Press. Stanford, 1996).

Lundgren, K., 'Why in Sweden? An Analysis of the Development of the Large Swedish International Firms from a Learning Perspective', *Scandinavian Economic History Review,* 2 (1995).

Naughton, B., 'Chinese Institutional Innovation and Privatization from Below', *American Economic Review: Papers and Proceedings* (May 1994).

North D., ' Institutions, Transaction Costs and Economic Growth' *Economic Inquiry,* XXV (1987).

North, D.C., *Institutions, Institutional Change, and Economic Performance* (New York: Cambridge University Press, 1990).

North, D.C., 'The New Institutional Economics and Third World Development', in J. Harriss, I. Hunter, J. Lewis and M. Colins (eds), *The New Institutional Economics and Third World Development* (London: Routledge, 1995).

Rawlin, T.G., 'Chinese Industrial Reform: Accomplishment, Prospects, and Implications', *American Economic Review. Papers and Proceedings* (May 1994).

Rohwer, J., *Asia Rising: Why America Will Prosper As Asia's Economies Boom* (New York: Simon & Schuster, 1995).

Rosenberg N. and L.E. Birdzell., *How the West Grew Rich: The Economic Transformation of the Industrial World* (New York: Basic Books, 1986).

Rosenberg, N. and C. Frischtak, *International Technology Transfer. Concepts, Measures and Comparisons* (New York: Praeger Publishers, 1985), p. 7.

Weitzman, M. and C. Xu, 'Chinese Township Village Enterprises as Vaguely Defines Cooperatives', *Centre for Economic Performance. Discussion Paper No. 155* (Harvard: Harvard University, 1993).

Williamson, O.E., *Markets and Hierarchies: Analysis and Antitrust Implications* (New York: Free Press, 1975).

Williamson, O.E., *The Economic Institutions of Capitalism* (New York: Free Press, 1985).
Williamson, O.E., 'Strategizing, Economizing, and Economic Organization', *Strategic Managemant Journal,* 12 (1991).
Wu, Yu-Shan, *Comparative Economic Transformations. Mainland China, Hungary, the Soviet Union, and Taiwan* (Stanford: Stanford University Press, 1994).
Zhang, Gang, *Chinese Rural Enterprises between Plan and Market.* Doctoral Dissertation (Stockholm: Stockholm School of Economics, 1997).

4
On Lao Tzu: His Impact on Chinese Thinking

Zhang Wei-bin

The most essential and, perhaps, most economic way to understand a culture is to digest the dominant philosophies created by the culture. These influence how people feel and what they do, shape how they socially and culturally interpret their behavior, and determine what rewards people receive from their behavior. In this sense, in order to understand both ancient and modern China, it is important to study I Ching, Confucius and Lao Tzu. Their visions have played an essential role in the formation of Chinese cultural characteristics, such as, the emphasis on the significance of intuition, the respect for rationality, the work ethic and the obedience to authority.

Chinese philosophical thinking emerged and developed during a long period of warfare that caused great changes in China's political and social structure. The period of the fifth to the third centuries BC is called the 'Period of the Warring States'. It is also appropriate to call the period 'the Period of the Philosophers' since never was speculative thinking so widely and freely practiced as in this troubled period. As a result of competition among various states and other social factors, schools and philosophers who could lay claim to any originality in ideas won preferment as well as prestige. The social environment, as a whole, was relatively free for thinkers to mediate and distribute knowledge. During this period, the 'Hundred Schools' were founded. But this wealth of schools did not survive. From the Han dynasty on, the only ones to remain active were Confucianism and Taoism.

Confucianism and Taoism have been the dominant philosophical schools in China's history. Confucianism has influenced official morality and public life, while Taoism has primarily affected the spiritual life of individuals. Throughout much of China's long history, these two rival approaches to life competed for dominance. Confucianism emphasizes reason, traditional morality, and rigid order in society (Zhang 1998, 1999). On the other hand, Taoism emphasizes intuition, identification with nature, and endless change and flux. The former developed a complex body of precepts and commentary; the latter found its natural expression in art, literature, and poetry. The two doctrines thus play different social and psychological roles affecting Chinese life. In this essay, I will attempt to explain the fundamental viewpoints of Taoism about Tao, man and society.

Lao Tzu and the *Tao Te Ching*

It was said that Lao Tzu retired from office as a keeper of the records because he saw how corrupt society had become. He put aside earthly ambition and retired from the world. He wrote a book, known as *Tao Te Ching* (*The Classic of the Way and Its Virtue*), at the request of his friend, the custom house officer at the frontier. The *Tao Te Ching* is often referred to as the Book of Five Thousand Characters. In fact, the length of the text varies from version to version. It is a small book even allowing for the fact that ancient Chinese was a very concise language. Irrespective of its limited number of words, the book laid the foundation for the philosophy now known as Taoism. No one can understand China without some knowledge of its contents, for it has modified Chinese life and thought throughout history. The book has influenced Chinese philosophy, religion, government, art, medicine, and even cooking. The Taoist spirit has contributed to the growth of graphic arts and many crafts. In China, restraint and simplicity have been regarded as the hallmark of true greatness. This is well reflected in the best of Chinese poetry. Love of the simple and the unassuming is much influenced by the intuitive perception of the nature of the Tao.

In *Tao Te Ching*, Lao Tzu is mainly concerned with man. Most of the little book is devoted not to the substance of Tao but to its function, particularly to its operation in society. A main subject is that of human affairs, including ethics, government, and diplomacy. Lao Tzu emphasizes the significance of peace of mind and tranquillity of the spirit.

Tao and its function

The key concept of Taoism is Tao. It serves not only as the standard for man but for all other things as well. In the words of Lao Tzu:

> There is a thing confusedly formed, born before heaven and earth. Silent and void it stands alone and does not change, goes round and

> does not weary. It is capable of being the mother of the world. I know not its name, so I style it 'the way'.

There is no word in the English language that describes Tao because conventional language is inadequate for such a purpose. It is best understood by inference. 'Tao' is often left untranslated as it is regarded as indefinable. If it is translated, it is usually called the Way.

Tao is traditionally interpreted as the highest attainment of primordial intuition. Tao is preontological experience, which is gained through the identification of the subjectivity of man and the objectivity of things. For Lao Tzu, Tao was no limited way or method, but the transcendental First Cause. The entity called the Tao existed before the universe came into being. It has an essence which is genuine, and this genuineness is vouched for by the existence of the universe which it has produced and continues to sustain. But we can say nothing about the Tao beyond this.

In Taoism the nameless is equivalent to non-being and the named is equivalent to being. The basic characteristics of Tao as the eternal, the nameless, the source, and the substance of all things are explicitly and implicitly affirmed. The meaning of Tao cannot fully be represented by words.

> The way that can be spoken of is not the constant way; the name that can be named is not the constant name. The nameless was the beginning of heaven and earth; the named was the mother of the myriad creatures. (Lao Tzu)

Modern philosophies of sciences and language also illustrate the depth of this paragraph. The 'genuine truth' seems to be beyond the ability of any existing language, such as music, mathematics, painting and common languages, to manifest. According to Lao Tzu, the real act of 'seeing' is that the unnamable and the namable are identified. When one sees something, one sees that within nothing, many things are simultaneously concealed and revealed. Being is simultaneously the formlessness of being and the wonder of non-being. When one sees being, one is limited to the form of being.

Lao Tzu's main concerns were related to the realm of human affairs, the natural and the metaphysical. The human is no longer the criterion of what is good or true. The traditional belief that a supernatural being, heaven, is the ruler of the universe is replaced by the doctrine that the universe exists and operates by itself. Although the Tao is the 'mother' and 'ancestor' of all things, in no circumstances can Tao be thought of or used as 'God'. In the concept of Tao, the limitations of the finite human mind are realized, practically and sensibly. The transcendental would no longer be transcendental if it could be described, formulated and named. Lao Tzu's (as well as Confucius') philosophy, has meant the problem of the existence of God has never become a major intellectual concern in China.

Needham (1956) equals Tao with the Order of Nature, saying that Tao 'brought all things into existence and governs their every action, not so much by force as by a kind of natural curvature in space and time.' According to Needham, to declare independence from the ethical judgment of men, in spite of the ethical character of the culture in which Taoism emerged and thrived, is the greatest achievement of the Taoist movement.

Lao Tzu holds that both being and non-being are of importance. They complement and produce each other. Non-being is not empty and devoid of everything. It is devoid of limitations but not devoid of definite characteristics. Tao as non-being is not only positive in character, but it is basic. It provides the basic principle of the unity of multiplicity. Although being and non-being are both mentioned, through being, the value of non-being is revealed. All forms, objects, and essences are inherent in the void, yet Tao itself is indistinct and ineffable. Tao is the reality of all these things. Tao is neither chaotic nor unpredictable. Tao is 'mysterious' only in the sense of subtlety and depth, not in the sense of irrationality. Instead of the will of Heaven or human desires, there is the law of Nature.

Change and order

For Taoism the essence of life is change. When things obey Tao, all parts of the universe will form a harmonious whole and the universe will become an integrated organism. Lao Tzu holds that the dialectical world is a world of endless movement between conflicting forces. When one reaches one extreme and yet is free from it, one enters the realm of the unity of opposites, in which both extremes are immediately and spontaneously identified. Tao means the identity of opposites. It may be worthwhile to remark, as well, that Hegel argues that reality is a dialectical process in which things pass over into their opposites (Hegel 1959).

In *The Turning Point*, Capra (1982), a physicist at University of California, Berkeley, discusses cultural values and attitudes by making extensive use of Taoist thinking. He writes:

> The Chinese philosophers saw reality, whose ultimate essence they called Tao, as a process of continual flow and change. In their view all

phenomena we observe participate in this cosmic process and are thus intrinsically dynamic. The principal characteristic of the Tao is the cyclical nature of its ceaseless motion; all developments in nature – those in the physical world as well as those in the psychological and social realms – show cyclical patterns. The Chinese gave this idea of cyclical patterns a definite structure by introducing the polar opposites yin and yang, the two poles that set the limits for the cycles of change: 'The yang having reached its climax retreats in favor of the yin; the yin having reached its climax retreats in favor of the yang.'

Man and society

One of the characteristics of Chinese philosophy is that man is at the center of its main concerns. Unlike ancient Greek speculation on nature and Indian contemplation on the spirit, Chinese philosophy, whether Confucianism or Taoism, grew as a result of the deplorable conditions of the time. In Chinese philosophy, man is not an absolute existence. Man is a part of nature. The study of universe is not separated from the study of man.

Lao Tzu was concerned with the origin and meaning of life but declared that no man's explanation of it is absolute. While Tao is common to all, it is what each thing has obtained from Tao that makes it different from others. One of Lao Tzu's main objectives is how to cultivate virtue. Virtue is Tao endowed in the individual things. In other words, virtue is the individualizing factor, the embodiment of definite principles which characterize things. To cultivate virtue, it is essential to perceive Tao. The superior man is one who finds Tao in himself and whose life is centered on it. Lao Tzu holds that nature provides a perfect example in her inactive activity. A life of sensation is a life of instability and non-accomplishment. Until the 'inner consciousness is understood', true peace is impossible, but when it is known, detachment from action for the sake of action will be the result. The sage lets objectivity happen as it happens and deals with things according to their nature.

Lao Tzu admired the intuitive wisdom of the common man and consistently advocated a return to the simple life, to a spontaneous and truer understanding of nature. Lao Tzu laid down no rigid laws for behavior. Men's conduct should depend on their instinct and conscience.

Lao Tzu emphasizes having no desires. Having no desires simply means having no impure or selfish desires, not having no desires at all. While desires should be few, good ones are to be fulfilled. In Chinese aesthetic practice, tea drinking, landscape painting, poetry, and landscape gardening, are not to be deserted but to be enjoyed in their simplicity. Ethically Tao stands for a simple life that is free from cunning and cleverness, is not devoted to the pursuit of profit or marked by hypocritical humanity and righteousness, but is characterized by plainness, tranquillity, and purity. The symbol of simplicity is the uncorked block which is not spoiled by artifice. It stands for the original purity and unity of Tao. Artifice and eagerness for power or riches are nothing to a sage. The cultivation of Tao is attained through being frugal, selfless and still. Lao Tzu holds that one should remain in quiescence all the time. When one looks inward, censors one's passions, and ceases one's thoughts, one's mind becomes tranquil. The adept cultivates stillness to obtain sublime perception of the Way. Knowledge in the sense of cleverness and cunning is to be discarded, but knowledge of harmony and the eternal, contentment, where to stop, and the self is highly valued. The highest attainment of Tao is to reach knowledge of no-knowledge

Lao Tzu was concerned with the lives of common people. Whereas other ancient recluses ridiculed reformers and retired to farms, Lao Tzu came forward with a comprehensive program for social and political reconstruction for the happiness of all. If the sage is singled out as the one fit to rule, it is because he has cultivated virtue according to Tao. Lao Tzu launched severe attacks on political institutions and social mores:

> The people are hungry, it is because those in authority eat up too much in taxes that the people are hungry. The people are difficult to govern, it is because those in authority are too fond of action that the people are difficult to govern.

Lao Tzu held that the only authority is the way of life itself. Organization and institutions interfere with a man's responsibility to himself. The more any outside authority interferes with a man's use of life and the less the man uses it according to his own instinct and conscience, the worse for the man and the worse for the society. He argued:

> Whoever takes the empire and wishes to do anything to it I see will have no respite. The empire is a sacred vessel and nothing should be done to it. Whoever does anything to it will ruin it; whoever lays hold of it will lose it. Hence some things lead and some follow; some breathe gently and some breathe hard; some are strong and some are weak; some destroy and some are destroyed. Therefore the sage avoids excess, extravagance, and arrogance.

The government will give free development to the spiritual life of each individual in the state. Lao Tzu creates a doctrine of *laissez faire*. The sage takes no action and does not interfere with the people, and they will transform spontaneously and the world will be at peace on its own accord. Lao Tzu says:

> When the empire is ruled in accordance with the way, the spirits lose their potencies. Or rather, it is not that they lose their potencies, but that, though they have their potencies, they do not harm the people. Govern the state by being straightforward; wage war by being crafty; but win the empire by not being meddlesome. How do I know that it is like that? By means of this. The more taboos there are in the empire, the poorer the people; the more sharpened tools the people have, the more benighted the state; the more skills the people have, the further novelties multiply; the better known the laws and edicts, the more thieves and robbers there are.

Hence the sage says:

> I take no action and the people are transformed of themselves; prefer stillness and the people are rectified of themselves; I am not meddlesome and the people prosper of themselves; I am free from desire and the people of themselves become simple like the uncarved block. The best of all rulers is but a shadowy presence to his subjects. Next comes the ruler they love and praise; next comes one they fear; next comes one with whom they take liberties. When there is not enough faith, there is lack of good faith. Hesitant, he does not utter words lightly. When his task is accomplished and his work done the people all say, 'It happened to us naturally.'

According to Lao Tzu, one should follow the basic teaching of tranquillity to govern the country. One attains tranquillity through *wu-wei*, or non-action, engaging in quiescence, non-interference, and non-ambition. Thus, one is spontaneously transformed, tranquil, wealthy, and returns to original simplicity. The ruler and the people are identified with each other. This is the essence of the teaching of tranquillity. For Lao Tzu, to bring people together is to be humble towards them. Thus, harmony is achieved through humanity. Humanity is basic to the dissolution of hostility between opponents. Lao Tzu holds that the sage leads the people but does not master them; the sage does not seek to enlighten the people but makes them ignorant. Lao Tzu says that if the worthy is not exalted, the people will not compete; and if people have too much knowledge, they will be difficult to rule.

> Not to honour men of worth will keep the people from contention; not to value goods which are hard to come by will keep them from theft; not to display what is desirable will keep them from being unsettled of mind. Therefore in governing the people, the sage empties their minds but fills their bellies, weakens their wills but strengthens their bones. He always keeps them innocent of knowledge and free from desires, and ensures that the clever never dare to act. Of old who excelled in the pursuit of the way did not use it to enlighten the people but to hoodwink them. The reason why the people are difficult to govern is that they are too clever.

In Tao Te Ching, there is neither evidence of collectivism, anti-feudalism, or opposition to merchants, nor any condemnation of kings and barons. What Lao Tzu advocated is a life of plainness in which profit, cleverness, selfishness, and evil desires are all forsaken. Lao Tzu was against the talk of benevolence, filial piety and loyalty that was characteristic of Confucians, saying that insisting on the need for them is a sure sign of them being in decline. Laws, he felt, merely lead to an increase in the varieties of crime. Lao Tzu spurned both religious and civil ceremony as misleading and harmful spectacle, his faith and conduct depending upon no outward prop but upon inner accord with the conscience of the universe. Moral restrictions arise when the great harmony of the universe is discarded. Taoism is not against moral values. Instead, it sees the fundamental ground from which moral behavior emerges. Lao Tzu says that getting rid of moral principles benefits the people.

> When the great way falls into disuse, there are benevolence and rectitude; when cleverness emerges, there is great hypocrisy; when the six relations are at variance, there are filial children; when the state is benighted, there are loyal ministers.
>
> When the way was lost there was virtue; when virtue was lost there was benevolence; when benevolence was lost there was rectitude; when rectitude was lost there were the rites. The rites are the wearing thin of loyalty and good faith and the beginning of disorder; for knowledge is the flowery embellishment of the way and the beginning of folly.

The man of great compassion reveals his simplicity, holds to his original nature, rids himself of selfishness, and casts away covetousness. He has no need of artificial moral claims such as benevolence and righteousness, and he is free from all anxieties.

Lao Tzu has the utopian conceptions of a model state. Everything is reduced to the purest simplicity and both rulers and the people obtain all they require by the abstract contemplation of an abstract good. Lao Tzu suggested to return to the life of a single and simple community where people do not use their utensils, weapons, or carriages, and where they grow old and die without visiting one another. Like Plato, he seems to have considered that until kings are philosophers, or philosophers are kings, cities will never cease from ill and that the study of economics, law, or finance are unnecessary qualifications for a legislator. He even suggested that the people should be ignorant. No education is necessary in the state. Spirituality rather than political economy is to be the basis of the 'state'. The social order is achieved not through militarism, but spiritual culture. Its central value is not man's hopes and fears, but the calm passionlessness of man's high natures. The utopian state is summarized as follows:

> Reduce the size and population of the state. Ensure that even though the people have tools of war for a troop or a battalion they will not use them; and also that they will be reluctant to move to distant places because they look on death as no light matter. Even when they have ships and carts, they will have no use for them; and even when they have armour and weapons, they will have no occasion to make a show of them. Bring it about that the people will return to the use of the knotted rope, will find relish in their food and beauty in their clothes, will be content in their abode and happy in the way they live. Though adjoining states are within sight of one another, and the sound of dogs barking and cocks crowing in one state will be heard in another, they grow old and die without having had any dealings with those of another.

The influence of Lao Tzu on the modern Chinese mind

If the reader is familiar with the philosophy of modern linguistics or with the natural sciences, she may immediately recognize Lao Tzu's importance. To illustrate the possible impact of Lao Tzu on modern China, let us consider two important issues, economic liberalization and democratization. I have argued that Lao Tzu believed that a 'no-active policy' is the best policy. This is nothing but *laissez-faire* in modern terms. There is no 'cultural resistance' to economic liberalization by either Taoism or Confucianism (Zhang, 1998, 1999). This Taoist principle has been manifested in varied forms in Chinese intellectual life, although not in an institutionalized form. The impact of Lao Tzu on China's democratization is more complicated. It is perhaps sufficient to state that Lao Tzu did not believe that any single authority can stand for the truth.

References

Capra, F., *The Turning Point – Science, Society, and the Rising Culture* (New York: Simon and Schuster, 1982).

Hegel, G.W.F., *Encyclopedia of Philosophy*, translated by Gustav Emil Mueller (New York: Philosophical Library, 1959).

Lao Tzu, *Tao Te Ching*, translated with an Introduction by D.C. Lau (London: Penguin Books, 1963).

Needham, J., *Science and Civilization in China. Vol. II, History of Scientific Thought* (Cambridge: Cambridge University Press, 1956).

Zhang, W.B., *Japan versus China in the Industrial Race* (London: Macmillan, 1998)

Zhang, W.B., *Confucianism and Modernization – Industrialization and Democratization of East Asia* (London: Macmillan, 1999).

5

Value Systems and Organization of Scholarship and Research in East and West

Martin Beckmann

East Asia is in transition. Along with the economies, the value systems and institutions are changing towards those of the West. To scholars with scientific contacts in East Asia, this change has been quite apparent. One can only marvel at the incredible speed with which it has been accomplished. It is increasingly harder to make a distinction between the value systems and institutions in East and West. All in all, this is no cause for regret. But a look backward may be rewarding, not just to historians – and historians of science – but for a broader perspective of the possible approaches to learning, the drive for innovation and the possession of knowledge that are revealed thereby.

This essay is also part of an ongoing study on the economics of knowledge – including the economics of science. To get a clearer view of the competitive processes that drive Western, that is, modern science everywhere, a closer look at the Confucian approach to learning and scholarship should provide new insight.

The transition that is manifest in science has accompanied, perhaps anticipated, that in economic activities. Their interaction is well known and the subject of another study concerning their mutual dependence: science in needing financial and motivational support from the economy and the economy in receiving ideas and even blueprints for innovation from science (Beckmann forthcoming). How well this interaction works depends largely on institutions. This points once more to the relevance of studying the institutional framework of science, as it is now and as it once was in Confucian China.

In Western society science must be considered an economic activity. Scientists are engaged in full-time work, nowadays invariably as members of organizations set up entirely, or in part, to the pursuit of scientific research. Scientists seek to make careers in their chosen occupation. Their advancement depends crucially on success in their work, namely the discovery of new results that have been accredited to them. For scientific results – new theorems, new measurements or newly discovered objects or relationships – cannot be traded for money but are communicated speedily and free of charge in return for recognition of 'priority'. This results in a highly competitive game or even race among ambitious individuals (sometimes teams) in search of fame. Riches are sought after, too, mainly in the form of research monies. It is a world far removed from the tranquillity and serenity of an ivory tower (Reif 1961).

The Confucian way

Picture, by contrast, the way of the cultivated scholar, embodied perhaps most distinctly in the 'superior man' of Confucian tradition. His motivation is not the acclaim of others or any fame derived from innovations. His is the disinterested search for truth, through the immersion in an existing body of knowledge. 'Wishing to become sincere in their thought, they first extend to the utmost their knowledge', and 'Thereby a calm unperturbedness may be attained' (Legge 1991, p. 3).

There emerges a canonized body of knowledge, laid down in the classics, which must be studied and thoroughly appropriated. 'If we wish to carry our knowledge to the utmost, we must investigate the principles of all things ... But so long as all principles are not investigated, man's knowledge is incomplete' (p. 9), but 'The study of strange doctrine is injurious indeed' (p. 75).

The ideal scholar is thus not a person who pursues knowledge for prestige gain or a livelihood. Scholarship is the optimal use of cultivated leisure, attainable by persons of independent means. The body of knowledge thus cultivated by gentlemen scholars need not be static, but may expand gradually through new ideas gained through better interpretation and sometimes extrapolation. Such growth is an unintended by-product rather than the object itself of learning and scholarship. (Technology, not being part of classical knowledge is improved through practice by men of affairs or workers, rather than by scholars.) Natural science growing out of philosophy may well be a part of scholarly knowledge – as in Aristotle – but is engaged in for its own sake, not with a view to applications.

There is something very attractive in this image of the distinguished gentleman scholar of old compared to that of the successful researcher embodied in the contemporary 'jet professor'. After all, consumption is better than production, and, in the simplifying language of economics, the pursuit of knowledge in modern Western societies is unabashed production; the learning of classical scholars in classical antiquity and the East, particularly in traditional Chinese society, is (without apology) consumption. Just as consumption is superior to production, so the untrammelled pursuit of knowledge for its own sake is preferable to the rapidly paced chase after innovation.

Even in ancient China, the pursuit of knowledge through scholarship and learning was not entirely disinterested. Scholarship attested by the passing of examinations became the entering gate to careers in the government service. Entry into the state bureaucracy opened the prospects of both prestige and income. The best analysis of this system is still that of Max Weber. This system has now been relegated to the past, although high esteem for learning appears to have survived. Bureaucrats are now recruited from the cadres of the Party. Not enough is known outside China about the details of this, so they cannot be discussed here. However, modern science in contemporary China is increasingly organized along Western lines.

Max Weber[1] on Confucianism

Max Weber's analysis of Confucianism and Taoism (1934) was part of his wide-ranging study of 'world religions' under the aspect of discovering the mental attitude needed to give birth to 'modern capitalism' – which he found to be ideally present only in certain types of Christian Protestantism: Calvinism, and the ascetic Protestant sects.

Although not a sinologist by training (he was an economist turned sociologist), he had read widely and thoroughly on the subject of Confucianism and Taoism. In the following, we excerpt his observations pertinent to our subject (my translation):

> Social rank was determined by knowledge (Bildung) as made evident by examinations. (p. 395)
> In the 'Annals' officialdom and its advancement by 'merit' is glorified. (p. 403)
> Notable was also the absence of 'arithmetic', and of science, geography and (foreign) languages. (p. 414)
> There is no 'speculation' no formal 'logic' such subjects being considered 'fruitless', improper and in danger of being 'innovative'. (p. 416)
> The aim is 'canonically perfect, beautiful achievements'. (p. 420)

> It is the carrier of 'prestige'. (p. 422)
> Not 'specialization' but 'universality' through a 'classical education' ennobles a person. (p. 448)
> Perfection is achieved only through a never-ending literary study including 'reflection'. (p. 451)

In order to place Confucianism into sharper perspective, Max Weber also examined its opposite, 'Taoism', that is, Lao Tzu's metaphysics and ethics (see Chapter 4). Max Weber goes so far as to say that 'While Confucianism may be fully accessible only to a Chinese, Taoism in the original meaning is, by contrast, alien to any correct thinking Chinese' (p. 471). The inner contradictions of Taoism led ultimately to a 'strengthening of Confucianism as the accepted state philosophy' (p. 471).

The main points of the controversy between Confucius and Lao Tzu concern the dismissal of rational knowledge as a means to the achievement of one's own and society's welfare (p. 475). Max Weber also refers to the 'gigantic encyclopedia of 1715' (p. 475). In his summary, Max Weber reiterates that 'philosophical literary knowledge (Bildung) based on the ancient classics was the universal means of perfection' whereas 'Insufficient knowledge is the basis of all vice and evil (Unheil)'.

> 'For the individual the ideal is the development of a harmonically formed, balanced personality, manifest in 'gracefulness and dignity' (Anmut und Würde). (p. 514)
>
> The Confucian ethics rejects 'specialization' (Fachmenchentum). The educated man is not a means to an end but the end in itself. (pp. 532/3)

Western institutionalization of knowledge

In the remainder of this chapter we take a closer look at the institutional setting through which the value system of the West is able to operate in the science establishment.

New knowledge is produced from existing knowledge and labor. This requires in particular:

1 that existing knowledge be organized so as to be accessible and usable;
2 that labor be recruited, supported (financed) and motivated.

The organization and preservation of knowledge have been the traditional task of archives and libraries. The importance of their classification systems for scholarly access cannot be over-emphasized. More recently, computer aided retrieval has become a valuable adjunct to this.

For access to current work, researchers rely on professional journals which tend to proliferate and become ever more specialized. Even so, overlap is inevitable, particularly since writers seek multiple outlets. This is the result partly of rejections and of an attempt to foil the dictates of editors and referees, and partly of the search for the most prestigious outlets.

As a flood of publications, even in narrow specialties, continues to rise – 'of the making of books there is no end' was complained of even in biblical times – the need for survey articles arises (de Solla Price 1963). In short-lived specialties, one such article or monograph or text will suffice, but in growing fields there is a periodic need for publications that digest and describe the state of knowledge. In spite of these efforts at systematization, the use of current knowledge depends still very much on personal ties and/or geographic and language proximity (Beckmann and Persson 1996).

I turn now to the labor side. It was thought at one time that only persons of genius, that is, of the highest intelligence, with an insatiable scientific curiosity could find their vocation in science. Along with other sectors of the economy, science has grown and broadened. It needs now whole armies of researchers, and some of their members tend to be of rather ordinary qualification. As de Solla Price has argued persuasively, large numbers are needed to bring forth a cadre of scholars of the highest ingenuity and productivity.

Recruitment of personnel relies on the high social prestige of science and scholarship even in the market oriented 'capitalistic' societies of the West, where in spite of a widespread belief to the contrary, 'money is not everything'. Thus, occupational prestige continues to prevail against a ranking based purely on income and wealth, and the learned professions rank high. Additionally, the world of science and learning offers security to a greater degree than is possible in the purely market-oriented economic sectors; this in spite of the fact that success in research is beset with a high degree of uncertainty. From this we must conclude that the rewards distribution in science is much less skewed than the distribution of actual discoveries, or of successful publications based on such discoveries. Few have perished, although many more have not published in spite of a much vaunted saying to the contrary.

But the motivation of scholars and scientists is supposed to be the search for results carrying prestige accorded on the basis of publications. Recognition of such results, and their attendant prestige, takes its most observable form in citation. Citation analysis can in fact be utilized to measure prestige by not merely counting but weighing citations (Beckmann 1996). However unprecise the awarding of scientific prestige may be, prestige serves as the principal gage in assessing a candidate's qualifications for positions in academia and in research organizations.

One highly visible form of prestige gain is through the award of notable prizes, among which the Nobel prize stands out. Of these prizes can be said what Schumpeter has remarked in *Capitalism, Socialism and Democracy* concerning the role of profits in the market economy: 'Extraordinary rewards are showered on a lucky few so that the rest of us is goaded into making ever greater efforts.' (Schumpeter 1946).

Thus prestige is ultimately converted to cash, and prestige, however satisfying in itself, is powerfully bolstered by monetary rewards. The intermediate role of prestige is mandated by the fact, insufficiently recognized except in economic circles, that pure basic knowledge has no market value. Its communication to other persons is never a sale. Even the teaching of existing and new knowledge cannot be considered a sale of particular pieces of knowledge each carrying a price tag, but is paid for on a time basis regardless of the items chosen for presentation by the teacher. Teaching is lucrative only of subjects deemed to have 'educational value'. Such value is often created artificially through the setting of examination subjects, the examinations being the gateway to desirable occupations – the principle raised to perfection in Ancient China.

That pure basic research is thus removed from the bustle of the market place allows it great freedom and independence, characteristics highly cherished by the scientific community. In this regard the distance between the gentleman scholar and the indefatigable researcher is not so large after all.

This brief analysis of the organization of production and communication in science shows that the institutions of scientific activity in the modern Western world are particularly well adapted to the facilitation of rapid progress in knowledge. And that societies, aiming at unperturbed values and a stable social system, are well advised to canonize their knowledge and guard it against unwanted disturbances through innovation with unpredictable results.

Note

1. 'Max Weber was a genius, the likes of whom has never existed in sociology before or since. He showed what was possible in the striving for objective knowledge' (Shils 1980, p. 411).

References

Beckmann, M., *Author's Evaluation Based on Citation,* unpublished manuscript (Stockholm: Institute for Futures Studies, 1996).

Beckmann, M., *Interaction in the Growth of Science and the Economy* (forthcoming).

Beckmann, M., and O. Persson, *Scientific Collaboration as Interaction Over Distance,* unpublished manuscript (Stockholm: Institute for Futures Studies, 1996).

Legge, J., (translator) The Chinese English Bilingual Series of Chinese Classics*: The Great Learning. The Doctrine of the Mean. The Confucian Analects* (Ching Xia Hunan, 1991).

de Solla Price, D. *Little Science – Big Science* (New York: Columbia University Press, 1963).

Reif, R., 'The Competitive World of the Pure Scientist', *Science,* December (1961).

Schumpeter, J., *Capitalism, Socialism and Democracy* (New York: Harper, 1946).

Shils, E., *The Calling of Sociology* (Chicago: University of Chicago Press, 1980).

Weber, M., *Die Wirtschaftsethik der Weltreligionen I. Konfuzianismus und Taoismus, Gesammelte Aufsätze zu Religionssociologie I* (Tübingen: JCB Mohr, 1934) pp. 276–536.

6
Illiberal Democracy in Southeast Asia

Jan Engberg

The unprecedented economic growth in East and Southeast Asia has not entailed a corresponding dynamic political change. While most of the high-performing economies in the region have chosen fairly similar paths towards economic growth, the political systems show much greater variety. Communist one-party systems, full-fledged democracies and different versions of authoritarian regimes are all represented in the area. To be sure, several authoritarian governments in the region have improved their position on human rights rankings, and some countries have recently taken decisive steps into the realm of democracies, but a Western-style *process* of democratization does not seem to take place. On the contrary, new self-assured Asian varieties of democracy and human rights are evolving. If there is such a thing as dynamic political change in East and Southeast Asia, it is to be found within the context of 'Asian' alternatives.

The recent financial crisis in many East and Southeast Asian countries highlights the crucial relationship between political and economic development. After the fall of communism in Eastern Europe, Francis Fukuyama claimed that the only remaining challenge to Western liberal democracy was the authoritarian form of state-controlled capitalism developing in East and Southeast Asia (Fukuyama, 1992). Maybe the current economic turmoil will intensify the political struggle between Western and Asian alternatives. At present, it is interesting that both adversaries and advocates of 'Asian' alternatives to liberal democracy may find reason to support their views. On the one hand, the crisis could be explained in terms of inefficient, corrupt and uninformed regimes with low levels of legitimacy. Western-style rationality built upon good governance and liberal democratic procedures would be a natural remedy for such shortcomings. On the other hand, it is a fact that the crisis has struck South

Korea and Thailand very hard – two of the most recent examples of political systems changing to Western-style liberal democracy. Thus, some would argue that too much democracy is detrimental to economic development, particularly for countries in East and Southeast Asia.

What then, might be the essence of 'Asian alternatives to democracy'? Generally speaking, it is about restraining the ability of civil society to perform its function as agents for democratic control, interest intermediation and political participation. In such a system, the state is not a neutral arena where independent interests compete over scarce resources and government policies. Rather, it is the other way around: the state attempts to control societal interests. There are of course, many political systems that share these characteristics. Sometimes they are called authoritarian, semi-authoritarian, quasi-democratic, state-corporatist or half-dictatorships. What makes the Asian alternatives particularly interesting in this context is the ability of the states to rule with public consent. In a number of reasonably fair elections, the electorates have supported parties who have an outspoken goal to restrain democracy. In the Southeast Asian context, Malaysia and Singapore are the prime examples of this kind of democracy while the Philippines and Thailand are more open societies and Indonesia, Vietnam, Brunei, Cambodia, Myanmar and Laos are substantially more authoritarian (*Freedom Review*, 1996).

It seems as if a different concept is needed in order to cope with restrained democracies, separating them both from more democratic varieties and more authoritarian ones. It is sometimes suggested that restrained democracies can be referred to as *illiberal democracies* (Bell and Jayasuria, 1995; Chua, 1995). They are *illiberal* because they limit the activities of civil society, while at the same time being *democratic* in the sense that they provide political rights which enable people to have a choice in determining the nature of the system and its leaders.

There are a number of reasons why illiberal democracies should be high on the agenda for political analysts. First, East Asian experiences may have an impact on our understanding of democracy and democratization. For instance, European ideas on the historical role of social classes for the development of democracy, seem to have little relevance in the Asian context. Perhaps the pace and mode of modernization in Eastern Asia tends to produce its own logic of political development.

Second, in trying to outline the underpinnings of Asian alternatives to democracy, the tendency of East and Southeast Asian countries to become role models for other 'emerging economies' should be emphasized. Sustained growth figures of five to 10 per cent annually create some argumentative leverage, particularly since the economic miracle of East

Asia tends to reduce income inequality, improve the conditions for women, make people live longer, enhance education, and generally increase the standard of living (World Bank, 1995). Despite the fact that these empirical findings are mostly related to economic activities, it has become commonplace for Asian political leaders also to stress the (positive) role of Asian political systems when miracle affairs are discussed. It is no surprise that many political leaders from developing countries study the development of East and Southeast Asia when new strategies for economic growth, political stability and social security are called for.

Third, illiberalism could be regarded as a solution, not only to economic growth, but also for ruling elites having problems with their own political legitimacy. The performance-oriented nature of illiberal politics could be attractive to political systems where other sources of legitimacy have failed. Thus, the attractiveness of illiberalism goes beyond economic measures. Illiberalism could become a stable authoritarian variety of democracy, much the same as there are different forms of democracy among liberal democratic countries. If there is something robust about illiberal democracy, then conventional theories on democratization will have to be modified. Illiberalism, in that case, is not a stage in a development sequence, but rather a distinct form of political organization. To what extent this is true for Southeast Asia is the main issue to be addressed in this essay.

However, before we can analyze the potential of illiberalism to become a democratic alternative, a number of initial questions have to be answered. How does illiberalism work? What are the mechanisms that seem to produce illiberalism? And, what are the challenges facing illiberal practice?

The focus of this essay will be on Malaysia and Singapore, since they are the prime examples of illiberal systems, but occasional references will also be made to other cases in East and Southeast Asia.[1]

Illiberalism at work

If states in East Asia are not neutral, what is it then that they are not neutral about? In short, it is about how conflicts between political interests should be settled. In the liberal tradition, political interests manage their disputes over resources, recognition and authority by way of an orderly and competitive process. They make their demands based upon power and influence; they negotiate, compromise or vote. In the Asian context, conflicting political interests are managed through a process of state guidance and direction, supported by an elaborate system of social controls.

The rationale behind the illiberal practice of restraining civil society reflects a feature within liberal democracy itself – democracy may coexist with different degrees of liberalism and *vice versa* (Zakaria, 1997). In the real world this means that a particular country may develop a very impressive system of free and fair elections, thus demonstrating the existence of *political rights* and, at the same time, limit a number of *civil liberties* concerned with the rule of law and the freedom of speech, assembly, religion and property. Furthermore, a political system may very well allow considerable civil liberties and at the same time restrict democratic processes. The first case illustrates a growing number of countries in the developing world – these are the illiberal political systems. The second example reflects European experiences, where for instance property rights and the rule of law were introduced much earlier than universal adult suffrage. In its extreme, the combination of civil liberties and restricted political rights may be referred to as a case of liberal autocracy (Hong Kong before 1997 may be a good example).

Using the rank ordering system of Freedom House, an American research organization where political rights and civil liberties are measured according to seven-point scales (lower points are better), it is possible to give the notion of illiberalism an empirical meaning. Any country where there are better provisions for political rights than civil liberties could, theoretically, be called illiberal (lower scores for political rights than civil liberties); but such an exercise would hardly be meaningful. If the emphasis were on the propensity for change towards democracy, only countries within a certain realm of rights and liberties would be of interest. Freedom House makes a distinction between countries that are 'free,' 'partly free,' and 'not free.' Among the 60 countries labeled as partly free, 21 have lower ratings on political rights than civil liberties. Thus, more than one third of those countries closest to becoming democracies could be referred to as illiberal. Using a broader category of countries, Zakaria (*ibid.*) demonstrates that since 1990, the proportion of illiberal countries among those involved in democratization tends to increase. Also, there are very few cases of illiberal democracies becoming liberal (*ibid.*). Malaysia and Singapore are not the only examples of illiberal political systems, but they are perhaps the most elaborate ones; therefore, it could be instructive now to turn to the question as to how these liberal systems work.

In the parliamentary arena, control is achieved first and foremost through the development of dominant party systems. These are not coalitions in a regular sense, but systems of authority that penetrate almost all aspects of society. Malaysia, Singapore and Indonesia all have dominant party systems and, up until quite recently, this was also the case for South Korea, Taiwan and Japan. In a dominant party system, party membership or active party support is a necessary condition for employment, government aid, business contracts, licenses, credits, educational opportunities, and access to governmental channels. Individuals, groups, and local communities who do not support the dominant party in elections face severe difficulties. Individuals may lose their jobs, housing facilities or career opportunities. Communities who vote for the opposition might find government support for local communications and education reduced or withdrawn. Paternalistic leadership and respect for authority become important features in illiberal democracies because societal control creates patterns of dependencies of a top-down nature. Therefore, in a dominant party system the relationship between the electorate and its representatives will be more of a patron–client type than a citizen–government relationship. Despite the fact that opposition parties sometimes get enough electoral support to acquire parliamentary seats, politics in illiberal democracies is more about controlling the electorate than the government.

Legal fine-tuning is another control mechanism at the disposal of illiberal governments. It refers to a practice whereby the rule *by* law replaces the rule *of* law as a judicial principle (Katzenstein, 1996). In real terms, it means that the government can outlaw any kind of behavior it dislikes. People are regarded as managerial problems and as such they can be manipulated in a number of ways. If co-optation, rewards or coercion does not work, then laws may be promulgated to deal with the problems. The intellectual heritage of this principle comes from the colonial powers, who gave themselves arbitrary power to suppress dissent through a variety of colonial emergency laws (Tremewan, 1996). In the modern world of Southeast Asia this tradition of administrative lawmaking has survived. Thus, in Singapore the Societies Act defines all action outside approved political parties as illegal and subversive. All associations of more than ten people must register and provide information about the aims, constitution and personnel of the organization. If the registrar should find the association to be undesirable or contrary to the national interest, it will, according to section 4 in the Societies Act, be rejected (*ibid.*). In Malaysia the Sedition Act regulates what can be discussed regarding ethnic affairs. The Official Secret Act prescribes what governmental information can be made official. In Malaysia the Internal Security Act provides the Minister of Home Affairs with the power to detain without trial anyone considered to be likely to act in any manner prejudicial to the security of Malaysia

(Crouch, 1992). Typically, laws of this nature are open-ended, which makes them work as pre-emptive legislation. Given the fact that judges and/or politicians can interpret the laws in an arbitrary way, potential dissidents may find it too costly to protest against government policies.

Societal control can also be very material in character. The Singaporean State owns 75 per cent of the land, provides almost all infrastructure, housing, health and facilities for education. It controls wages and labor unions and regulates the supply of labor. It dominates the domestic financial market and runs state corporations and joint ventures (Tremewan, *ibid.*). A state with this kind of position will have a unique opportunity to create patterns of dependencies, where ordinary citizens will find it extremely difficult to find other sources of material and social security than those provided by the government. In Malaysia the dominant party, UMNO, has been instrumental in creating a new Malay middle class through a policy of affirmative action, whereby Malays are given precedence in business, education and administration over the economically dominant ethnic Chinese population. The purpose of the policy is to satisfy Malay demands for more power and wealth, thereby trying to defuse conflicts based on ethnic inequality. In order to implement the program a massive re-allocation of resources was conducted. First, the government forced established Chinese and foreign enterprises to restructure in such a way that at least 30 per cent of the shares would be owned by Malays – either government agencies acting on behalf of the Malay community or private Malay businessmen (Crouch, 1992). Second, the Malay-dominated government launched a huge program for the establishment of large state-owned corporations in heavy industry, energy, transportation and agriculture (Gomez and Jomo, 1997). These economic transformations, combined with other measures of societal control, have undoubtedly been instrumental in creating a Malay middle class that perhaps is more a product of public policies than of modernization itself.

A popular strategy by governments trying to control civil society is to use pre-emptive and co-optative strategies. Typically, most literature on the subject refers to European welfare states, where all-embracing governments try to pre-empt conflicts by building new institutions, programs and organizations. The strategy is to control the agenda and the activity of potentially problematic groups by inviting them to an orderly form of interest intermediation. If there are no consumers' organizations, no associations for foreign workers, or no women's groups, the government may allow budgetary means for such organizations to develop. Or, the government can establish new public offices with the purpose to represent under-represented segments of the population. In illiberal democracies, pre-emptive and co-optative strategies flourish. In the case of Singapore, this is evident in the construction of parapolitical institutions such as Community Centres, Citizens' Consultative Committees, Residents' Committees, and Town Councils. In all these cases the government is providing both the rules and aims of the organization and the candidates for leading positions. The general purpose of parapolitical institutions seems to be twofold: 'to disseminate information to the people about government policies and to provide feedback on local opinions by means of which the government is able to assess local support' (Hill and Fee, 1995).

For as long as Malaysia and Singapore have been independent states, the dominant parties have had an overwhelming support from a majority of the electorate. In Singapore, the Peoples' Action Party (PAP) has ruled since 1965 with very few incidents of opposition politics. The first opposition Member of Parliament was elected in 1981. The electoral support for the PAP has been 63 per cent in 1988, 61 per cent in 1991 and 65 per cent in 1997. The slow decline in the 1991 election caused many observers to predict the coming of a new era in Singapore with a greater role for opposition parties. However, moving into the 1997 electoral campaign, the PAP excelled in illiberal measures by changing electoral boundaries in favor of the incumbent, by promising to upgrade Housing and Development Board (HDB) estates in constituencies that supported the ruling party, by issuing a very short (9 days) campaign period, and by using the judicial system to bankrupt the opposition (after the election) (Chin, 1997). The strategy was successful as the PAP made its best election since 1984. But the massive support for the PAP should not be regarded as representing total electoral homogeneity. By looking into results in different constituencies it becomes clear that class, religion and ethnicity play a role in Singaporean politics. The inability of those cleavages to become important political forces does say something important about the strength of illiberal politics.

The dominant party in Malaysia, the United Malay National Organization (UMNO) has a less secure position in terms of electoral support than is the case for the PAP in Singapore. This is evident in the history of UMNO, where clear dividing lines between different factions within UMNO can be observed. Since 1986 and the split within UMNO, open competition between parties has become more important. The government in Malaysia is composed of the 14-party coalition, Barisian Nasional (National Front), which is dominated by the UMNO. The coalition is largely built upon ethnic and regional cleavages and represents an effort to harmonize (and control) potentially conflicting interests. In the 1990 elections, UMNO and the Barisian Nasional for the first time had to fight against a coalition of opposition parties. Even though the ruling coalition won the elections in terms of seats in the parliament, its electoral support was reduced to 53.4 per cent compared to 57 per cent–61 per cent in the past (Crouch, 1992). However, order was restored in the 1995 election when the ruling coalition won a landslide victory, securing 64 per cent of the votes (*Keesing's Record of World Events*, 1997).

How is the electoral arena to be evaluated in illiberal political systems? On the one hand, the restrictions imposed by illiberal practice makes the democratic content of the elections highly questionable. On the other hand, electoral processes, the nature of opposition politics, the growth of Non-Governmental Organizations (NGOs), incidents of cultural resistance, the sometimes critical role of the mass media and the voices of independent intellectuals, make the political climate much more interesting in illiberal democracies compared with more authoritarian regimes. The strong electoral support for dominant parties in Malaysia and Singapore cannot totally be explained as a result of successful illiberal practices. Sustained economic growth is a very strong argument on any electoral arena and, in the case of Malaysia and Singapore, economic growth has been impressive for more than two decades. Moreover, supporting a dominant party for economic reasons is not a novel feature of Southeast Asian politics. However, the extent of the support for the PAP and UMNO would be unheard of in a Western democratic context, which indicates that additional explanations are called for. A typical argument would be that, in East and Southeast Asian political history, there are few examples of grand coalitions or political compromises involving opposing ideologies. This indicates that notions of pluralism and tolerance would be less common in the Asian context.

East and Southeast Asian states never did draw the 'lesson' that political systems must be founded on general principles to widely different moral outlooks and interests groupings, much less the idea that the state ought to be neutral between all conceptions of the good life. Instead, East and Southeast Asian political understanding places great value on substantive moral consensus that denies or suppresses moral pluralism and social diversity (Bell and Jayasuriya, 1995, p. 8).

If there is a widespread public sentiment that 'moral pluralism' is threatening and possibly disruptive for society as a whole, then it is hardly surprising that political parties that advocate such views and, at the same time, demonstrate an ability to pursue stability and well-being, also receive sustained electoral support.

Challenges to illiberalism

According to mainstream modernization theory, economic growth and technical achievements tend to create new interests and new loyalties. When a sufficient number of people are able to define such common interests, they will mobilize and organize in order to maximize their goals. They will do so in competition with other interests and with traditional authorities. In that process, patterns of loyalties change from vertical to horizontal, from authoritarian forms of hierarchy to collective identities. These identities define a civil society, which in a theoretical sense is located between the private sphere and the state. Empirically, social classes will form the most important part of civil society and, depending on the distribution of resources and ability to mobilize people, classes will define a new political system. Whether this system is oriented towards a revolutionary or reformist order has very much to do with the strength of the middle class. Traditionally the middle class is the only social entity that can successfully mediate between modernist demands for democracy and greater participation on the one hand, and traditional values and practices on the other. Furthermore, the middle class has, because of its relative affluence, a vested interest in a productive society characterized by order and stability. Thus, a growing middle class involved in rapid modernization will, owing to self-interest and societal pressure, pursue a change toward liberal democracy. At least this is the way modernization theorists usually read their history.

What is the relevance of the modernization/middle-class hypothesis in East Asia? To begin with, the middle class is a growing phenomenon. It is estimated that around 2010 there will be 700 million people in China, India and Indonesia who will enjoy a living standard comparable to that of the average Spaniard (*Economist,* 1994). Another estimate claims that around the turn of the century, Asia will have 259 million people or 79 million households with incomes of US$18 000 (calculated at purchasing power parity) (*Fortune,* 1994). Regardless of measure or statistical source, there is definitely a new middle class emerging in Southeast Asia; but it is quite another matter to establish what political impact this new class carries. In the wider Asian context it appears that intellectuals and middle-class businessmen have been quite instrumental in the recent transformations to democracy in Taiwan, South Korea and Thailand. It is probably safe to say that the new NGOs that are emerging in the region, particularly in Thailand, Indonesia and Malaysia are dominated by middle class members but it is difficult to assess their impact. In Singapore, there are few records of middle-class activity with political underpinnings (Rodan, 1996). It seems as if the symbiosis between economic growth and illiberalism is a system that the middle-class actually thrives on.

Maybe the key to understanding the ambiguous and passive nature of the East Asian middle class, when it concerns political activity, has to do with the character of state–society relationships. The fact that the governments of, especially, Malaysia and Singapore have intervened in almost all aspects of the economy throughout their short history of nationhood, may have had profound effects also on the relationship between the citizens and the state. If the state were regarded as the guarantee for economic growth and prosperity, then the middle class would have few incentives to complain. In analyzing the role of the political opposition in Malaysia, Jesudason (1996) introduces the concept of the syncretic state. He writes:

> The syncretic state operates at a multi-dimensional level, mixing coercive elements with electoral and democratic procedures; it propagates religion in society as it pursues secular economic goals; it engages in ethnic mobilization while inculcating national feeling; and it pursues a combination of economic practices ranging from liberal capitalism, state economic intervention, to rentier arrangements.
> (Jesudason, 1996, p. 131)

In practice, every group, interest or elite in a syncretic state has an incentive to be subordinate, low-tuned and supportive of the ruling order because of the benefits that are provided and because of the potential for repression. In that sense, illiberal democracy is built upon an intricate web of patron–client relations that structure state–society relations. This is particularly evident in the way the economy is organized in Malaysia. There seem to be different economies for different segments of citizens:

> There is a rentier segment for accumulating resources for political patronage, a protected sector for politically important small and aspiring business men, a quasi-monopolistic segment for well connected business men and large state companies, and a sizeable competitive arena comprising multinationals, local Chinese companies, and a few Malay companies to ensure national competitiveness.
> (*ibid*., p. 135)

Typical forms of interest formation such as class, ethnicity, religion, age and locality would have a hard time to develop opposition roles in such a system. Every effort to construct horizontal loyalties needed in a process of political mobilization would be hampered by the fact that potential members of such causes would find themselves in different (vertical) segments.

Illiberal systems tend to structure their political and economic systems in a way that counteract independent political mobilization – not just middle-class opposition. It is true that the middle class in East and Southeast Asia, as in any other place in the world, has more resources to use for political purposes, but the role of the middle class in a historical perspective is not homogeneous. Whenever middle-class interests are threatened, some kind of political reaction can be expected, but it is not altogether easy to predict to what extent actions will be left or right, democratic or authoritarian.

A second challenge for illiberalism could be a variety of international pressures and external conditions. It seems as if Western governments, and particularly the United States are launching more and more campaigns against Asian countries for alleged human rights violations. This is a recurrent issue in international negotiations and bilateral talks. There is also a growing movement in Western countries which addresses questions relating to labor rights in Asia. Here the background could be less virtuous, since labor in Europe and North America is competing for jobs with their Asian colleagues. The Asian response to international pressure on matters of democracy and human rights is quite interesting. Typically, an authoritarian state would deny any accusation of human rights violations and would put much effort into proving that violations were not taking place. Not so with illiberal democracies. Knowing that they have substantial popular support for their views on rights and duties, illiberal elites are launching a counter-offensive that sometimes is labeled the Asian Way.

Senior minister Lee Kuan Yew in Singapore, Prime Minister Mahathir bin Mohamad in Malaysia and former president Soeharto in Indonesia are the major proponents of this offensive strategy. They claim that Western ideals of individualism, pluralism, democracy and welfare statism are inferior to Asian values and generally unsuitable in the Asian context. The Singaporean alternative is formulated in a White Paper on Shared Values, presented to the parliament in January 1991. It has several components but the major invention reads: 'Nation before community and society above self.' It stresses the importance of the family as the basic building block of society and emphasizes consensus instead of contention when it comes to resolving major issues (Chua, 1995). Generally speaking, advocates of the Asian Way are trying to reconstruct Asian values, inspired by some version of

Confucianism and from neo-conservative notions of communitarianism. Taken together, the perspective leads to a society where the individual is subordinated to various collectives: the family, the community and the state; and where the collectives themselves are supposed to be led by virtuous and paternalistic leaders. Interestingly, president Soeharto's rejection of IMF demands for economic liberalization during Indonesia's recent economic crises was motivated in terms of 'Asian values'. Apparently, the constitution of Indonesia was not in concord with liberal (individualistic) capitalism: Soeharto argued that the economy of Indonesia was to be founded on 'family values' (*Dagens Nyheter*, 1998).

Another form of external challenge to illiberal democracies could derive from the integrative processes that Southeast Asian countries are involved in. The Association of Southeast Asian States (ASEAN) has not achieved much in terms of integration, but represents a first element in an evolving pattern of interstate cooperation. Looking at the charter of the ZOPFAN declaration (Declaration on the Zone of Peace, Freedom and Neutrality), which is a part of ASEAN's security undertakings, the overall impression is that the member states should not interfere in each other's internal affairs. Instead, all cooperation is expected to take into account national sovereignty and national identities (Luhulima, 1995). Given these typical formulations from states who do not want discussions about internal affairs, it is interesting to observe that other, more involving, forms of integration are taking place within ASEAN. Several cases of subregionalism, often referred to as growth triangles, have been established. These triangles define a border region between different states as growth areas, where the complementarity of capital, labor and land is to be optimized (Thambipilla, 1991). Already the southern triangle between Singapore, Johor in Malaysia and the Riau archipelago has been declared a success in terms of investments, dividends and spin-off effects on local economies. A northern triangle is projected to combine northern Malaysia, southern Thailand and eastern Sumatra (Thant and Tang, 1996). Another triangle is proposed to encompass Brunei and parts of Indonesia, Malaysia, and the Philippines. Interestingly, it seems as if the triangles have had some impact also on other policy areas, apart from matters of investment and production. It appears as if border conflicts, communication issues, military cooperation and other foreign policy areas are easier to discuss at a subregional level (Weatherbee, 1995; Bridges, 1997). At the same time, owing to increased subregional cooperation, it becomes more difficult to separate domestic from international affairs. Thus, Southeast Asian leaders may have to accept more political issues relating to sovereignty, political legitimacy and regional disparities.

External pressures and effects of subregional integration could be a challenge for illiberalism to handle because the issues at stake create new agendas. The East versus West debate provokes Asian national leaders to dichotomize a political arena that up until now has been dominated by harmony and consensus. By talking about them and us and by making distinctions between good and bad values, the whole concept of the East Asian Miracle has changed. Anti-communism, sovereignty and economic growth are no longer sufficient as core values. The political repertoire has expanded.

A third challenge to illiberalism is information and knowledge of rights and duties. Through internationalism, information technology and improved levels of education, it has become increasingly difficult for political elites to provide 'monolithical' truths. Trying to impose Asian values on a Chinese population which has no word for Asia could be a rather difficult operation. Talking about communitarian values in economies that thrive on individualism must be confusing for most people. Using Confucianism for the purpose of establishing new values ought to be disturbing for people who know that Confucianism, like Protestantism, can be used both to defend modernity and to reject it, to advocate subordination as well as to propose individual freedom. Legal fine-tuning, as a way to control people, will become increasingly difficult to use in a global culture where knowledge of international standards of rights and duties are well known. Manipulating ethnic groups for the purpose of achieving social harmony can be difficult in times when the right to self-determination has gained a new international meaning. Again, each individual curiosity or contradiction may not be all that important but, taken together, they could destroy the legitimacy of illiberal democracy.

The future of illiberalism

Illiberal democracy is probably as old as the notion of democracy itself. Political elites have always tried to compensate for their lack of legitimacy and popularity with intriguing combinations of rewards, punishments and controls. In that sense, it is not really surprising that the ruling elites in illiberal systems are trying to invent an ideology – The Asian Way – to support their own power ambitions and to resist foreign influence. But illiberal regimes in East and Southeast Asia are under increased pressure from their own hierarchies, their constituencies and from foreign sources, to reconstruct and reformulate their political systems towards liberal democracies. This is particularly true in a situation where East and

Southeast Asia are enduring severe economic crises with ramifications all over the world. The economies in the region are dependent on markets governed by liberal democratic systems to such a degree that any ideological challenge, followed by investment and trade disturbances, would result in a gigantic loss of profit and state revenues. In such a case major investors, political elites and local middle-class interests might find a mutual interest in pursuing democratic change. Maybe Huntington was right when he wrote:

> For three hundred years on every continent, economic development has been the central force generating conditions favorable to the emergence of democratic regimes. In East Asia, paradoxically, a slackening of economic growth, such as may be occurring, could be the force generating transition from Asian-style dominant party democracy to Western-style competitive party democracy.
>
> (Huntington, 1993, p. 42)

Western countries are not the only ones to contest illiberal politics. The democratic achievements made by South Korea and Taiwan create a new argumentative leverage in the region. This is particularly important since role models have always been important in East Asian politics. And maybe, in the aftermath of the financial crisis, new role models will emerge. Taiwan (and China, for different reasons) seems to be mysteriously unaffected by the economic crisis that has struck Indonesia, Thailand, Malaysia and South Korea with such vigor. It appears as if Taiwan has been able to handle the effects of over-heated economic growth much more rationally than other 'tiger economies'. The *Economist* (1998) maintains that Taiwan probably has the best 'economic fundamentals in Asia: large foreign exchange reserves, a current-account surplus, little foreign borrowing and a healthy banking sector'. Perhaps the miracle story will change location. The forecasts for 1998 indicate that China will have a GDP growth of 6.3 per cent and Taiwan 5.0 per cent. The 1998 forecasts for Indonesia, Malaysia and Thailand are less inspiring: –5.2 per cent, 1.6 per cent and –4 per cent respectively (*Economist, ibid.*).

Going back to the initial question about illiberal democracy being a distinct variety of democracy, or a stage in a process of democratization, the arguments so far seem to support a process character of illiberalism. International pressure, domestic elitist demands, the anachronistic nature of culturalist demands and the rise of new role models, would all point towards the demise of illiberal democracy. This conclusion would also be in concord with mainstream theory on democratization.

Thus, Huntington (1991) questions the ability of East Asian systems that combine Western procedures with Confucian values to last during prolonged economic downturn. Mancur Olson (1993) maintains that autocracies 'rarely have good economic performance for more than a generation' (*ibid.*, p. 567). According to Olson, this is so because the security of property and contract rights is necessary for economic growth, and democracy is the only political system that can facilitate these rights. In a recent study covering 43 societies, Inglehart (1997) demonstrates with an impressive empirical record that democratic values, economic development and cultural change go together in a coherent and even predictable way. 'With rising levels of economic developments, cultural patterns tend to emerge that are increasingly supportive of democracy' (*ibid.* p. 330).

If these empirical and theoretical considerations almost invariably point towards poor prospects for illiberal democracy, why is illiberalism a growing phenomenon? So far the discussion about illiberal political practice has focused on 'emerging economies', or countries in 'transition' in relation to full-fledged democracies – Western style. Maybe this is unfortunate. Whenever democratic conditions or democratization is analyzed, the point of departure is usually an *ideal type* of Western democracy. This is perfectly right as long as the ideal type at least rudimentarily corresponds with the *real type*. If this is not the case the analysis will be regarded as anachronistic if not obsolete. Perhaps this is the perception that many political leaders in the developing world have of liberal democracy; and there is probably some truth to it. Western democracy as a point of departure for evaluating political systems is increasingly becoming a moving target. First of all, the ability of liberal democracy to deliver that which it is supposed to deliver – namely material well-being, social security and political stability – is very much put into question. At least this is true for an increasing number of people who are unemployed, disabled, aging, single parents or immigrants, or worse, any combination thereof. These groups of citizens are also politically weak, as their political representation is almost absent. Second, liberal democracies are suffering from systemic problems that concern low voting turnouts, difficulties in recruiting new party members, increased tension between citizens and non-citizens, inability to adapt political ideologies to changing cleavage structures and problems in defining spheres of autonomy and nationality in a transnational world.

These are uncertainties that ruling elites and citizens, in emerging economies and transition countries, can relate to in different ways and it is not self-evident that liberal alternatives will succeed. The attractiveness of *illiberal* democracy in developing and transition countries could be that it appears to facilitate effective governance in a historical situation where few other sources for such governance are to be found. Effective governance implies, among other things, the absence of corruption, an emphasis on meritocracy and education, the rule of law and generally an ability to make rational decisions in response to challenges and to implement what has been decided. In that sense, effective governance is about managing the difficult tension between stability and change.

In political settings where effective governance is made particularly difficult through border conflicts, ethnic strife or chronic usage of political violence, it must be tempting to restrain whatever seems to facilitate social unrest and government inefficiency. Thus, interest formation and mobilization and other important aspects of civil liberties would often run the risk of being defined as problems and not as creative features of political life. If, at the same time, a repressive (illiberal) formula can be combined with a potential for economic growth, then the imagined 'hazard' associated with elections and political rights can be accepted by elites who normally would resent democracy. Thus, the attractiveness of illiberal politics – the practice of allowing for political rights *and* limiting civil liberties – is on the rise, since such a scheme forebodes political efficiency and stability at locations where such qualities are unheard of or severely contested.

Notes

1. Although the emphasis is on Southeast Asia, 'East Asia' will be used when matters of interest for the whole region are discussed.

References

Bell, D.A. and K. Jayasuriya, 'Understanding Illiberal Democracy: A framework'. In D.A. Bell, D. Brown, K. Jayasuriya and D.M. Jones, *Towards Illiberal Democracy in Pacific Asia* (Oxford: St Martin's Press 1995).

Bridges, B., 'Beyond Economics: Growth Triangles in Southeast Asia', *Asian Perspective*, 21 (1997) 55–77.

Chin, J., 'Anti-Christian Chinese Chauvinist and HDP upgrades: the 1997 Singapore general election', *South East Asia Research*, 5 (1997) 217–41.

Chua, B.H., *Communitarian Ideology and Democracy in Singapore* (London: Routledge, 1995).

Crouch, H., 'Authoritarian trends, the UMNO split and the limits to state power', in J. Kahn and K.W. Lo (eds), *Fragmented Vision-Culture and Politics in Contemporary Malaysia* (Honolulu: University of Hawaii Press, 1992).

Dagens Nyheter, 8 March, 1998.

Economist, 15 October 1994.

Economist, 7 March 1998.

Fortune 29 May 1994.

Freedom Review No. 1, 1996

Fukuyama, F., *The End of History and the Last Man* (London: Hamish Hamilton, 1992).

Gomez, E.T. and K.S. Jomo, *Malaysia's Political Economy: Politics, Patronage and Profits* (Cambridge: Cambridge University Press, 1997).

Hill, M. and L.K. Fee, *The Politics of Nationbuilding and Citizenship in Singapore* (London: Routledge, 1995).

Huntington, S.P., *The Third Wave: Democratization in the Late Twentieth Century* (University of Oklahoma Press, 1991).

Huntington, S.P., 'American Democracy in Relation to Asia', in R. Bartley, C.H. Chee, S.P. Huntington and S. Ogata (eds), *Democracy & Capitalism – Asian and American Perspective* (Singapore: Institute of Southeast Asian Studies, 1993).

Inglehart, R. *Modernization and Postmodernization: Cultural, Economic and Political Change in 43 Societies* (Princeton: Princeton University Press, 1997).

Jesudason, J.V., 'The syncretic state and the structuring of oppositional politics in Malaysia' in G. Rodan, (ed.), *Political Oppositions in Industrialising Asia* (London and New York: Routledge, 1996).

Jones, D.M., K. Jayasuriya, D.A. Bell and D. Brown, 'Towards a Model of Illiberal Democracy'. In D.A. Bell, D. Brown, K. Jayasuriya and D.M. Jones (eds) *Towards Illiberal Democracy in Pacific Asia* (Oxford: St Martin's Press, 1995).

Katzenstein, P.J., 'Regionalism in Comparative Perspective', *Cooperation and Conflict* 31 (1996) 123–59.

Keesing's Record of World Events, 41 (1997) No. 4.

Luhulima, C.P.F., 'ASEAN's Security Framework', *The Asia Foundation's Center for Asian Pacific Affairs* (CAPA) *Report No. 22* (1995) pp. 1–11.

Olson, M., 'Dictatorship, Democracy and Development', *American Political Science Review*, 3 (1993) 567–76.

Rodan, G., 'State Society Relations and Political Opposition in Singapore' in G. Rodan, (ed.) *Political Oppositions in Industrialising Asia* (London and New York: Routledge, 1996).

Thant, M., and M. Tang, (eds), *Indonesia–Malaysia–Thailand Growth Triangle: Theory and Practice* (Manila: Asian Development Bank Publication, 1996).

Thambipilla, P., 'The ASEAN growth triangle: the convergence of national and sub-national interests', *Contemporary Southeast Asia*, 3 (1991) 122–44.

Tremewan, C., *The Political Economy of Social Control in Singapore* (Oxford: St Martin's Press, 1996).

Weatherbee, D.E., 'The Foreign Policy Dimension of Subregional Economic Zones', *Contemporary Southeast Asia*, 16 (1995) 421–33.

World Bank, *Human Development Report 1993* (Oxford University Press, 1995).

Zakaria, F. 'The Rise of Illiberal Democracy', *Foreign Affairs,* 76 (1997) 22–44.

7

Beyond Dire Straits? Transnationalization and Renationalization in the Southern Growth Triangle

Niklas Eklund

> Nothing can function in isolation. Everything reacts to its surroundings. What one entity does will affect others. This principle holds true for economic development. There is a link, for instance, between development and government.
>
> Mahathir bin Mohamad, 1994

In most parts of the world, governments are facing challenges from transnationalizing tendencies in economic and social life. The political impact of such tendencies, however, varies between regions and individual countries. In Europe, the management of transnational partnerships, business opportunities and infrastructural links entails a slow evolution of new institutions and organizations. In Asia Pacific, it is generally held that intergovernmental relations dominate. Governments in this region do not envisage political institutions specially adapted to transnationalization, nor do they seem to find them desirable.[1] It is in this light, however, that the growth triangle phenomenon becomes interesting.

The aim of this chapter is to present some preliminary ideas and lay the foundation for further study of transnationalizing tendencies and political legitimacy in the Southern Growth Triangle (JSR[2]) between Singapore, Malaysia and Indonesia. While overwhelmingly economic and consensus-based in nature, the JSR can be defined as neither an international political institution, nor a sub-unit to the ASEAN. As noted by several Asian analysts, economic growth and stable security arrangements within the ASEAN framework seem to be necessary, but not analytically sufficient, determinants of growth triangles.[3] The active pursuit of national goals is a vital driving force behind the phenomenon, whereas the mechanisms that actually make the triangle work, such as private enterprise and investment, are transnational. In effect, the JSR can be seen as an attempt to create politically manageable transnationalization. Consensus-seeking and informal politics[4] are key factors in the effort, on the one hand, to support cross-border investments and trade while, on the other hand, sustaining the stability and legitimacy of national political systems. It has been suggested in principle that an analysis of the JSR is equal to an analysis of how national decision-makers and economic managers cooperate in order to meet the need for national adaption to global economic change.[5] But what is the relationship between transnationalizing tendencies and national political legitimacy in a growth triangle? Do growth triangles also entail new political pressures from below?

Development and characteristics of JSR

The growth triangle between Singapore, Malaysia and Indonesia was first formally conceptualized in December 1989. Singaporean prime minister Goh Chok Tong was the first to announce the concept officially, having tested the political ground for a joint international approach to investment activities and development efforts in the region. Singapore, the peninsular city region of Johor, and the Riau archipelago centered on the island of Batam were indentified as the territorial units to be involved. Malaysian prime minister Mahathir bin Mohamad and Indonesian president Soeharto gave their official consent and support for the idea in June 1990.[6] A new approach to development in the region was launched by 'steps to create more liberal and open economic environments with greater reliance on market forces for pricing and investment decisions.'[7]

The development of the JSR appears to have gone through four distinct developmental phases and is currently entering a fifth phase.[8] The first might be called the *conceptualization phase* of 1989–90, during which a top-level political consensus on the desirability of the initiative was reached. Jakarta and Kuala Lumpur decided to support the Singaporean idea after intense diplomacy and personal interaction between national leaders. This initial, and very important, low-key political process was then followed by a *process phase* between 1991 and 1993. This period involved the fleshing out of practical administrative detail while economic investments and other activities were gaining in pace and scope. The political 'nod' from top national leaders gave credibility to the project and helped make Johor and the Riau attractive areas for investment. This phase also involved shuttle diplomacy between politicians and administrators on different political levels in order to sustain political and social stability during the build-up, and to forestall any social opposition and unrest. Importantly, during this phase the JSR was still based on the premises of informal agreement and understanding.

The year 1994 represented the *formalization phase*. The vital Memorandum of Understanding (MOU) was signed by political leaders, thus giving the JSR institutional status. Several steps were taken to ensure the so called 'win–win' character of the project by emphasizing its nature as a positive-sum game for all actors involved. Johor, for example, was to be compensated because much investment had gone into the Riau. The industrial park on the island of Batam was now fully functional and the attention of infrastructure planners was directed northwards. For instance, plans for a second causeway between Singapore and Johor were brought up on agenda. 1995–96 represented a *maturing phase*. Batam industrial park was turning dividends which spawned ideas and efforts to further development in adjacent areas (Malacca, Negri Sembilan, and Pahang). By and large, however, real estate development was soon declared a failure, not least on Batam outside the industrial park proper. During 1996, Singaporean actors seemed increasingly to begin shifting their attention to other potential areas within the ASEAN context.[9] The concept of growth triangles had spread across Asia Pacific, well into eastern Russia, the northern parts of China, Japan and Korea.

During 1996 it seems that the JSR entered a *renationalization phase*. The transnationalizing tendencies of the early years seemed almost to disappear. Beginning with the failure to realize further expansion and economic take-off in the Riau, less of an economic spillover from Batam could be envisaged by Indonesian leaders. Although officials and managers continued to make use of transport facilities between Singapore and Batam, real estate investments were in decline. Singapore continued to be the highly developed economic engine in the triangle, as has been suggested elsewhere, perhaps in line with Singaporean national strategy.[10] From the Malaysian side, actors began to voice discontent concerning developments in the Johor city area. National competitiveness was back on the agenda. For example, Malaysia went ahead with its projected deep-sea harbor development just north of Singapore, with an eye to making Malaysia more competitive in shipping and has continued in accordance with the national Vision 2020 program. In the summer of 1997, there was a real downturn in the relationship between Singapore and Malaysia, harsh language and accusations flying from both sides. In parallel, however, the ministers of finance from the three countries concerned continued talks on how to increase flows in the triangle, particularly concerning tourism, and how to continue eliminating obstacles to transnational mobility, such as unnecessary degrees and levels of bureaucracy. Also, the JSR was expanded territorially in two steps, eventually to encompass two more regions in Malaysia and another five in Indonesia. Interestingly, the current standing seems to be one of parallel developments illustrating what one Asian analyst has called an inherent contradiction in the process:

> [O]n the one hand these countries wish to achieve a technologically advanced information society, on the other hand they are ready to isolate themselves culturally and politically if deemed necessary in order to legitimate national sovereignty.[11]

Looking deeper into the nature of the JSR, certain characteristics seem to dominate. First of all, the project seems to be firmly rooted in the notion of economic complementarity between countries. Complementarity essentially evolves around the three major economic factors of land, capital and labor.[12] It is therefore not surprising that the first initiatives at developing transnational economic and infrastructural links between the three territories came from Singaporean actors, private as well as public, in the form of industrial and financial groups and the Economic Development Board. Whereas the geographically minuscule state of Singapore had plenty of investment-ready capital in the 1980s, its shortage of land and labor was becoming acute. By the late 1980s, a spontaneous movement of small enterprises into Johor was emerging in an effort from private business to alleviate the labor shortage. These activities were welcomed by Johor, envisaged to further boost economic life in that part of Malaysia which was already the richest. For land, however, Singaporean actors looked south. The first steps towards what was later to become the Industrial Park of Batam were taken because land was readily available in the Riau, by boat only some 40 minutes away from the main Singaporean offices. Indonesia being a densely populated nation, labor could be supplied from other parts of the country, mainly from Java, also in accordance with the transmigration policy in Indonesia. It would probably be realistic to say that Singapore managed to solve two of its major economic factor problems, that is, shortages of land and labor, by beginning to actively promote transboundary economic development across to Johor and Riau. Furthermore, it is likely that Singapore had a hidden agenda in the process since good ties with its closest neighbors would also ensure access to other vital resources. The major issue here is what has been termed the 'water politics' of Singapore. Given that a successful balance could be kept in relations with Indonesia and Malaysia, Singapore might also be able to eliminate the risk of one-sided dependency upon the federal state of Malaysia.[13]

Briefly comparing the JSR with other political efforts at creating transnational economic spheres, for example, the Internal Market in Europe, important differences stand out. Whereas the driving force behind the JSR is complementarity, it is the conscious creation of freedoms that drives transnationalization in Europe. Likewise, the process factors are different. The Internal Market initiative in Europe is about the transnationalization of four major economic factors: capital, labor, goods and services. Since the project is ultimately aimed at creating a 'level playing field' for all four factors, the political agenda has been heavily burdened with social aspects of mobility and competition.[14] More often than not, European nations have managed to opt out of total factor mobility on grounds that transnationalization has adverse effects on national growth and welfare. Moreover, the Internal Market project is wholly directed towards facilitation and creation of transnational *mobility*. Land, therefore, does not enter into the picture. The JSR process, on the other hand, starts from a different concept, in which capital (to some extent involving services) is the only transnationally mobile factor. Land is naturally immobile also in the context of the JSR but, importantly, labor mobility by and large remains a national issue.

In the European setting it is possible, perhaps arguably, to discern elements of over-formalization in political institutions and processes, sometimes an over-representation of political interests. Moreover, the political, legal and economic aspirations of the European Union on the supranational level are nowhere paralleled in the Southeast Asian setting. The JSR is first and foremost projected as a pragmatic scheme for the realization of positive values between nation-states and private industry:

> Although Johor, Singapore and the Riau Province are in different countries, it is the goal of the three governments to cooperate in order to enable companies to view the area as effectively one investment region so that the advantages of each area can be maximised.[15]

Importantly, the JSR does not indicate any supranational or other integrative ambitions among the participating states. In effect, one Singaporean political scientist has crossed out any parallels between European or North American experiences; for instance, in the form of neofunctionalist integration theory and state-centric realism. He has allowed for the possible analogy with the early transactionalist model of Karl Deutsch, which stipulates the emergence of new security communities between countries in regions signified by growing economic and social interaction across state boundaries.[16] From this point of view, however, the ASEAN would appear to be the relevant unit of analysis, not emergent subregional entities such as the JSR.

Indeed, investments and development prospects were well under way in what is today the JSR area before the official government endorsements of 1989–90.[17] Importantly, there seems to be current scholarly agreement that the vital distinguishing feature of growth triangles in a *political* sense is that governments have a reactive, as opposed to proactive, role and involvement in their development. Comparison between, for example, the JSR and the Special Economic Zones of Southern China (Zhuhai, Shenzen, Shantou and Xiamen) show that transnational economic expansion hinges upon a plurality of actors, mainly firms and business interests, and the extent to which they are allowed to exploit the complementarities and opportunities of each respective area.[18] Governments play a reactive, or 'facilitating', role in both cases, in the sense that they monitor needs for infrastructural development and support and, also, attempt to change systemic rules in order to facilitate mobility across national boundaries.[19] One striking example of the latter is the introduction of a smartcard in 1991 for business people traveling between Singapore and Batam. Importantly, however, this potential transnationalization of labor does not involve unskilled labor.

The JSR seems to involve a minimum of formal arrangements and political representation. Also, the arrangement seems to have been immediately productive for the involved actors, governments and organizations alike. More than anything else, it seems to be a concept that allows for far quicker, and far more efficient, adaption to economic needs than, for instance, the process in Western Europe. For example, full-factor mobility is not a stated political goal. Importantly, transnational mobility has no supranational regulatory body, supervision or even guarantee.

Aspects of political legitimacy

A prerequisite for any political system is that the majority of its citizens and social actors abide by its common laws and practices. This, however, does not imply that the rules citizens follow in a given political system are legitimate. Following the tradition of Max Weber, political analysts have tended to look upon the concept of legitimacy as complex.[20] The reason for abiding by rules and accepting prevalent political institutions can be one of several. In theory as in real life, there are two possible extremes; legitimate and illegitimate. There is a wide range between the former, characterized by ideal normative agreement between the ruler and the ruled, and the latter, which represents a relationship based on coercion and violence. As suggested by David Held, such extremes on an imagined theoretical continuum are unusual in the real world. Political analysis must also come to grips with such mechanisms as apathy, tradition or pragmatic acquiescence.[21]

> Thoroughgoing repressive societies are a limit, on one end and 'thugocracies' of competing gangs the limit on the other end of the continuum of organized threat and use of force that underlies all state structures.[22]

Transnationalization further complicates this discussion since it dissolves established relationships between territory and function in a given country. At least in theory, transnational legitimacy structures emerge in its wake; for example, cultural and interest group networks.

> The idea that consent legitimates government and the state system more generally has been central to nineteenth- and twentieth-century liberal democrats. These democrats have focused on the ballot box as the mechanism whereby the individual citizen expresses political preferences, and citizens as a whole periodically confer authority on government to enact the law and regulate economic and social life. (...) Whose consent is necessary and whose participation is justified in decisions concerning, for example, AIDS, or acid rain, or the use of non-renewable resources, or the management of economic flows? What is the relevant constituency: national, regional or international? To whom do decision-makers have to justify their decisions? To whom should they be accountable?[23]

However, the nature of political legitimacy can change over time. In the long run, government is dependent upon its own values, norms and tastes being congruent with those of individuals and groups in society.[24] Transnationalization entails an analytical challenge in that it calls for a more dynamic legitimacy concept. But it is far from certain that the best way to meet this challenge is by taking for granted that alternative commonalities, that is, alternative actors and strata in social life simply erode the legitimacy of states. Indeed, who are the agents of such new commonalities? It has been suggested that the temporal perspective be expanded in order to make better use of historical political patterns and dynamics that precede nation-states.[25] Medieval transaction patterns in Asia Pacific, however, seem to have little bearing on the current political and economic situation.[26] The need for a more current, dynamic perspective remains.[27]

The concept of legitimacy must encompass more than the relationship between the rulers and the ruled in a well-defined geographical setting. The subdivision suggested here would illustrate two dimensions of the concept of political legitimacy. To begin with the systemic dimension, it represents such aspects of political life as institutional structures, procedural rules of the game and slow developmental processes, such as long-term adaption to economic and social change. In this perspective, the goal is the sustainability of the political system. Different degrees of political legitimacy are defined or judged on the basis of intangibles such as 'good government', collective realization of values, and social and political rights. Social debates over ideological differences and long-term goals, such as 'the good society', are also assumed to belong to this dimension. The managerial dimension, on the other hand, represents a part of the concept of legitimacy, which is connected with practical government action, policies and intervention in social and economic life, national as well as transnational. The goal is political efficiency and a government is judged on the basis of how well or badly it manages economic and social change. Short-term goal attainment, for example, in improving the national budget or in increasing or decreasing infrastructural investments, are the focus of attention. A government is judged as more or less legitimate based on how it performs regarding tangibles, for example, taxes or real interest policies. Performance related to economic output, savings and dividends are crucial to political efficiency on this dimension.[28]

Again, to the extent that the concept of political legitimacy is reduced to questions about the systemic dimension, there seems to be little room for dynamic change. Indeed, systemic legitimacy could then be seen in opposition to managerial legitimacy. It would seem more productive, however, to look at it as contingent on both managerial and systemic aspects.[29] Situations defined by complexity, short-term actions by government such as, for instance, temporary economic interventions, would otherwise seem to fall out of the picture.[30] Importantly, as depicted in Figure 7.1, this conceptual approach views politics as a matter of both tangibles and intangibles. The managerial dimension represents an understanding that political systems are not immune to short-term

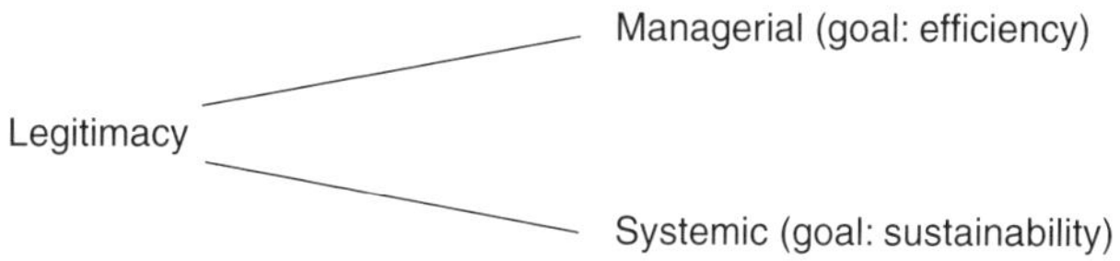

Figure 7.1 Two dimensions of political legitimacy

changes in, for example, economic life. Furthermore, governments are forced to act on such changes in order to preserve or increase their legitimacy. The JSR in itself illustrates how political decision-makers seek active involvement in projects aimed at economic management. In simple terms, national decision-makers and officials must be ready to be evaluated by their constituents and by organized interests on the basis of their performance both in systemic and managerial terms. The relationship between the systemic and the managerial aspect of political legitimacy is complex. Political philosopher John Stuart Mill once observed that political governance by the state makes the decisions and activities of political institutions multi-faceted and diverse.[31] In this perspective, it follows that the political legitimacy of a government is contingent on two major links with society. One is the systemic link, which involves the elite-mass dimension according to which modern societies have embraced the one citizen–one vote principle as a core value. Modern democratic government will be evaluated in a process in which national systemic rules, issues of citizenship and democratic rights come to the fore in political analysis. Another systemic aspect, perhaps less frequently observed and embraced by analysts of democratic governance, is the relationship to organized interests in society. Organized interests may, for instance, represent both corporate and local-territorial interest groups in their political interaction with democratic government; albeit relationships vary in both form and intensity by country and over time.

Active involvement with or reliance upon organized interests, nevertheless, draws government towards the managerial side of political life. Tangibles and short-term issues become vitally important for governments in order to sustain political legitimacy. In the case of the JSR, what has been termed the *facilitating role of government* signifies a direct and important link between three distinct national governments, the economic-corporate world and the transnational sphere. As such, the JSR can in large parts be regarded as an effort to create and manage transnationalization in a particular geographical setting. Thus, each government enters a process in which political legitimacy must be sought from other spheres than the national, and from other actors than 'the people'. Political legitimacy in the JSR would seem to hinge on whether the governments concerned can handle the tension between systemic and managerial legitimacy.

Transnational linkages and bones of contention

Looking at the extensive news press material that covers the development of the JSR, it appears that the bulk of reports made on the phenomenon are from the years 1991–94. These years coincide with what we have termed the *process phase* and the *formalization phase*. Interestingly, in 1995 and 1996 the number of articles and mentions of the JSR in the press falls drastically. For example, the total number of articles for 1995–96 does not add up to even half those published in 1991 alone. In the current *renationalization phase*, interest seems to have dropped even further. This would seem to support the view taken here that the years 1991–93 indeed represented a *process phase*, during which different forms for cooperation were tested and the various details of experience were fleshed out between actors in the venture. The *process phase* was then followed by the *formalization phase* in 1994, at which time coverage in the press was still intense and comprehensive. In the last phase, the coverage amounts to odd articles and mentions.

One example from the *process phase* illustrates how social tensions build up around otherwise peaceful economic and social transnationalization. Thai newspaper *The Nation* reports on 'Troubled times for Johor' (18 January, 1991). Johor, already being the richest of the federated Malaysian states, is beginning to experience an economic upsurge resulting from the new opportunities of the growth triangle at this point in time. Whereas the projected growth rate for Malaysia as a whole is 9.4 per cent this year, the predicted rate for Johor has an upper limit of 12 per cent. The JSR is related as an excellent opportunity for Johor to speed up its successful route to becoming 'the next growth pole in national economic development in the 1990s', not least as a result of the heavy influx of regional investment and tourism.

According to statements by local politicians, intellectuals and residents, however, the bright prospects are heavily shadowed by problems of 'inflation, rising property prices, crime and pollution.' The article actually refers to a vicious circle of economic and social forces emanating from transnationalization: the weaker Malaysian currency makes Johor, particularly the city area of Johor Bahru, an attractive spot for Singaporean investors and tourists. The service sector enjoys a boom and expands rapidly, increasing levels of economic transactions and the need for infrastructural repair and investment, which further boosts the economy, and so on. Transactions are taking place and expanding on several levels, from the individual tourist spending money on goods and services up to firms and organizations cashing in on business opportunities. However, the rapid growth of the tourism industry also leads to higher price levels. The spending by cash-strong Singaporeans drives prices upwards to levels that Johoreans cannot afford. The result is what might be termed socio-economic segregation, which is also quietly lamented by local residents in the referred article. Even more serious comments are made about the pricing of real estate which, also surging upwards to levels difficult for Johoreans, 'could eventually drive them out of their own state.' Business focuses upon Johor as an investment spot for heavy, capital intensive industry, not only adding to the already heavy pollution by transnational car traffic, but also causing tensions between Johor and its neighbors inside the Malaysian federation. In Penang and Selangor, investments are reported to be expanding mainly in the (environmentally less adverse) electronics sector.

The article simply asks: 'Is boom a bust?' Relating to crime, violence and worsening economic and environmental living conditions, it takes a rather grim view of the future. Obviously, prospects for economic expansion are good. The fear of social unrest, however, is clearly present in a rhetorical mention of the freshwater treaty between Malaysia and Singapore. The recently signed water treaty states that Malaysia will supply Singapore with fresh water up until 2061. The rhetorical observation by local politician G.S. Nijar, however, is that 'about one fourth of the Johor population is without piped water supply.' It is one of several indicators in the media coverage that social tension indeed is a complicating factor in the initial process of legitimating the JSR.

Another example revolves around the planned second causeway, between Tuas in Singapore and Gelang Patah in Malaysia. In an entry on 21 January, it is reported that Malaysian information minister and member of parliament Mohammed Rahmat refuses to attend a seminar on the subject of problems related to the construction and subsequent use of a second causeway. The minister had been invited by an action committee, which claimed to represent 3000 residents eager for more information about the infrastructural project. The action committee was allegedly looking forward to the participation of top regional politicians and university staff. A short recapitulation of the event ends with the statement that the minister simply refused to attend the seminar on grounds that he was not elected representative of the citizens of the

Gelang Patah area. His comment was that a local initiative such as this 'has nothing to do with me'.

These reports seem to hint at a political dimension in the JSR *process phase,* which relates to the problem of political legitimacy. First of all, in the last part of the article, an important aspect of real politics in Malaysia flashes by. The minister explains that local initiatives such as that of the action committee are unnecessary and 'should be channeled to the action committee set up by the government'. Furthermore, this central committee (headed by a regional assemblyman appointed by central government and involving experts from the Johor Economic Planning Unit) was allegedly soon to arrange a seminar 'to explain the project to the people'. According to the article, an important aspect is that the whole idea of the second causeway is to alleviate problems of air pollution and traffic congestion in several other localities in Johor. This can, nevertheless, be interpreted as a signal to local interests and potential opposition to the project. In the perspective of this chapter, it seems that central and regional government in Malaysia perceives a task of actively promoting transnationalization in the *process phase,* which might at least hold one key to a better understanding of political legitimation processes in the JSR.

To give another example, and turning attention over to the current *renationalization phase,* the picture becomes less clear in terms of who is for and who is against the JSR. It appears that the pragmatic, low-key approach of the governments involved is showing some cracks, and the nature of the project as a positive-sum game based on principles of economic complementarity is being questioned. On the other hand, an interesting tension in the national–transnational dimension occurs. Above all, the JSR is brought high up on national agendas.

On 6 June, 1997, Singaporean newspaper the *Straits Times* reports on major JSR developments since March. Beginning with a speech by senior minister Lee Kuan Yew, in which he commented on problems with high crime rates in Johor, bilateral relations between Singapore and Malaysia took a downward turn. According to the paper, the speech and ensuing negative reactions from the Malaysian side had brought the bilateral relationship almost to the freezing point. Five 'waves in Malaysia–Singapore relations' are identified in the article, in which different issues are seen as the cause of the problem. All of them, potentially at least, could result in a severing of the good ties between the governments of Singapore and Malaysia.

Initially, the dispute apparently revolves around the allegations of Lee Kuan Yew and the ensuing reactions from Malaysian officials. According to the article, the immediate reaction from the Malaysian side was to question an agreement to develop land sites around a joint railway project. At one point, even the validity of written agreements from earlier in the 1990s were put into question. Reference is also made to earlier reports in the media that the Malaysian Cabinet had proclaimed a freeze on bilateral ties. Much confusion also stemmed from the fact that some bilateral activities were indeed canceled at the same time as Kuala Lumpur denied having made any statement to freeze relations.

After the first two waves, according to the *Straits Times*, the ensuing three waves broke around three similarly fuzzy political events. At one stage in the development, threats to cut the supply of fresh water were made from the Malaysian side, as a result of follow-up reports in the Singaporean press on crime in Johor. Another incident occurred when a Malaysian official accused the government of Singapore of having issued a directive to Singaporeans against visiting Johor, even as tourists. Finally, what the article calls the fifth wave starts when new and more time consuming immigration checks in Johor at that point kept Singaporeans, on their way home from Johor, waiting for several hours at the border. The whole period March–June 1997 apparently is one marked by high politics and international tension between Malaysia and Singapore.

On 2 June, the *Straits Times* reports on how there had been demands for forceful retaliation against Singapore from the UMNO Youth in Malaysia immediately after the senior minister's speech in March. The incident as such, together with its possible international repercussions, was also covered by international media. For example, the *Economist* discussed it as a definite matter of competition between two nations in its 22 March issue:

> Now comes Malaysia's challenge. It is building new ports, so that less of its trade will be shipped through Singapore. Kuala Lumpur's new ariport, to open next year, is advertised as the biggest in the region. The Malaysian capital also wants to become a financial centre; and the prime minister, Mahathir bin Mohamad, is drumming up support for a 'multimedia super-corridor' intended in part to divert information-technology business from Singapore. (p. 33)

In this much heated climate of international accusations and conflict between two of the founding nations of the JSR, it would seem hard to imagine that transnationalization could still be part of the picture. What in 1996 had seemed like a continuing positive expansion of the triangle, with the inclusion of Malacca and Negri Sembilang, now seemed destined to be overrun by intergovernmental bickering. Perhaps surprisingly, however, the *Straits Times* reported on 10 June 1997 on continuing 'Growth Triangle talks'. In a meeting between the ministers of finance from Indonesia, Singapore and Malaysia, a joint decision to expand the JSR was taken. Another five provinces on the Indonesian side were now to be included, thus doubling the 'market size' of the JSR and substantially increasing its territory to encompass 34 million people. The inclusion of Bengkulu, Jambi, Lampung, South Sumatra and West Kalimantan was envisaged by officials to enhance the opportunities for growth and, specifically, to expand the market for tourism in the JSR. Echoing the cordial political language from the early phases of JSR development, the national ministers went very far in their expansion of transnational ties but, as the article reports, 'took a back seat to the private sector, which they said should continue to lead its economic development.' Quite contrary to the earlier political events of spring–summer 1997, ministers of international trade, industry, production and distribution from the three countries involved now agreed that it was time to reduce the obstacles to transnational mobility in the area. Malay minister of International Trade and Industry is quoted as saying: 'On our part we have asked our regional, provincial and state governments to look into how red tape at the local level can be cut out . . . to develop hassle-free travel for visitors and businessmen.'

These examples from an ongoing study of the regional press are presented here to illustrate political changes in the JSR, possibly in accordance with the suggested developmental phases. By comparison, the first example seems to represent a phase in which political arguments are focused on mutual benefits and how all participants in the project will eventually benefit from the development of infrastructure and an expansion of transnational flows inside the growth triangle. Evidence of local opposition in the early stages seems to indicate that there was social and political opposition to transnationalization, which might have more to tell us about the general theoretical question concerning the social and political effects of such processes. Furthermore, the material indicates hidden attempts at legitimation from political decision-makers involved in the managerial side of the process. At least in the *process phase*, local opposition seems to have been made to understand that if one locality opposes the process, it will make things worse for others. An example that stands out is the discussion about environmental problems around the causeway. In other words, the provincial government has a self-appointed task of legitimating the causeway by making arguments about benefits for the whole area in localities where, apparently, no prior or spontaneous legitimacy for the project exists. As far as central government is concerned in the example, represented here by the Malaysian minister of Information, the effort seems concentrated on the international level as illustrated by the fact that he would not attend meetings or rallies initiated on the local level.

The other example, from the *renationalization phase*, seems to make the picture less clear. Ostensibly, it indicates that the JSR is highly sensitive to high politics between the national centers. It could perhaps be argued that the legitimacy of the whole project *per se* begins and ends with either a nod or a shake of the head from leading politicians in the respective national centers of the three countries concerned. From this perspective, the problem of political legitimacy seems to pertain to (national) systemic phenomena inside national boundaries. High politics aside, however, the expansion and development of the JSR nevertheless continue. Geographical expansion means bigger markets but also an increased number of actors and more managerial complexity, new social groups becoming concerned as well as new private and corporate actors. The *renationalization phase* looks almost contradictory on the face of things. The delicate political balance between national interests contrast sharply against the seemingly untouched cooperation and development of the JSR.

An experiment in dynamic political legitimization?

The development of the JSR over time illustrates how the 'facilitating role of government' has changed. Or perhaps better, how the prerequisites for that role have changed. Politicians and high-level officials seem to have been able to manage trade, growth, infrastructural development and other transnational interaction in the JSR. An area for economic investment, trade and development that stretches across the boundaries of the three countries has been achieved. National politicians have stayed in the background, allowing private actors and interests to spearhead the development. Only in the last stages of the development have the national leaders stepped back in to remind actors about the sensitivity and high-political roots of the project.

Interestingly, in the *renationalization phase,* signs appear that transnationalization is subjecting the three countries to demands for autonomy. At the same time as there is a top-level dispute between Singapore and Malaysia threatening to overthrow the whole process and to chill relations, the JSR is actually expanded upon, involving more localities and more people. According to those local newspapers surveyed the negotiations over expansion were held in the same cooperative and respectful atmosphere as that which was evident in the early 1990s. The mutual respect and low-key negotiation techniques of national leaders, however, are no longer prerequisites for transnationalization. The JSR continues to grow and to produce new economic opportunities. At least to some extent it seems that the JSR has passed a political threshold in its development and become a transnational setting for transnational investments and interaction in its own right.

Another possible interpretation is that the JSR is becoming an alternative source of political legitimacy. There seem to be enough vested interests to make it survive even fighting and bickering among top national politicians. The interest of non-governmental actors, not least transnational investors, could be an important factor since the managerial legitimacy of the JSR is heavily dependent on economic opportunity, growth and successful development of the infrastructure. Furthermore, it might be hard for either government in Singapore or Malaysia to motivate a severing of ties. Particularly Johor, and other federated parts of southern Malaysia, stand to lose much. In effect, the JSR can be seen as a vital factor in the growth and development of southern Malaysia and, by extension, as a factor in the systemic legitimacy of Malaysia.

Nevertheless, it is hard to speculate about outcomes. If the current expansion of the JSR is successful, all three of the involved states might increase their managerial legitimacy. It would seem particularly difficult for Malaysia to develop alternatives for its southern periphery within national boundaries. The Riau, however, is a different thing. Doubtless, any economic or developmental argument that applies to Johor equally applies to the Riau. Taking the recent economic and political developments in Indonesia into consideration, however, speculation would seem dubious at best. The Riau has been developed for the sole purpose of joining the JSR. It has been successful as far as production and industry is concerned. On the other hand, the current expansion of the JSE specifically targets tourism, a sector in which the Riau by and large has been a failure. Above all, the Riau is not strongly linked to the systemic aspect of political legitimacy in Indonesia. In the light of recent events, it must be added that any speculation about the future of the JSR would also need to take the possibility of continued economic decline in the region into account.

However, as illustrated by the quarrel between politicians in Singapore and Malaysia, national leaders can at any point in time decide to substitute the transnational for the national. This would be equal to seeking an enhancement of systemic legitimacy at the cost of managerial legitimacy. Whether it is done in terms of religious–cultural orthodoxy, nation-building, a glorious past or an envisaged prosperous future, does not make a difference in this perspective. In a transnationalizing setting, however, it is possible that those structures and symbols that legitimate national political systems turn into historical liabilities in future stages of economic development. Systemic political legitimacy is challenged by transnationalization. Transnationalization, nevertheless, is sought and encouraged by national political leadership, not as an ideology but for reasons of economic opportunity and potential gain.

Transnationalization makes managerial legitimacy more important for national leadership. Particularly if the development of transnational ties and interaction is successful, the need to legitimate why and how the process unfolds in a certain way increases. Efforts to build up systemic legitimacy in a similar situation might well backfire if the 'win–win' spirit is lost. Questions about who pays for what, and who gets the profits would seem inevitable with potential, more serious public conflicts between actors to follow. After all, an assymmetrical triangle is still a triangle. A triangle that loses one or two of its points is no longer a triangle. The relationship between managerial and systemic legitimacy is theoretically interesting. For the future, it would be particularly interesting to follow up on how actors in the JSR try to balance the managerial and systemic aspects of political legitimacy. It could be that managerial legitimacy proves to be more important than its systemic variant in overcoming the problems and meeting the challenges raised by transnationalization.

Notes

1. Ganesan, N. 'Conceptualising Regional Economic Cooperation: Perspectives from Political Science', in Toh, M.H. and Low, L. (eds), *Regional Cooperation and Growth Triangles in ASEAN* (Singapore: Times Academic Press, 1993) p. 6.
2. The abbreviation JSR to connote the Johor–Singapore–Riau Growth Triangle is suggested by Thant, M., Tang, M. and Kakazu, H. (eds), *Growth Triangles in Asia* (Oxford and New York: Oxford University Press, 1994) p. xxi ff.
3. Toh, M.H. and Low, L. (eds), *Regional Cooperation and Growth Triangles in ASEAN* (Singapore: Times Academic Press, 1993) p. 224. Further, they write: 'Without conducive political factors and leaders with a common vision, growth triangles can be stillborn or aborted. It is also imperative that political factors should be given their due recognition wherever relevant to provide a multi-disciplinary approach.'
4. Informal politics as a *national* political phenomenon is discussed for example in the March 1996 issue of *Asian Survey* with particular reference to China, Japan, Taiwan and South Korea.
5. Thambipillai, P., 'The ASEAN Growth Triangle: The Convergence of National and Sub-National Interests', *Contemporary Southeast Asia*, 13 (1991) 299–313. See also Scott, A. (ed.) *The Limits of Globalization* (London: Routledge, 1997) pp. 1–15.

6. Ahmad, M., 'Economic Cooperation in the Southern Growth Triangle: An Indonesian Perspective', in Toh and Low *op. cit.* p. 93.
7. Tang, M., Thant, M. and Kakazu, H., (eds), *Growth Triangles in Asia – A New Approach to Regional Economic Cooperation* (Oxford: Asian Development Bank and Oxford University Press, 1995) p. 6.
8. The developmental phases of the JSR are my own idea and, importantly, still under discussion. They are included here for descriptive purposes. For other overviews of the development, see for example Toh and Low *op. cit.*; Thant, Tang and Kakazu *op. cit.*; Thambipillai *op. cit.*
9. It would seem equally proper to regard current developments as part and parcel of an *expansion phase* which involves the conscious development and expansion of the SIJORI concept in other parts of Asia Pacific. This, however, falls beyond the scope of this paper and is also the topic of the parallel studies by Janerik Gidlund and Jan Engberg.
10. Rodan Garry (ed.) *Singapore Changes Guard: Social, Political and Economic Directions in the 1990s* (Melbourne: Longman Cheshire, 1994) *passim.*
11. Poon, J. 'Handelsblock i Asien och Europa' in *Framtider* no. 1 (1998) p. 26 (author's translation).
12. My thanks go to Professor Linda Low at the NUS, Singapore, for pedagogically pointing this basic fact out to me in an interview, which led me not only to look at the literature from a new angle but also to discard any *prima facie* analogies with European and other Western experiences in regional integration.
13. The facts in this paragraph are adapted from interviews.
14. See for instance Clesse, A. and Vernon, R. (eds), *The European Community after 1992: A New Role in World Politics?* (Baden-Baden: Nomos Verlag, 1991).
15. Quoted from the Keynote address in Toh and Low *op. cit.*, p. xi.
16. Ganesan, N. *op. cit.*, pp. 1–8.
17. Ahmad *op. cit.*, p. 92ff.
18. Tsao Yuan, L. 'Sub-Regional Economic Zones in the Asia Pacific' in Toh and Low *op. cit.*, pp. 12–21.
19. See for instance Tang, M. and Thant, M. 'Growth Triangles: Conceptual Issues and Operational Problems', Asian Development Bank, Manila, Staff Paper No. 54, 1994. Also: Abonyi, G., 'The Institutional Challenges of Growth Triangles in Southeast Asia', MPP Working paper no. 3, August 1994, Public Policy Programme at the Centre for Advanced Studies, National University of Singapore.
20. Björkas, K.-J., *Legitimitet och entropi i samhällsprocesserna*. Ph.D. Dissertation, Åbo Akademi, Finland (1980).
21. Held, D., *Political Theory and the Modern State* (Cambridge: Polity Press, 1989) pp. 101–2.
22. Nash, M., *The Cauldron of Ethnicity in the Modern World* (Chicago: University of Chicago Press, 1989) p. 58.
23. Archibugi, D. and Held, D. (eds.), *Cosmopolitan Democracy* (Cambridge: Polity Press, 1995) p. 102.
24. Goldmann, K. *et al.*, *Statsvetenskapligt Lexikon* (Stockholm: Universitetsforlaget, 1997) s.144–5.
25. Bull, H. *The Anarchical Society: Study of Order in World Politics* (London and Basingstoke: Macmillan, 1977). Professor Bull writes of a system of overlapping authority and multiple loyalty', p. 104.

26. Berggren, H., *En okänd värld. Malaykulturen och ASEAN-länderna* (Stockholm: Wahlström & Widstrand, 1990). He wrties about 'the Malay factor' in the seaward parts of Southeast Asia. Also, ASEAN as a possible modern counterpart to the Malay factor is discussed, pp. 306–43.
27. Agnew, J. and Corbridge, S. *Mastering Space-Hegemony, Territory and International Political Economy* (London: Routledge, 1995) pp. 79–80.
28. *Ibid.*
29. Lui, T., 'Efficiency as a Political Concept in the Hong Kong Government: Issues and Problems', in Burns, J. (ed.), *Asian Civil Service Systems: Improving Efficiency and Productivity* (Singapore: Times Academic Press, 1994) p. 46ff.
30. This notion echoes some of the classics in the field, such as Robert Dahl and Karl Friedrich. In his *Modern Political Analysis* from 1963, Dahl describes political legitimacy as the 'belief that the structures, procedures, acts, decisions, policies, officials, or leaders of government possess the quality of "rightness", propriety, or moral goodness and should be accepted because of this quality irrespective of the specific content of the particular act in question.' Quoted in Sahlin, M. *Neo-Authoritarianism and the Problem of Legitimacy* (Stockholm: Rabén & Sjögren, 1977) p. 141.
31. Mill, J.S. 'On the Influence of Government' in *Principles of Political Economy Books IV and V* (Harmondsworth: Penguin Books, 1985) pp. 145–52. Mill specifically builds his reasoning around the central argument that: 'In attempting to enumerate the necessary functions of government, we find them to be considerably more multifarious than most people are at first aware of, and not capable of being circumscribed by those very definite lines of demarcation, which, in the inconsiderateness of popular discussion, it is often attempted to draw around them', p. 146.

References (Interviews)

17/4/1996, w/ Lim Sak Lan, Deputy Chief Executive Officer (International) at Jurong Town Corporation, Singapore.

17/4/1996, w/ Birgitta Malmwall, Counselor at the Embassy of Sweden, Singapore.

18/4/1996, w/ Lam Sheng Wei, Marketing Executive at Sembawang Industrial Group, Vietnam–Singapore International Marketing Pte. Ltd., Singapore.

18/4/1996, w/ Sanjay Natarajan, Senior Officer, Strategic Planning at the Economic Development Board, Singapore.

18/4/1996, w/ Peter Soh, Senior Officer, Strategic Planning at the Economic Development Board, Singapore.

18/4/1996, w/ Szu Wei Soh, Assistant Head, International Business Development Division ASEAN at the Economic Development Board, Singapore.

19/4/1996, w/ Shirley-Ann Ting, Marketing and Communications Executive at Batamindo Industrial Management Pte.Ltd., Singapore.

23/4/1996, w/ Dr Linda Low, Department of Business Policy at the National University of Singapore.

24/4/1996, w/ Dr Martin Perry, Department of Geography at the National University of Singapore.

8

Land-Use Controls and Economic Freedom: the Diverging Histories of Singapore and Taipei

David E. Andersson

Conventional rankings of economic freedom focus on factors such as impediments to international trade, government spending as a share of GDP, and the regulation of foreign direct investment (FDI). According to these conventional criteria, Hong Kong consistently ranks as the world's freest economy, while Singapore – with equal consistency – ranks as the second freest economy (Gwartney *et al.*, 1996). However, traditional definition of 'economic freedom' may be relevant for multinational corporations contemplating investments in new markets, but it is far less useful at the level of the individual citizen.

Prevailing construction of economic freedom indices relates to *de jure* statutory laws concerning trade, investment regulations, and taxation. According to these criteria, a relatively free economy is characterized by free trade, a level playing field for foreign investors, an absence of artificial monopolies, and low levels of (non-distortional) taxation. The benefits of such economic freedoms are articulated in terms of the ease of migration, availability of economic information, and decentralization of economic decision-making.

However, current economic freedom indices fail to consider the role of governments in suppressing the autonomous economic activities of individual citizens. In this chapter I attempt to show, through the examples of Taipei and Singapore, how differences in governments' use of land-use controls can affect our understanding of the term 'economic freedom'. In addition to traditional measures, I propose two other factors that need to be considered, namely the market for land, and, the impact of law enforcement.

Economic freedom in the market for land

Important indices in the market for land include the existence and severity of zoning ordinances, building codes, and plot-area ratios. A relatively free economy should exhibit a spatial distribution of land uses that approximates the distribution that would arise from the operation of a free market with well defined and stable property rights. A further measure of *effective* economic freedom could be the dispersion of land ownership. Widely dispersed land ownership (with limited land-use regulations) provides an important element of economic freedom at the level of the individual citizen. It does this by providing opportunities for entrepreneurship and self-expression. Dispersed land ownership also serves as a protection against the potentially adverse effects of relying exclusively on market interactions.[1]

Impact of law enforcement on economic freedoms

This is perhaps the most difficult component to assess regarding the impact on effective economic freedoms. Pertinent aspects include tax collection, corruption and *de facto* land-use regulations. The main problem in evaluating law enforcement is that it may cut both ways with respect to economic freedom. The non-enforcement of land-use regulations or immigration controls may lead to more opportunities for land-use conversions and a freer flow of labor, thus increasing economic freedom. Also, *some* corruption may enable commercial ventures to escape punitive tax rates. Conversely, arbitrariness in law enforcement and excessive corruption may distort the allocation of resources and suppress otherwise profitable economic activities.

In discussing the role of land-use regulations below, I will disregard traditional measures of economic freedom as these measures have been comprehensively discussed in Gwartney *et al.* (1996).[2] The objective here is to briefly describe the economic theory of land use, with an emphasis on the location of households. I then speculate on the consequences of the planners' and politicians' (mostly spurious) interpretation of the theory. Subsequently, land-use regulations in Taipei and Singapore are discussed. The discussion is an illustration of how an approach to economic freedom that accounts for land-use regulations differs from a traditional approach. As for my overall conclusions regarding Singapore and Taipei, it is still uncertain whether they are in proportion to some prospective quantitative index.

Economic theory and urban land use

An appropriate starting point for a discussion about the distribution of urban land uses is the well known monocentric model (Alonso, 1964; Muth, 1969). The Alonso–Muth model is simple, elegant and its empirical support is strong, at least by economic standards (e.g. Andersson, 1994; Cheshire and Sheppard, 1995; Andersson, 1997).

The Alonso–Muth model assumes that households value housing services, H, with price $P(A)$. The price P is a function of accessibility A which is a function of the distance d to the city center, where $\delta A/\delta d$ is assumed to be negative. In this model, the desired level of housing services is predetermined and the accessibility function A is a decreasing function of the distance to the center. Household i incurs transport costs, $T(A)$, as a function of its accessibility. Increases in the accessibility function A (and thus decreasing distances) imply increased house prices, $H(P)$, and decreased commuting costs $T(A)$. Moreover, a household consumes other goods and services. A composite consumption good, (C), which has been normalized with a price of one, accounts for these other goods and services. Household i then faces the problem of maximizing the utility function $U_i = U(H_i, A_i, C_i)$, subject to the income constraint $Y = C + P(A)H + T(A)$. The utility function is assumed to be concave and differentiable at least twice. The Lagrangian optimization problem becomes:

$$\max L = U(C, H, A) - \lambda(C + P(A)H + T(A) - Y) \tag{8.1}$$

The first order conditions with respect to C, H, and A are thus

$$\delta L/\delta C = (\delta U/\delta C) - \lambda = 0 \tag{8.2}$$

$$\delta L/\delta H = (\delta U/\delta H) - \lambda P(A) = 0 \tag{8.3}$$

$$\delta L/\delta A = (\delta U/\delta A) - \lambda(\delta P/\delta A)H - \lambda(\delta T/\delta A) \tag{8.4}$$

Substituting (8.2) into (8.3) and (8.4) yields

$$(\delta U/\delta H) - (\delta U/\delta C)P(A) = 0 \tag{8.5}$$

$$(\delta U/\delta A) - (\delta U/\delta C)[(\delta P/\delta A)H + (\delta T/\delta A)] = 0 \tag{8.6}$$

Rearranging (8.5) and (8.6):

$$(\delta U/\delta H)/(\delta U/\delta C) = P(A) \tag{8.7}$$

$$\delta U/\delta A)/(\delta U/\delta C) = (\delta P/\delta A)H + (\delta T/\delta A) \tag{8.8}$$

shows that the marginal rate of substitution between housing and other consumption must equal the price of housing (equation (8.7)) at the optimal level of housing consumption. Equation (8.8), finally, shows that a household is in locational equilibrium when the marginal rate of substitution, between increased access to the center and other consumption, equals the sum of the marginal increase in house prices (as a function of distance) and the marginal decrease in transport costs. (An additional implication of the theory is that there is trade-off between quantity and location relative to the center. Hence, a fixed utility level generates an indifference curve that shows how greater quantity must compensate for lower accessibility.)

The above formalization of the monocentric model given in this section is an adaptation of Alonso's model for studying the location choices of households. In addition, Alonso's land-use theory implies spatial specialization of land uses as a consequence of the operation of the free market, *if and only if* the individual utility functions (or profit functions for profit-maximizing firms) associated with each activity are relatively homogeneous compared with the corresponding functions of other activities. As an illustration, this could, for example, imply a separation of residential households' utility functions from the profit functions of car dealerships. The less (more) the bid–rent curves of individual households differ from each other, and the more (less) the bid–rent curves of households differ from the bid–rent curves of other activities, the more (less) households will tend to locate away from other activities. An overall pattern of spatial specialization rests on the assumption that different economic activities require differing needs of land, transport, and communication facilities per unit of output.

The emphasis on utility-maximizing households, rather than profit-maximizing firms, in the exposition above is a deliberate one. It is only by disregarding the intrinsic potential for heterogeneity associated with individuals' utility functions that we can make any predictions of spatial separation of land uses as the inevitable outcome of free market processes. But this disregard for households seems to have been the clinching feature of the enthusiasm for enforced separation of land uses among planners of the modern era.

Another feature that the prediction of spatial specialization overlooks is what Jacobs (1961) has called 'secondary diversity.' This term refers to the myriad of activities that depend for their survival on highly localized access to 'primary activities' (that is, the profit-maximizing firms of the monocentric model). Examples of secondary diversity include household services (e.g., restaurants or convenience stores) as well as business services (e.g., consultancies or libraries)

The question thus arises why mid-twentieth-century city planners, and by extension the politicians whom they advised, bothered with exclusionary zoning proposals if they believed that the market would ultimately deliver the desired results. One reason may have been that they wanted to accelerate and bring order to the perceived inertia of an unregulated market. An additional reason, about which there can be little doubt, was that they thought they could identify and legislate against external diseconomies, without affecting the overall efficiency of an urban economy.

However lax their understanding of the market for land, it is in governments' attempts at 'internalizing' externalities that planners have wreaked the most havoc. An airport is usually considered an environmental disamenity to households and thus, according to the logic of orthodox urban planning, it must be separated from 'incompatible' land uses such as housing. However, this line of reasoning overlooks the capitalization of (valued) environmental amenities and disamenities in land values. In addition, it is yet another example of the failure to observe the potential heterogeneity of individuals' utility functions. (One implication of economic theory is that individuals receive compensation for the noise from airports through lower house prices. Moreover, the voluntary nature of market transactions ensures that the utility levels of the buyer and seller both are greater than before the transaction. Defensible attempts to avoid external diseconomies thereby reduce to prevention of unanticipated diseconomies affecting established property owners, although this would require a knowledge of *unobservable* utility functions.)

Foldvary (1994) has shown how the elimination of undesirable external diseconomies and the supply of territorial public goods both can be secured in a purely voluntary setting. He does this by explaining how condominiums and voluntary communities in the United States have provided public goods and regulations analogous to those that governments provide. For example, condominiums provide territorial public goods such as swimming pools, parks, elevators and security services, as well as abatement of external diseconomies through littering and noise regulations. The difference between such private settings and a political entity is that the former has to stand the test of the market. This means that they have to offer a package that individuals voluntarily pay to obtain.[3] Foldvary envisions a competitive market for urban environments that reconciles the efficiency of profit-maximizing cities (as measured in land values) with the diverse preferences of individuals in their role as consumers of urban environments.

By shifting the focus from firms' profits to individuals' utilities, it becomes evident that the 'efficiency' of an urban economy is a more elusive idea than seems at first sight. Only voluntary transactions can achieve proven utility gains. The nature of government coercion *guarantees* that the utility gains resulting from government regulations or tax-funded expenditures are impossible to ascertain. It is only by removing obstacles to voluntary transactions that we can provide opportunities for efficiency gains from the non-paternalistic vantage point of methodological individualism. A polity that permits a wide variety of land-use patterns, land-use conversions, *and* land-use regulations is thus, in the sense of providing opportunities for proven utility gains, a more efficient polity.

Perhaps the most surprising revelation of a focus on land values is that the common dichotomy between 'economic freedoms' and 'personal freedoms' is far from obvious. If an individual values freedom of speech or legalization of homosexual marriages, she will be willing to pay more for urban environments that include these attributes than for more puritanical environments.

Land use in Taipei and Singapore[4]

For a present-day traveler going from Taipei to Singapore, the differences between the streets of the two cities are stunning. Whereas the typical street in Taipei comprises first-story business establishments mixed with dwellings on the upper floors, Singapore consists of a number of functionally dissimilar districts. A Central Business District of North American appearance is situated across a river from a shopping and entertainment district, while the ubiquitous 'HDB estates'[5] predominate in outlying areas. These are the planned residential neighborhoods of big apartment houses in which over 85 per cent of the population lives.[6]

In view of present dissimilarities, it is surprising perhaps to discover that Taipei and Singapore once had several urban traits in common. In the 1950s, both cities were medium-sized communities with land-use patterns derived from the traditional urban layout of southern China.[7] This was a high-density environment of narrow lanes with two-to-three-story shophouses, covered walkways, and a lack of any clear spatial division between residential and non-residential functions (McGee, 1967). The migrational roots of the Chinese in the two cities also are similar, even though they are not in geographical proximity to one another.

Land-use patterns and their effect on economic freedom in Taipei

Taipei was originally inhabited by Malayo-polynesian aborigines of the Ketagelan tribe, whom the Hokkien[8] majority later assimilated. The first settlers from the Chinese mainland arrived around the sixteenth century, most of whom were Hokkien peasants from the southern part of Fujian. Over the next 400 years, successive waves of settlers followed. The predominant local language, before 1949, was Hokkien (*Minnanhua*), with the Japanese colonial government imposing Japanese as the official language between 1895 and 1945. Unlike the other ethnic groups,[9] the Japanese were a society apart from the rest of the population, and virtually all Japanese left the island at the end of the Second World War.

With the Nationalist defeat on the Chinese mainland in 1949, soldiers in the Nationalist army and *Kuomintang* supporters from all parts of mainland China arrived *en masse* in 1949. These recent arrivals are currently referred to as 'mainlanders,' and they now amount to roughly 20 per cent of the population of the conurbation.

Chiang Kai Shek and his *Kuomintang* supporters subsequently went on to impose a somewhat unusual type of dictatorship which was unusual in two respects. On the one hand it was heavily dependent on American support, which required it to retain a semblance of political pluralism and freedom. Still, perhaps more crucial, was the 'outward' orientation of its utopian tendencies (utopianism being what politicians of an authoritarian disposition have in common). Insofar as there was no perceived threat to the supposedly shared objective of an anticommunist *Kuomintang*-led reunification of Taiwan with the Chinese mainland, there were few incentives to circumscribe domestic economic freedoms.

In addition, the massive redistribution of land ownership resulting from the Land to Tiller Act of 1952, of which the primary aims were to raise the productivity of land and support Taiwan's nascent industrialization,[10] had as its most lasting effect the expansion of the economic opportunities of the rural majority of the population. The Land to Tiller Act drew some of its inspiration from the homesteading principle, with land to be claimed by the people who cultivated the land. In the following decades, it also provided the extraordinarily large number of people migrating from rural to urban areas with the means of exchanging urban for rural land.

As regards land-use regulations, the government inherited a Japanese approach to city planning. As has been noted by Whyte (1988), Japanese land-use regulations have always been much more tolerant of mixed land uses than their American counterparts. As in Japan, the Taiwanese legal definition of 'residential zone' permits commercial activities to take place on the first floor (and sometimes the second floor) of any residential structure. Also in opposition to current American practice (Davis, 1990), there are no minimum lot-size requirements, and plot-area ratios have been generous enough to allow an extremely high population density.

For a political leadership that was bent on emphasizing the 'provisional' status of Taipei as the capital of the Republic of China, it comes as no surprise that urban policy initiatives, with the aim of presenting Taipei as a showcase capital, were half-hearted at most. The *de facto* implications of Taiwan's land-use regulations and policy initiatives on the economic freedoms enjoyed by its citizens have, as a consequence, been largely beneficial.

As an example of Taipei's typical pattern of urban development, we may look at the area surrounding the campus of Academia Sinica on the eastern outskirts of Taipei. Initially being a remote rural area of paddy fields, it has experienced a remarkable spontaneous transformation into an increasingly urbanized area over the past three decades. At the outset, this transformation consisted of the construction of streets and simple dwellings as well as the appearance of hawkers on the streets. Street hawkers have always been part of the informal economy of Taiwan,[11] and as such they are *de facto* exempt from rents and taxes. The transition from small-scale agriculture to informal retailing in this case represents the initial phase of a process of asset accumulation through entrepreneurship.

With no rents, no taxes, and often with some ownership of land, it became possible for successful street hawkers to accumulate the means of switching to more formal economic activities. They could do this by, for instance, converting their land from purely residential use to mixed use (for example, by converting the first floor of a dwelling into a convenience store or a noodle shop). A flexible implementation of licensing laws aided the opportunities for entrepreneurship. While business licenses have been difficult to obtain before the establishment of a business, it has been common for the Taiwanese authorities to license businesses after an initial period of informal operation. This posterior approach to licensing has doubtless assisted entrepreneurship in its role of being a discovery process, by enabling entrepreneurs to make repeated attempts at business formation. It has also had the effect of securing a higher level of economic freedom, in that it has reduced the start-up costs of new businesses and facilitated the identification of profitable locations for voluntary exchanges.

The resulting land-use pattern near Academia Sinica, as elsewhere in Taipei, is decidedly multi-functional. Densely populated apartment houses intermingle with more or less formal first-story commercial establishments,[12] hawkers on the streets, parks, and educational institutions. Unregulated opening hours, minimal building codes (a generous plot-area ratio and quality requirements that are limited to fire safety regulations), and widespread tax evasion augment the low cost of land-use conversions. If we focus on the freedom of (urban[13]) individuals to conduct voluntary transactions in locations of their own choosing, it would, arguably, be difficult to find a more liberalized economy in Europe or North America.[14]

Singapore's land-use policies as an expression of utopian paternalism

Singapore was, until the early nineteenth century, a sparsely inhabited island with a small population of Muslim Malays. With the expansion of the British Empire in the nineteenth century, a British official, Sir Stamford Raffles, in 1819 proposed the establishment of a British-controlled city on the island. His initiative finally resulted in the 1824 Treaty of London between Britain and Holland, which united Singapore with Penang, Province Wellesley, and Melaka under the Straits Settlements government of the English East India Company. In 1867 the Straits Settlements were transferred to direct colonial rule.

The rationale for controlling an island off the southern tip of the Malay peninsula was the strategic advantage of controlling the shortest route between the Indian Ocean and the North Pacific. Apart from the small group of British administrators and traders, most of the first settlers in Singapore after 1824 were Hokkien traders from the Malay peninsula.

In nineteenth-century China, there was no shortage of poor, young, and landless men willing to seek their fortunes overseas. Because of the familiar cultural features of Singapore's Hokkien pioneers, large numbers of people arrived in Singapore, mainly from Fujian and Guangdong. As in Hong Kong, the British governed with little interference or interest in Asian customs, preferring to let the various Asian communities conduct their internal economic interactions independently. As a result, the most numerous segment of the population constructed houses and streets reminiscent of their ancestral homes in southern China.

As in Taipei, land in the Chinese neighborhoods consisted of narrow lanes with multi-use shophouses. The shophouses typically had family-run businesses on the first floor with dwellings above. While the Chinese neighborhoods of cities such as Taipei and Singapore were – apart from some local idiosyncracies in their architecture and use of material – virtually identical as late as the 1950s, subsequent political developments in Singapore led to a radical divergence in land use, scale, and visual appearance.

The People's Action Party (PAP), which gradually evolved from a left-wing alliance between 'moderates' and communists into an authoritarian political party under the leadership of Lee Kuan Yew (Turnbull, 1989), had ideological traits that were very different from the *Kuomintang* of Chiang Kai Shek. While the latter was essentially a branch of the armed forces with Chinese nationalism and anti-communism as its only tools of internal cohesion,[15] the PAP developed into an instrument for the party's ideologue. This included a puritanical lifestyle, a socialist belief in planning and social engineering, and a technocratic preference for economic growth and the symbols of economic progress.

Later developments, such as the departure of the communists from the PAP to form a new party (*Barisan Sosialis*) in 1961, have purged many of the egalitarian components of socialism from the ideology of the PAP (Turnbull, 1989). Nevertheless, it seems likely that its socialist roots explain the PAP's embrace of extensive land-use planning and social engineering. The Singapore government, for example, has been an ardent advocate of 'Asian Values' which extol social order over individual freedom, explaining perhaps its proclivity towards social engineering tools of taxation, regulation, and prohibition.[16]

The PAP has used planning tools to create a reflection of its ideological construct. The priority given to public housing, as well as to the creation of large government-linked corporations, have also enabled the PAP to entrench its political control. According to Rodan (1996): 'the opposition ranks tend to be over-represented by marginalized people with comparatively little to lose, or self-employed people who have comparative independence, such as small business people or lawyers.' The government has also realized that truly unsupervised land-use decisions by individual citizens, in the long run, runs counter to the authoritarian aim of a shared ideology. Singapore-style city planning is therefore in marked opposition to current American practice, where even the most inflexible exclusionary zoning, none the less, mainly serves as a framework for the private property market.

The wholesale demolition of old neighborhoods in the 1960s and 1970s exemplifies the Singaporean approach to planning. Large portions of what is now the Central Business District once consisted of a mixed-use residential and commercial area divided into small lots. Meanwhile, businesses in the area were moved to large single-use shopping centers owned by property developers. In this way, the great majority of Singaporeans now live in – socially and demographically engineered – single-use high-rises set in vast expanses of grass. Previously, Singapore was a city where (bottom-up) market transactions mostly decided land-use patterns. Currently, it is a city where the bureaucratic elite shapes these patterns. The government not only decides how much land is allocated to each land use, but also the precise location of the various uses and minimum lot sizes. By way of example, if an individual entrepreneur wants to set up a new shop in Singapore, he must typically bid for allocated space in a centrally located shopping mall. Moreover, he must adhere to licensing requirements and the regulations of the shopping mall, which are partly shaped by the government.

The suppression of the spontaneous market process of continuously evolving land-use patterns, the prohibition against small lots, and the reduction of individuals' autonomous decisions as consumers and entrepreneurs, together amount to a severe curtailment of economic freedom. From the individual's standpoint, therefore, there is much less scope for truly voluntary exchanges and much less decentralized decision-making in Singapore than in Taipei.

Conclusion

In this chapter, I have argued that Singapore and Taipei represent two extreme examples of the effects of land-use controls on economic freedom. The type of land-use regulations currently popular in American cities, such as Los Angeles, represents an intermediate level of economic freedom. An interesting corollary of Singapore's planning regime is that the government has managed to reconcile the competitive rigors of awarding lots to the highest bidder with utopian city planning social engineering. It is unfortunate that many advocates of economic development have overlooked the interdependencies between land-use regulations, opportunities for entrepreneurship, and utility gains from trade. This may have led governments – democratic as well as authoritarian – to the excessive application of land-use regulations in the belief that this would be the best way to improve efficiency or environmental quality.

Notes

1. The potentially adverse effects of market interactions in the absence of land ownership has been noted by Buchanan (1993).
2. These measures include predictability of monetary policy, relative size of government consumption and government redistribution, severity of impediments to international transactions, and conscription.
3. Even if the aggregate change in land values can be estimated for public sector investments, it remains impossible to calculate the opportunity cost. Besides, land values do not measure the 'attachment' component of the utility of established land owners.
4. My account of the historical developments and resulting land-use policies and land-use patterns draws on a wide variety of formal and informal sources. As a resident of Taipei and as a frequent visitor to Singapore over the past eight years, I have had the opportunity to explore the two cities and observe their

land-use patterns. I have also benefited from discussions with academics, entrepreneurs, employees, and expatriates in both cities. In particular, Professor Chung-Hsin Yang of the Institute of Economics, Academia Sinica, Taipei, provided me with a wealth of information on laws and law enforcement in Taiwan. My printed sources include the Census of Population 1990 (Department of Statistics, Singapore), Singapore in Facts and Figures, Urban and Regional Development Statistics 1991 (Urban and Housing Development Department, Council for Economic Planning and Development, Executive Yuan, ROC), and news reporting in the *China News*.

5. Housing and Development Board.
6. Census of Population 1990, Department of Statistics, Singapore.
7. Over 70 per cent of Singapore's population are Chinese.
8. Hokkiens from Taiwan are usually, and somewhat misleadingly, called native Taiwanese or *bendiren*, 'people of this locality,' in Taiwan. They make up roughly 70 per cent of the population. The remainder primarily consists of 'mainlanders,' Hakkas, and aborigines. The ethnic identification is strictly patriarchal.
9. I prefer to equate ethnic group with language rather than the peculiar concept of race. Particularly in China, the concept of the Chinese race has been used for manipulative political reasons. (What better way to expand a nation than to convert neighboring peoples into a shared identity?) There is also, I think, a political reason for calling mutually unintelligible languages, such as Hokkien and Cantonese, dialects rather than languages.
10. Industrialization was supported by compensating the former quasi-feudal landlords with shares in confiscated Japanese firms.
11. Estimates of the size of the informal economy range from 30 to over 50 per cent of GDP.
12. It was recently reported by the *China News* that only about 30 of the estimated 6000 karaoke lounges in Taipei City are licensed.
13. The urban qualification refers to the strict enforcement of laws against conversions between agricultural and non-agricultural land.
14. It is, however, uncertain whether the extraordinary economic freedoms enjoyed by Taipei's residents will remain in intact, in view of the determination of the present city government to enforce licensing requirements and building codes.
15. The Three Principles of the People, formulated by Sun Yat Sen, and the ideological rationalization of the *Kuomintang*, is a curious attempt to reconcile various streams of thought popular in political movements at the beginning of the twentieth century, notably nationalism, liberal democracy, and socialism.
16. Emmerson (1995) has criticized the concept of 'Asian Values' for being misleading, owing to the diversity of Asian cultures and philosophies.

References

Alonso, W., *Location and Land Use* (Cambridge Ma.: Harvard University Press, 1964).

Andersson, D.E., 'Households and Accessibility: An Empirical Study of Households' Valuation of Accessibility to One or More Concentrations of Employment and

Services,' *Discussion Papers in Urban & Regional Economics No. 97* (Reading: University of Reading, 1994).

Andersson, D.E., *Hedonic Prices and Center Accessibility: Conceptual Foundations and an Empirical Hedonic Study of the Market for Condominium Housing in Singapore* (Stockholm: KTH Hogskoletryckeriet, 1997).

Buchanan, J.M., 'Property as a Guarantor of Liberty,' in C.K. Rowley, (ed)., *Property Rights and the Limits of Democracy* (Aldershot: Edward Elgar, 1993).

Cheshire, P.C., and S. Sheppard, 'On the Price of Land and the Value of Amenities,' *Economica*, 62 (1995) 247–67.

Davis, M., *City of Quartz: Excavating the Future in Los Angeles* (London: Vintage, 1990).

Emmerson, D.K., 'Singapore and the "Asian Values" debate', *Journal of Democracy*, 6 (October, 1995) 96–100.

Foldvary, F., *Private Communities and Public Goods: The Market Provision of Social Services* (Aldershot: Edward Elgar, 1994).

Gwartney, J., R. Lawson, and W. Block, *Economic Freedom of the World 1975–1995* (Vancouver: Simon Frazer Institute, 1996).

Jacobs, J., *The Death and Life of Great American Cities* (London: Penguin Books, 1961).

McGee, T.G., *The Southeast Asian City* (London: G. Bell & Sons, 1967).

Muth, R.F., *Cities and Housing* (Chicago: University of Chicago Press, 1969).

Rodan, G., 'State–society relations and political opposition in Singapore,' in G. Rodan, (ed)., *Political Oppositions in Industrializing Asia* (London: Routledge, 1996).

Turnbull, C.M., *A History of Malaysia, Singapore and Brunei* (North Sydney: Allen & Unwin Australia, 1989).

Whyte, W.H., *City: Rediscovering the Center* (New York: Doubleday, 1988).

Part II

Environmental and Economic Constraints

9
Ecological Sustainability

Finn R. Førsund

> A sustainable development is a development which meets the needs of the present without compromising the ability of the future generations to meet their needs.
>
> *Our Common Future*, WCED (1987)

The popularized version of sustainable development above is, of course, too vague for practical policy purposes, and also difficult to give a precise theoretical interpretation. Economic interpretations are usually based on a Hicksian concept of sustainable income, with a sharp distinction between income used for consumption as a flow concept, and capital, as a basis for income, as a stock concept (Hicks 1946). Consumption is sustainable if the stock of capital is left intact. This leads us to the general economic definition of sustainability as a non-decreasing consumption path over time.

Since consumption of exhaustible resources obviously does not leave the capital intact, the use of such resources implies the accumulation of some other type of capital capable of generating a sufficient yield. Such capital may be real capital in the conventional sense, knowledge capital, or even cultural capital. We have arrived at the core of the economics of sustainability: the role of substitution.

The environment is influenced by economic activity, but there are no obvious substitution possibilities for keeping a constant level of environmental quality. No man-made goods necessarily compensate for environmental degradation by pollution, reduced stocks of biological resources, or less pristine land. Pollution load increases may be compensated by a reduced number of people, but this is hardly a realistic road to travel.

For a development to be sustainable the utility level must be non-decreasing. We may have some scope for substitution within a utility function between man-made goods and environmental quality. This depends on the marginal utility of environmental quality as it declines. But the role such substitution should be allowed to play within the concept of sustainable development is hotly debated. Hard-core environmentalists claim that the environmental quality should not be allowed to decrease, that is to say, that man-made goods cannot be substitutes for environmental quality. Swimming pools, zoological gardens, parks, adventure parks, and so on, cannot compensate for the loss of 'the real thing.' But there seems to be a general agreement that the use of exhaustible resources such as minerals and fossil fuels can be substituted by man-made real or human capital.

Green accounting

If a development path should exist that satisfies sustainability, we still have the problem of how to measure to what extent such a path corresponds to the current development path. There have been attempts to measure whether a development path is sustainable based on an extension of the national accounts. The general idea is that the consumption path may be sustainable if the total sum of natural capital and man-made capital is constant (this is the so-called Hartwick rule, see Hartwick, 1977). However, there are many pitfalls for empirical applications of this Hicksian approach. Different types of man-made and natural capital must be made comparable, which is impossible without detailed knowledge of future price developments of natural and man-made capital. It is not necessarily the case that an increase in the total capital using current prices implies that the current consumption path is sustainable (Asheim, 1994, 1997), that is, that saving more than the market value of the resource depletion implies sustainability. Comparing the current value of commercial exhaustible resources and total capital formation is neither here nor there as to sustainability.

Rate of discount

Since sustainability is a long-run consideration, the magnitude of the rate of discount is often brought up. Should the rate of discount be smaller for long-term projects than for short-term ones? Can the rate of discount be zero? Our concern for the future is expressed through our decisions about inheritance. A higher rate of discount would correspond to attaching less importance to inheritance and more importance to current consumption. This indicates that the long-term view implies a relatively small rate of discount. But, if we consider investments undertaken by the present generation with a positive present value, a reduction of the discount rate to zero would have unlimited value. Carrying out all investment projects with positive present values may indeed leave the present generation rather poor. A positive rate of discount is therefore compatible with sustainability, but the rate should probably not be constant along an optimal path, but declining.

Current environmental policy

A successful environmental policy will imply that adverse environmental impacts of economic activities are internalized in current decision-making. However, this does not imply that the development is necessarily sustainable if only current evaluations of the environmental effects are taken into consideration. We face the same problems regarding future evaluations as for capital.

Multi-dimensional games

The discharge of pollutants only benefits the current generation, but pollution abatement may only benefit future generations, as is the case for global warming. At the same time as we have intergenerational conflicts in each country about global pollution reduction, we also have conflicts between different countries. The following simple example of two countries and two generations may illustrate the nature of the game (the example is borrowed from Asheim, 1995) (Table 9.1). The question is whether pollutants should be discharged in the first period (the lifetime of the first generation) or not. The payoff matrix is organized with the payoff to country 1 as the first entry, and to country 2 as the second entry after the slash.

The generation headings apply to both countries at the same time. The first generation acts selfishly if it discharges pollutants, inflicting costs on the next generation. If both countries curb pollution in the first period, both

Table 9.1 Payoff matrix: country and generation game

Country 1	*Country 2*			
	No pollution *Generation 1*	*Generation 2*	*Pollution* *Generation 1*	*Generation 2*
No pollution	4/4	4/4	3/6	3/3
Pollution	6/3	3/3	5/5	2/2

the first and the second generation enjoy a welfare level of four for both generations. If both countries pollute in the first period, the first generation in both countries enjoy welfare levels of five, but the second generations enjoy welfare levels of only two. If country 1 pollutes in the first period, but country 2 acts altruistically, the first generation in country 1 enjoys a welfare level of six, while the generation bearing the costs in country 2 only enjoys a level of three. Country 1 benefits from the pollution abatement of country 2 in the first period. The second generation in the short-sighted country 1 enjoys a welfare level of three, the same as the second generation in the altruistic country 2. The benefit of the abatement efforts of country 2 in the first period accrues equally to both countries' second generations. Who said the world is just? Reversing the roles of the two countries in the first period results in symmetrical payoffs.

Without any international cooperation or concern for the next generation, the non-cooperative Nash solution is pollution in both countries in the first period, resulting in welfare levels of five units for the first generation in both countries and a much lower level of two units for the second generations. Full bilateral cooperation and altruistic behavior of the first generations yield pollution clean-up in the first period in both countries, and a welfare level of four for both generations in both countries. For this to be the outcome there must be some ethical preferences at play.

Optimal growth theories

Humankind must have faced problems with the utilization of limited resources and environmental degradation since the dawn of civilization. Some written records to that effect have survived from ancient Egypt, Greece, and Rome. These show that the resolution of free-access-commons problems by a concentration of property rights is an old institutional solution. But the social skills of early humankind or primitive tribes in husbanding biological resources are probably overrated. A guess would be that the hunting or harvesting technology was not productive enough to threaten reproduction. There is archeological evidence that the productivity of chasing herd animals over traps, for example, over cliffs, leads to many more animals being killed than could be utilized.

The long-term view was common among economists at the onset of the industrial revolution. The steady state envisioned by Malthus, with its balance between population and food production, and Ricardo's iron law of wages that predicted poverty as the rule, do not, however, seem particularly attractive as sustainable states.

The neoclassical heritage

Neoclassical aggregated growth theory as popularized by Solow (1957) has greatly influenced modern economic thinking about growth. The focus is on the steady state level of *per capita* consumption. At first glance this may seem interesting, from a sustainability perspective, but the opposite is actually the case. There is neither any constraint on the availability of physical resources, nor is there any restriction against residual discharges or any environmental considerations in general. Utility is only derived from the consumption of man-made goods. The problem of resource depletion and the link between the use of resources and environmental degradation is absent, as is the recognition that the state of the environment has direct impacts on people's utility levels.

Instead, the key concept of neoclassical growth theory – 'the golden rule of capital accumulation' – is found by maximizing consumption per head with respect to the capital–labor ratio. A result of neoclassical growth theory is, furthermore that the accumulation of capital should be conducted at such a pace that the marginal productivity of capital per worker is equal to the population growth rate in steady-state equilibrium. This implies that the savings rate is equal to the ratio of the marginal productivity of the steady-state capital per worker, and the average production per worker. Since capital must increase at the same rate as labor in steady state, this total capital accumulation is exactly enough to maintain a constant capital–labor ratio. On the terms of the model itself, the development is sustainable; a constant consumption per head can be maintained forever.

In defense of neoclassical growth theory, it should be said that it has not been seriously intended as a theory for really long-term growth. It is too obvious that exhaustible resources will run out in finite time if the extraction rate is positive. This type of model grew out of an interest in long-term employment problems, such as the balance between capital accumulation, job creation, and population growth. The long run is also definitely not infinity, but something between a five-year and a fifty-year perspective.

Growth and pollution dynamics

A very simple two-period model will bring out some essential features of the problems we face with accumulating pollution. Let all interactions between the environment and the economy be captured by a partial two-relationship model consisting of monetized damage functions, D_i, being strictly convex, and benefit functions, B_i, being strictly concave. P_i represents the pollution level and the periods, i, are indexed t and $t+1$:

$$D_t = D_t(P_t), D_{t+1} = D_{t+1}(P_t + P_{t+1}), D'_i > 0, D''_i > 0 \tag{9.1}$$

$$B_i = B_i(P_i), B'_i > 0, D''_i < 0 \tag{9.2}$$

The partial character of the model is obvious, not showing explicitly the trade-off between environmental quality and man-made goods. The case of pure accumulation of pollutants is shown in the damage function for period $t+1$, the initial level of accumulated pollutants being included in the functional forms. There is no decay of the pollutants. The benefit function is based on the value to the consumer of man-made goods and least-cost ways of reducing the discharge of the pollutant, including conventional purification and reduction of production.

The social planning problem is to find the discharge of pollutants that maximizes benefits minus damage costs. This procedure *implicitly* takes care of the linkages including the generation of pollutants and physical environmental impacts through dose-response relationships, that is to say the trade-offs between environmental quality and man-made goods.

Let us start by solving the decision problem for the first period. Since accumulation occurs, the future period damage must also be taken into account.

$$\text{Maximize}_{\,Pt}\{B_t(P_t) - D_t(P_t) - D_{t+1}(P_t + P_{t+1})\} \tag{9.3}$$

Two important lessons can be drawn from this simple model formulation. First, the discharge in the future period must also be decided upon in period t in order for the problem to have a solution. Thus, society faces a *simultaneous* multi-period problem. Second, accumulation implies that the concept of the marginal damage of current pollution must be extended to cover not only the current period marginal damage, but also the future period marginal damage.

The relevant social planning problem is therefore:

$$\text{Maximize}_{\,P_t, P_{t+1}}\{B_t(P_t) + B_{t+1}(P_{t+1}) - D_t(P_t) - D_{t+1}(P_t + P_{t+1})\} \tag{9.4}$$

yielding the first-order conditions:

$$B'_t = D'_t + D'_{t+1}, B'_{t+1} = D'_{t+1} \tag{9.5}$$

These are two equations in the two endogenous variables having a solution under our assumptions. A third general lesson can be learned by the nature of the conditions: For constant functional forms the discharge in period t must obviously be less than the discharge in period $t+1$. In the general case of changing functional forms, only a sufficiently strong positive shift in the benefit function and/or a sufficient negative shift in the damage function can reverse this feature of an optimal discharge policy. Casual empiricism, however, indicates *positive* shifts in the damage function, and an inconclusive direction in the shift of the benefit function.

The green golden rule

The definition of sustainability that utility, which is a function of both current consumption and environmental qualities as functions of stock concepts, should be non-decreasing, is termed the *green golden rule* in Heal (1995). The main idea here is that among development paths that are environmentally feasible in the sense that stocks of environmental resources are not run down, one attempts to find the path that maximizes long-run utility. Heal's idea requires that the stock of pollutants should not be allowed to grow, that biological resources are kept at a constant level corresponding to the maximum sustainable yield, and that congestion is kept at bay. To meet the last requirement any population increase must be compensated by regulating access to natural environments and/or by increasing the land area devoted to natural ecosystems.

The key concept for sustainability of environmental resources, including global resources such as the climate and the ozone layer, is the critical load. It is rather obvious that, in order to secure long-term sustainability, we cannot allow more pollution than that which corresponds to the absorption capacity defined as the critical load in a dynamic setting. But, note that if there are some capacities that are not fully utilized in the first period, utilizing them now would leave future generations worse off, and this would not satisfy the strict definition of sustainability. However, if we are currently overloading nature, and the environmental quality is deteriorating, as is perhaps the case with global warming, reducing the loads to be within natural depreciations and less than the critical loads may lead to a sustainable path.

Conclusion

In view of the rate of discovery of new exhaustible resources, and the trend of technological progress in decreasing the unit use of resources, it is the various environmental quality constraints that are likely to make up the most important management problems in the future. These environmental problems range from mere nuisances to potentially life-threatening problems.

Accumulation of pollutants, such as greenhouse gases, belongs to the rather threatening problems, while reduced air and water quality, in general, may be more local negative amenities that may be best solved at the local level. The extinction of species is perhaps also a passing discomfort: Who cares about the Do-do bird that got killed off in New Zealand around 1700? The possibility of preference changes poses a deep ethical problem. It is possible to envision an environment completely engineered by humans with very little in the way of pristine natural habitats. This would be desirable if our preferences were to match such a state, and provided ecological life-supporting systems, such as photosynthesis, are not destroyed.

The concept of a sustainable path is hardly operational. All future prices of man-made capital, natural capital, and irreversible environmental amenities have to be known at the outset. Therefore, a *standards approach* seems to be the only feasible option. The international community should take responsibility for international environmental resources, and set physical utilization limits and promote institutions and instruments to make countries, firms, and individuals comply. International agreements are necessary for keeping cross-border pollution sufficiently in check to secure sustainability, including pollutants that cause global warming, and for managing biological resources in free-access international commons.

However, there are serious distributional issues involved, both between countries at various development stages, and between present and future generations. Placing restrictions on the present generation is an investment for future benefits, but while current hardships are real and observable, the success of such investments are highly uncertain, and we do not even know if future generations will be grateful at all.

There are social norms, often in the name of religion, that make people behave in a way that naive utility maximization cannot explain. Maybe such social norms may be introduced as a protection against the consequences of each person pursuing individual goals.

References

Asheim, G.B., 'Net national product as an indicator of sustainability', *Scandinavian Journal of Economics* 96 (1994) 257–65.

Asheim, G.B., 'Adjusting green NNP to measure sustainability', *Scandinavian Journal of Economics* 99 (1997) 355–70.

Hartwick, J., 'Intergenerational equity and the investing of rents from exhaustible resources', *American Economic Review* 66 (1977) 972–74.

Heal, G., 'Lecture notes on sustainability', *Memorandum* from Department of Economics, University of Oslo, No. 16, May 1995.

Hicks, J., *Value and Capital* (Oxford: Oxford University Press, 1946).
Solow, R.A., 'Technical change and the aggregate production function', *Review of Economics and Statistics* 39 (1957) 312–20.
WCED (The World Commission on Environment and Development), *Our Common Future* (Oxford: Oxford University Press, 1987).

10
Pollution Transitions and Economic Growth in Asia

Hua Chang-i

The rapid economic growth occurring in most parts of Asia has caused widespread concern over the increase in pollution levels in the region. This concern is apparent if we consider the following questions: China has a population which is five times greater than the US, and India's population is rapidly approaching the same size. If the *per capita* incomes of these two countries were to increase to a level close to that of the western countries, would the total amount of CO_2 emissions created by the necessarily huge production stifle world economic development? Or will these latecomers to industrialization generate less pollution per unit of output? Further, will the pollution generated from Asia's development reach a maximum before leveling off or even declining? This chapter attempts to address all of these questions.

Consistent and comparable data among Asian countries are hard to come by. Our data include only total emissions of one pollutant, namely carbon dioxide (P) in metric tons, total economic output (Q), in constant US dollar of gross domestic product, and population (N) for India, China, South Korea, and Japan. The four countries are at different levels of development which make them relevant for comparative purposes. On the other hand, our data cover only the 19 years from 1973 to 1991, which is a short time span in the course of economic development. This limits our ability to generalize from the analysis. None the less, a study of the pollution dynamics over these 19 years should help shed light on the relationship between pollution levels and economic growth in Asia.

Pollution transition in East Asia: theory and data

To most people, sustainable development refers to the cessation of economic growth (for a representative position, see Daly, 1990). However, to many scholars, especially many mainstream economists, this is the wrong prescription. As there is empirical evidence pointing to a correlation between poverty and environmental degradation in developing countries, the cessation of growth may only make things worse (MacNieill, 1989). A big push would therefore be needed to rapidly increase people's incomes, since rising incomes have historically been associated with environmental improvement.

Among the proponents of growth, Baldwin (1995) emphasizes the intervening variable of population, and argues that people make pollution while poverty makes people. Most interestingly, he proposes an ecological transition to echo the well known demographic transition: just as population growth rate is the net result of the birth rate and the death rate, so the effective *per capita* pollution is the net result of incipient *per capita* pollution and the *per capita* abatement. The original descriptive demographic transition with time as the horizontal axis has often been extended to a theory by the 'Big Push' school of development economics using *per capita* income to substitute time. Consequently, a bell-shaped curve has been proposed to describe the behavior of *per capita* pollution over time (Baldwin, 1995) with theoretical rationale premised upon the works of Becker *et al.* (1990) and Grossman (1995).

To address Baldwin's hypothesis, Figures 10.1 and 10.2 plot P, Q, and N, in natural logarithmic scale, against time for each of the four countries. The graphs show several interesting trends:

1 Pollution and production indeed go together in tandem in each country, while population growth may be regarded as running a separate course.
2 While the increase in CO_2 emissions persisted in both India and South Korea, it seems to have slowed down in China and Japan. Yet, a leveling off of total emissions is not yet in sight.
3 The ratio between pollution and production varied widely among countries, and it also changed over time, in different directions within each country. If it measures efficiency, then China is least while Japan is most efficient. Furthermore, while China, Korea, and Japan all improved on this score, India regressed during this period.

Let $g = P/N$ measure *per capita* pollution of CO_2 and $y = Q/N$ *per capita* income. Furthermore, let $f = P/Q$ measure the pollution per unit of output. These three derived quotients are plotted in Figure 10.2 against time for

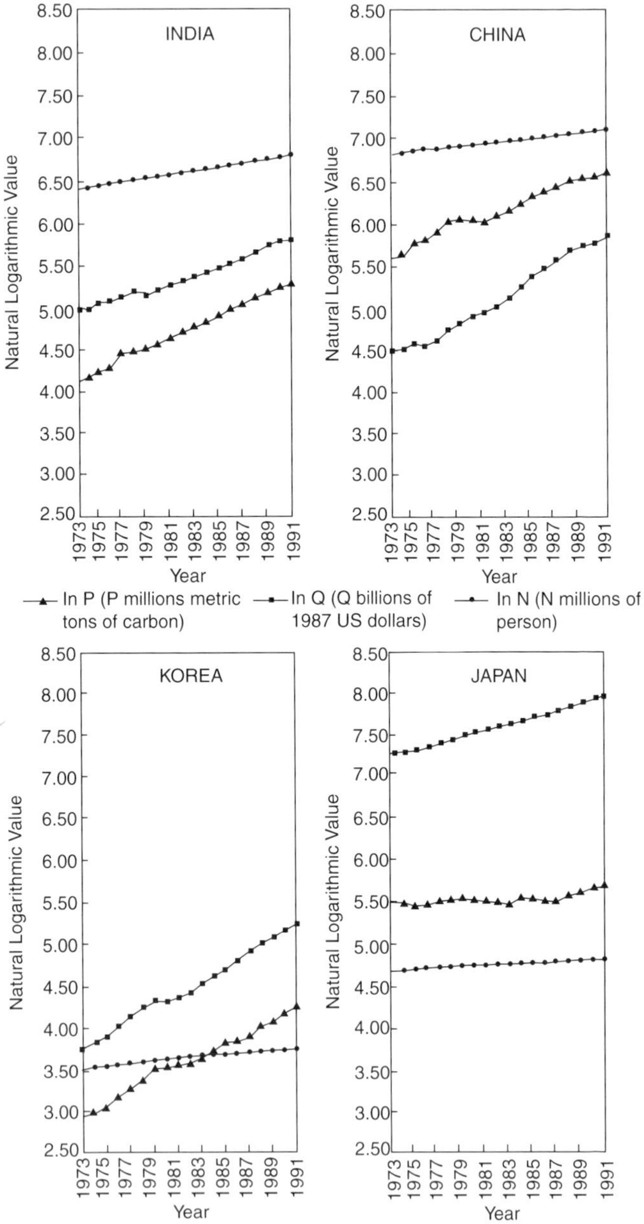

Figure 10.1 CO_2 emissions in metric tons (*P*), economic output (*Q*) and population (*N*)

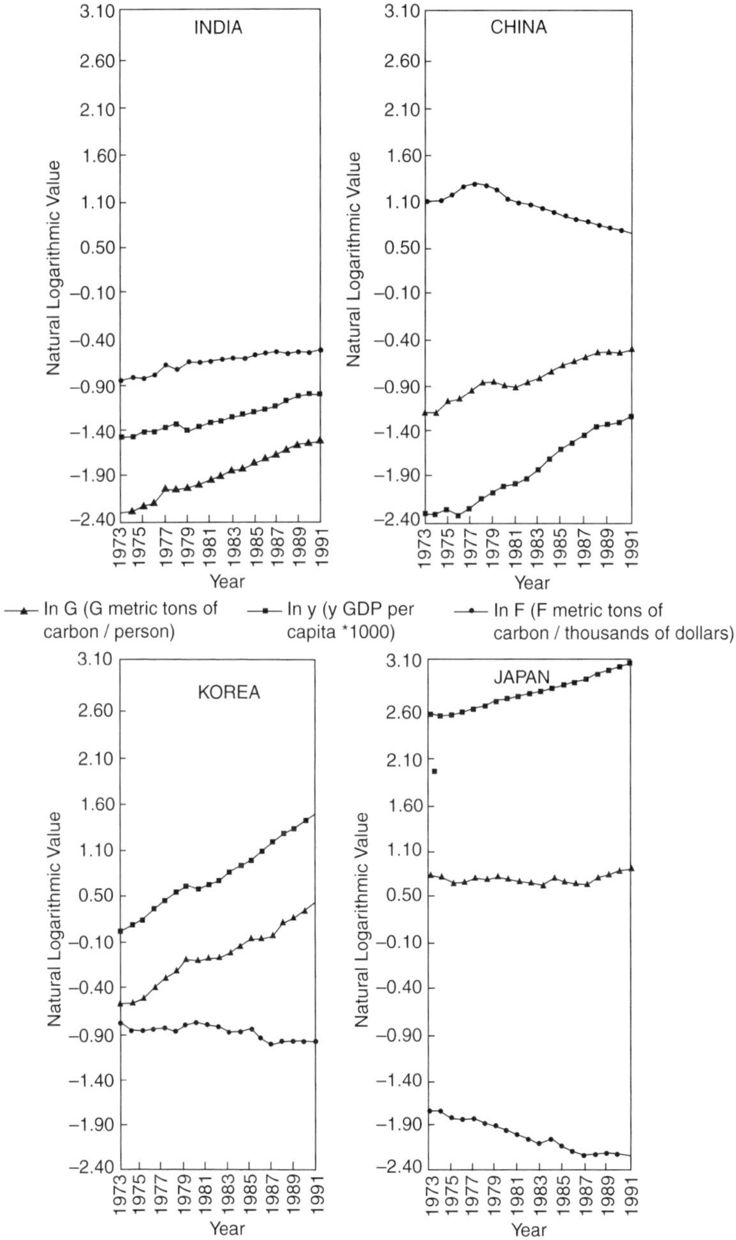

Figure 10.2 CO_2 emissions by *per capita*

each of the four countries. Figure 10.2 provides us with more meaningful information than Figure 10.1:

1. As is well known, all of the four Asian countries saw their *per capita* income continuously increase in this period. The increases in China and Korea were much faster than in India and Japan, who in their turn grew faster than most European and American countries.
2. *Per capita* CO_2 emissions also increased in India, China, and Korea, but declined in Japan. It is not clear, however, if the other three countries would exhibit declining quotients, such as Baldwin's ecological transition model would imply, after their *per capita* incomes reached that of Japan's.
3. In terms of CO_2 emission per unit of output, again China was the least efficient country, but seemed to have reached its peak around 1980.

The pollution and economic trends, so far, would seem to suggest that there is a maximum level of *f*, which is represented by an inverted U curve, over the long run in economic development. This represents another transition, which may be termed the output quality transition.

The total pollution of a country or a region can, as proposed by Cohen (1995), can be decomposed into:

$$\begin{aligned} P &= (P/Q)\,(Q/N)\,N \\ &= fyN \end{aligned} \qquad (10.1)$$

This equation is useful for identifying the sources of pollution change. The three components in the equation can be viewed as dimensions that measure different aspects. The first term on the right side, *f*, measures the output quality with respect to generated pollution; the second term, *y*, the economic welfare of residents; and the third term, *N*, the population size. Equation (10.1) implies that the rate of pollution change is the sum of the rates of change in these three components:

$$.P/P = .f/f + .y/y + .N/N + e \qquad (10.2)$$

In the equation, *e* covers the interaction terms ($.f/f\ .y/y + .f/f\ .N/N..y/y\ .N/N + .f/f\ .y/y\ .N/N$). Our data can be used to compute 18 annual rates of change for each term in the equation for each of the four countries. They are tabulated below with their respective percentage distribution in parentheses (Table 10.1).

Clearly the growth of pollution in these countries during the 1973 to 1991 period was mainly the result of the *per capita* income growth, but was

Table 10.1 Annual rates of pollution change

	India	*China*	*Korea*	*Japan*
$\dot{p}/P$	0.061(1.00)	0.051 (1.00)	0.070 (1.00)	0.009 (1.00)
$\dot{f}/f$	0.017 (0.28)	–0.022 (–0.43)	–0.019 (–0.27)	–0.030 (–3.33)
$\dot{y}/y$	0.024 (0.39)	0.056 (1.09)	0.056 (1.09)	0.030 (3.33)
$\dot{N}/N$	0.021 (0.34)	0.015 (0.29)	0.013 (0.19)	0.007 (0.78)
e	–0.001 (–0.01)	0.002 (0.04)	0.007 (0.10)	0.001 (0.11)

also substantially abated by the improvement of output quality. In the case of Japan, the latter just about fully compensated for the former. The population growth effect, however, was a minor one except for India.

Cohen has further proposed extending equation (10.2) to:

$$P(y) = f(y)yN(y) \qquad (10.3)$$

which contains

$$g(y) = f(y)y \qquad (10.4)$$

From equation (10.3), an extreme value may be given at P′(Y) = 0 such that:

$$fN + (Nf' + f\,N')y = 0 \qquad (10.5)$$

Cohen argues that since both $f'(y)$ and $N'(y)$ are negative, at least when y is very large, the above equation indicates that if the magnitude of $(Nf' + fN')\,y$ exceeds fN, then $P(y)$ can be represented as an inverted U-shaped curve. This is unnecessarily restrictive, however. The demographic transition does not include $N' < 0$, and empirically $N' < 0$ has only occurred in a few countries during the period following the demographic transition, a phenomenon so new that its long-run implications are yet to be examined. Thus, $N' > 0$ should be taken as the normal case, which is also indicated in Figure 10.1.

To generalize, equation (10.5) is the condition for an extreme value of $P(y)$. Since $P(y)$ is increasing before this point, it is indeed an inverted U-curve, at least within a certain local range, and equation (10.5) indicates where maximum pollution occurs. Whether $P(y)$ is before or after this point depends on whether $Nf' + fN' > -fN/y$, which can alternatively be expressed as

$$E_y^f > -(1 + E_y^N) \qquad (10.6)$$

where E_y^f is the elasticity of f with respect to y and E_y^N the elasticity of N with respect to y. Before the negative growth of population, pollution *can* decline as long as the first elasticity is large, or f' is steep enough. We differ from Baldwin and Cohen because we show that it is the output quality transition that is important in turning the tide of pollution generation.

If $P(y)$ is indeed an inverted U-curve, then there is a pollution transition. Let $P/N = g(y)$, and further assume it is an inverted U-curve to represent the ecological transition, as Baldwin argues. Furthermore, as we shown above, there is an inverted U-curve of $f(y)$, which is also hinted in Figure 10.2, with China representing the case with a turning point. Taken together, there are actually three transitions.

Given equation (10.3), it can be shown that there is a logical sequence (see Appendix): the peak of $P(y)$ is preceded by the peak of $g(y)$, which is in turn preceded by the peak of $f(y)$. This sequencing is important. One cannot expect the emission of pollutants to decline unless a country has passed the turning point of the ecological transition. And one cannot expect the latter to be the case unless one knows that the country has gone through the worst stage of the output quality transition. In short, the output quality transition is the necessary condition for a pollution transition.

To operationalize the model, the following rationales are made in order to capture, first, a functional form amounting to an inverted U-curve, and, second, the aggregation based on equation (10.3):

$$\log f = a_1 + b_1 y + c_1 y^2 + e_1 \tag{10.7}$$

$$\log N = a_2 + b_2 y + c_2 y^2 + e_2 \tag{10.8}$$

In the two equations, e_1 and e_2 are stochastic terms. From this have

$$\log g = a_1 + b_1 y + c_1 y^2 + \log y + e_1 \tag{10.9}$$

$$\log P = (a_1 + a_2) + (b_1 + b_2)y + (c_1 + c_2)y^2 + \log y + (e_1 + e_2) \tag{10.10}$$

The parameters in equations (10.7) and (10.8) can be estimated by the standard regression method (Table 10.2).

The estimated performance of model (10.8) is impressive. For each country, the regression coefficients are all very significant, and the overall coefficient of determination is high. It is impressive in that these four countries are quite different in their patterns of population growth, yet all can be explained simply by the *per capita* income alone. During this period of 19 years, India is in the fast demographic growth phase and its total population grew by 45.4 per cent; China, on the other hand, under a strictly enforced birth-control policy, grew by 30.5 per cent. South Korea grew by 26.5 per cent when its income was increasing most rapidly. Finally, Japan, with a rather mature economy, grew by only 13.8 per cent. One can see that all of the four countries were in a decreasingly growing

Table 10.2 Regression results based on equations (10.7) and (10.8)

	a_1	b_1	c_1	R^2	a_2	b^2	c_2	R^2
India	–3.26	15.8	–22.8	0.84	4.75	9.95	–12.3	0.96
	(–6.4)	(4.6)	(–4.1)		(16.8)	(5.3)	(–4.0)	
China	1.53	0.88	1.88	0.88	6.59	2.68	–4.02	0.96
	(9.9)	(–1.8)	(0.4)		(1.63)	(5.6)	(–3.1)	
Korea	–0.75	–0.044	–0.004	0.67	3.29	0.299	–0.028	0.97
	(–9.1)	(–0.7)	(–0.3)		(1.35)	(11.9)	(–8.3)	
Japan	0.441	–0.235	0.005	0.96	4.20	0.0534	–0.0011	0.97
	(1.6)	(–7.6)	(5.9)			(8.4)	(–6.6)	

(*t*-statistics in parenthesis)

population path with *per capita* incomes explaining both the growth rates and the decreasing speed.

In contrast, the statistical performance of model (10.7) varies widely among the four countries. The case of India is close to what is expected: b_1 is positive and c_1 is negative and both are significant. Thus, f is indeed increasing at a decreasing rate and a maximum value of f can be computed. In the cases of China and Korea, the signs of the two coefficients are, although insignificant, not as expected. For Japan, we have a significant negative b_1 and a significant positive c_1. From this, a minimum value of f can be computed, although this would be difficult to interpret with the model.

We therefore must conclude that model (10.7) is not satisfactory. This is perhaps not too surprising considering that there may well be many factors besides the *per capita* income that affects the pollution per unit of output in a country. Before we speculate on what these factors are, one implication is that models (10.9) and (10.10), since they are based on model (10.7), are of questionable validity. So while both ecological and pollution transitions may occur, they are not explained by the change of *per capita* income alone.

On the other hand, we argue that the output quality transition is a prerequisite for the other two transitions. This may be further demonstrated by decomposing Grossman's model into two factors:

$$f_t = P_t/Q_t = {}_i a_{it} s_{it} \qquad (10.11)$$

where subscript t indexes time and i the economic sector (or other finer ways of classifying the economy). a_{it}, a technological coefficient, is the pollution generated by a unit of output from sector i; $s_{it} = Q_{ti}/Q_t$, a structural coefficient, is the share of output deriving from sector i. Hence, the change of f reflects both the change in the composition of the economy and the change in the technology of pollution abatement.

Since goods from the primary and tertiary sectors of an economy generate less pollution per unit of output, then as *per capita* income increases over time, the distribution of goods and services across an economy should change (Syrquin, 1989). This would result in changes in the composition of pollution.

A numerical example may serve to illustrate this. Consider a matrix of s_{it} representing the structural change in a three-sector economy over three stages,

$$s_{it} = \begin{matrix} 0.8 & 0.3 & 0.1 \\ 0.1 & 0.5 & 0.3 \\ 0.1 & 0.2 & 0.6 \end{matrix}$$

The first column represents the distribution of output in the initial stage when most output comes from the primary sector. The second column represents that in the industrializing stage when the secondary sector takes command. The third column represents the post-industrial stage, when most output comes from the tertiary sector. Next, assume that the pollution generated by each unit of output in each sector is measured as

$$a_i = (1 \quad 5 \quad 1)$$

Multiplying the row vector a_i with the matrix of s_{it} we have $(P/Q)_t = (1.4 \quad 3.0 \quad 2.2)$. This demonstrates the rise and probable fall of P/Q during the three stages of development. The technological coefficients a_i are here assumed to be stationary during the three stages. If we further let them decrease over time, then the three resultant P/Q values will become a distinctly inverted V.

Summary and conclusion

This chapter sets out to explain, both theoretically and empirically, the trends in CO_2 emissions, economic output, and population for India, China, South Korea, and Japan from 1973–91. Each of the four countries experienced decreasing rates of positive population growth. Population changes in the four countries can all be statistically explained by the *per capita* income alone. On the other hand, only a small portion of the pollution growth in the four countries can directly be attributed to population growth.

Per capita income can be viewed both as an explanatory variable of pollution and as an argument of people's welfare function. Yet, the output quality should be the focus of our attention since decreases in the pollution quotient of output is the prerequisite for a pollution transition. This quotient was observed to be declining in China, Korea, and Japan, but ascending in India.

The change of this quotient in a country can be traced to both structural changes in the economy and technological improvements. To the extent that the income level is related to these two factors, it is associated to the course of pollution. More meaningfully, both structural changes and technology improvements are subject to policy measures. Emphasizing the tertiary sector in an economy and the rapid transition from the secondary sector to it would reduce total pollution. Shifting investment from consumption goods to pollution abatement would improve the technology. These policy measures are matters of choices and in most cases involve tradeoffs. They reflect the collective values of a society. The value question is not independent of the income level of a country, however. Thus, the idea that faster economic development will eventually bring down pollution cannot be rejected, especially when the intervening variable of output quality is taken into consideration.

Appendix

Since $P(y) = g(y)\ N(y)$, we have $P' = gN' + Ng'$. When P/N reaches its maximum, $g' = 0$. Substituting this into the last equation entails $P' = g\,N' > 0$ if we take the normal case $N' > 0$. That is, P is still increasing. On the other hand, when P reaches its maximum, $P' = 0$. Substituting this into the same equation entails $g' = -\ (N'/N)\ g < 0$. That is, P/N is already declining. Combining these two results, we conclude that there is a lag between the two inverted U-curves $P(y)$ and $g(y)$ and that the latter leads the former.

In a similar way we can analyze the courses of $f(y)$ and $g(y)$. From equation (10.4), we have $g' = y\,f' + f$. When P/Q reaches its maximum, $f' = 0$. Substituting this into the last equation entails $g' = f > 0$. That is, P/N is still increasing. On the other hand, when P/N reaches its maximum, $g' = 0$. Substituting this into the same equation entails $f' = -f/Y < 0$. That is, P/Q is already declining. Thus, we conclude that there is a lag between the two inverted U-curves $g(y)$ and $f(y)$, and that the latter leads the former.

References

Baldwin, R., 'Does Sustainability Require Growth?', in I. Goldin and L.A. Winters (eds), *The Economics of Sustainable Development* (Cambridge: Cambridge University Press, 1995).

Becker, G., K. Murphy and R. Tamura, 'Human Capital, Fertility, and Economic Growth', *Journal of Political Economy*, 96 (1990) S12–S37.

Cohen D., 'Discussion (On R. Baldwin's 'Does Sustainablity Require Growth?)', in I. Goldin and L.A. Winters *op. cit.*

Daly, H.E., 'Toward Some Operational Principles of Sustainable Development', *Ecological Economics*, 2 (1990).

Grossman, G.M., ' Pollution and Growth: What DO We Know?', in I. Goldin and L.A. Winters, *op. cit.*

MacNieill, J., 'Strategies for Sustainable Economic Development', *Scientific* American, 261 (1989) 154–65.

Syrquin, M. 'Pattern of Structural Change', in H. Chenery and T.N. Strinivasan, (eds), *Handbook for Development Economics, Vol. 1* (Amsterdam: North-Holland, 1989).

World Resource Institute, *World Resources 1990–1991* (New York: Oxford University Press, 1990).

11

Social Security Systems in Southeast Asia: Are They Sustainable?

*Mukul G. Asher**

This chapter provides an assessment of the sustainability of the formal social security arrangements in five Southeast Asian countries, namely, Indonesia, Malaysia, Philippines, Singapore, and Thailand. There are several reasons why the provision on a sustainable basis of a socially adequate and equitable retirement protection system, while simultaneously minimizing adverse effects on economic efficiency, incentives, and international competitiveness, is of major importance to these countries.

First, as a result of economic growth and accompanying industrialization and urbanization (Table 11.1), these countries are experiencing an erosion of the informal system, based on family and community, which has traditionally taken care of the aged. The importance of the formal system for individuals and for the economy is, therefore, set to increase in the future, and requiries policy response.

Second, these countries are expected to experience both individual aging (reflected in higher life expectancy at birth) and population aging (reflected in increasing share of the population above 60 years of age) (Table 11.2). The Elderly Dependency Ratio (EDR) is expected to rise significantly in all five countries but, particularly, in Singapore and Thailand (Table 11.2). As women generally live longer than men, many older persons will be women. Indeed, in all five countries, women already outnumber men among the old-old, that is, those above 75 years of age (Bos *et al.*, 1994). But, typically, women have a lower degree of exposure to

* This paper has benefited from the thoughtful comments of Robert Palacios, G. Shantakumar, Joseph Delfico, and an anonymous referee. I would also like to thank Krishnamoorthy Viswanathan for research assistance. They are, however, not responsible for errors, omissions or the views expressed in the chapter.

Table 11.1 Southeast Asia: economic and urban indicators

	GNP (US$ millions)	*GNP per capita (US$)*	*Annual real rate of growth*	*Share of Mfg in GDP*		*Urban population as percentage of total population*		*Average annual growth rate*
	1995	*1995*	*1985–95*	*1980*	*1995*	*1980*	*1995*	*1980–95*
Indonesia	198 079	980	6.0	13	24	22	34	4.8
Malaysia	85 311	3 890	5.7	21	33	42	54	4.3
Philippines	74 180	1 050	1.5	26	23	38	53	4.9
Singapore	83 695	26 730	6.2	29	27	100	100	1.8
Thailand	167 056	2 740	8.4	22	29	17	20	2.6

Note: The World Bank classifies Singapore as a high-income country, Malaysia as an upper-middle-income country, while the other three are classified as low-middle-income countries.
Source: World Bank, *World Development Report 1997*, p. 209; Table 1, pp. 214–15; Table 9, pp. 230–1, and Table 12, pp. 236–7.

the labor market and a lower level of earnings than men. Social security arrangements in Southeast Asia will need increasingly to take this into account.

During the 1990–2000 period, except for Singapore, the population in Southeast Asia grew at a faster rate than the working age population (Table 11.2). As a result, rapid labor force growth could be potentially relied on as an avenue for rapid economic growth. This situation may be termed the demographic gift (Asian Development Bank, 1997, para. 14.2). Reliance on this gift, however, would need to be gradually reduced: during the 2030–50 period, it is projected that all five countries will experience a demographic burden, where the rate of growth of working-age population will lag behind that of the total population. One of the ways these countries could capture the benefits of favorable demographic trends is to set up sustainable social security arrangements before the demographic gift turns into a burden.

Third, individual and population aging, along with modernization, neglect of the environment, and higher income are expected to lead to a convergence of the morbidity (i.e., nature of illnesses affecting the population) and mortality profiles of East and Southeast Asia towards those currently obtained in the industrialized countries resulting in a substantial increase in demand for health care (Heller, 1997).

Fourth, with increasing *per capita* income, demand for economic security by individuals in Southeast Asia is expected to increase.

Table 11.2 Southeast Asia: selected demographic and labor force indicators

Country	*Average annual rate of population growth*			*Annual average rate of labor growth*			*Total fertility rate (TFR)*[a]		*Proportion of population above 60*[a]		*Elderly dependency ratio (EDR)*[b]	
	1990–2000	2000–30	2030–50	1990–2000	2000–30	2030–50	1990–95	2025–30	1990	2030	1990	2025
Indonesia	1.5	1.0	0.5	2.4	1.1	0.2	2.93	2.16	6.4	14.1	11.3	19.3
Malaysia	2.1	1.3	0.7	2.6	1.6	0.5	3.50	2.08	5.7	14.5	10.3	20.8
Philippines	2.3	1.5	0.8	2.7	2.0	0.7	4.05	2.11	5.3	13.5	8.9	16.2
Singapore	1.6	0.8	0.0	1.5	0.3	–0.1	1.80	2.05	8.5	29.4	12.6	43.9
Thailand	1.4	0.8	0.4	1.4	0.8	0.1	2.21	2.11	6.0	18.0	10.0	23.1

Note: [a] TFR is the average number of births per woman in the population. A TFR of 2.1 maintains a stable population, assuming no net migration takes place. TFR of slightly above 2 is needed to account for women who may die before reaching the fertility age.
[b] EDR is defined as persons 60 years and above/persons 15–59.

Source: World Bank, 1994 Tables A1 and A2, pp. 343–53; and Bos *et al.*, 1994 Table 10, pp. 30–3.

Moreover, if international experience is any guide, continued economic growth and westernization are likely to bring about an attitudinal shift towards more individualistic life-styles and consumption patterns. One of the consequences would be to make parents less willing to live with their children in their old age and *vice versa*. Increasingly, deeper integration of the Southeast Asian economies with the world economy will necessitate provision of adequate social safety nets if these countries are to sustain the necessary internal social cohesion and political support for globalization.

Fifth, currency and stock-market turmoil set off by the devaluation of the Thai baht on July 2, 1997 has significant implications for social security arrangements in Southeast Asia. Not only is the medium-term economic growth expected to slow significantly, but many unpopular and painful reform measures would need to be undertaken. To ensure social cohesion, it is essential that burden-sharing required to cope with the aftermath of the turmoil is perceived by the population as equitable, and that the heightened anxiety of the population of these countries concerning their future economic well-being is addressed (Sato, 1998).

Not only have the currency and stock-market values declined sharply, but several weaknesses in corporate governance, and in financial sector lending and regulatory practices have also become evident in Southeast Asia[1] (Claessens and Glaessner, 1997; *Economist*, 1997). As a result, investing accumulated balances in defined-contribution provident and pension funds, much preferred by the Southeast Asian policy-makers, in a prudent yet remunerative manner, would be even more of a challenge than is usually the case.

Options for financing social security

The main tasks of any social security system are to alleviate poverty, prevent a significant and abrupt fall in the standard of living upon retirement, death, or disability, and to make adequate level of health care accessible and affordable to individuals in their old age. Governments are usually involved in provision of social security because of market imperfections, the need for income redistribution, and paternalism (Diamond, 1995). In addition to informal family or community-based arrangements, there are three broad options for financing social security. The first is the pay-as-you-go (PAYG) system. It is usually publicly managed, mandatory, universal (those satisfying the requisite criteria are automatically entitled to the benefits), earnings-related (formulae determining retirement income flows are related to individual earnings histories), and defined-benefit (DB) type in which a certain level of benefits is prescribed. This system is most commonly found in the developed countries, and until recently in Latin America. Under this system, today's workers are taxed (usually a payroll tax is used) to pay for the prescribed benefits to the current retirees. The system is unfunded, that is, no accumulation of funds is undertaken to help meet the future pension liabilities. This is, however, not inherent in the PAYG system, as partial pre-funding can be easily incorporated in its design.

The benefit formulae are designed to redistribute income in favor of the lifetime poor, make adjustments for inflation and longevity risks, and provide survivors' benefits. Therefore, both social insurance and redistribution elements are present in the PAYG system. Redistribution, however, creates incentive problems. Since insurance may be viewed as redistribution from an earlier time, it also creates incentive problems. In its initial stages, this system has a strong tendency to redistribute to early cohorts of retirees, thus creating intergeneration redistribution (Diamond, 1996, pp. 88–9). However, once the system has been in place for some time, the scope for such redistribution is much less. This also implies that the benefits of a shift from a mature PAYG system to other types of arrangements are also likely to be less.

A major accomplishment of the system has been to considerably weaken the historically strong correlation between old age and poverty. It has thus enabled the social question (that is, the tendency of the free market to result in considerable income inequalities and income volatility thereby threatening equitable and harmonious social relations) to be addressed in a reasonably satisfactory manner. The system, however, is vulnerable to the populist political tendencies promising over-generous benefits, to significant changes in individual and population aging trends, and to macroeconomic parameters such as growth, unemployment, labor force participation, and inflation rates.

The second option for financing social security is the mandatory defined contribution (DC) system which involves individualized accounts. Individuals' balance at retirement equals contributions made during the working life, plus accrued interest on accumulated balances, less any permitted pre-retirement withdrawals for housing, health care, and so on. Since benefits and contributions are, in principle, fully linked, there is full funding and no intentional redistribution. This implies that the lifetime poor may be left with inadequate retirement income protection. The main political advantage of the DC system is that it establishes property rights of workers to the accumulation of contributions and returns obtained on them.

This system could be administered either on a centralized basis as in Malaysia and Singapore, or on a decentralized basis under which retirement provision is the mandated responsibility of firms, which, in turn, could use private sector financial institutions for investments and for administration, as in Chile and Australia. It is also possible to separate administration. Unlike the DB system, investment risk under the DC system is borne by the individual. Investment performance, in turn, has a major bearing on the adequacy of the retirement benefits. Investments may be undertaken by individual choice among approved pension fund companies (e.g., as in Chile) or by the authorities themselves (as in Malaysia and Singapore). In either case, prudential regulatory structure and a reasonably well-functioning capital market are essential (Vittas, 1996; James, 1997). To the extent that government exerts direct or indirect control over investment funds, political risk is present under this system.

Accumulation of balances into an individual's account raises the issue of converting such accumulation into retirement income flows and the minimum age at which such conversion is to be permitted (Diamond, 1996, p. 85). Two integral features of this system, uniform saving rate, and uniform retirement age create inefficiencies for rational individuals who have differing needs and rates of time preference (pp. 84–6). Explicit provision also needs to be made for inflation protection and for longevity under the DC system as private annuity markets, even when available at reasonable cost, are unlikely to provide them at an affordable price. Permitting lump sum withdrawal of accumulated balances at a specified age runs counter to the main rationale for mandating saving, that is, the myopic nature of the individuals and the problem of moral hazard lessen incentives for self-financing.

The mandatory DC system (with the Chilean type of decentralized investment arrangement to minimize political risk and attain investment efficiency) has received considerable attention as a result of the World Bank's strong preference for it over the PAYG system (1995). A shift from the PAYG to the mandatory DC system, however, involves transition costs as implicit pension liabilities of the government (benefits entitlements which the retirees and the present contributions have accumulated) would need to be paid off. As a result, pension reform involving such a shift is much more difficult and costly than when the PAYG system is absent.

The World Bank's preference for fully-funded DC system is based on its potential (as compared to the PAYG system) for realizing higher economic growth because of the favorable impact on saving, investment, and work incentives (James, 1997). It is, however, too early to regard the arguments in favor of replacing the PAYG system with the fully funded mandatory DC system as being conclusive. High administrative costs, difficulties involved in securing diversified portfolios, imperfections and high costs of annuities markets, high transition costs, cost of providing tax incentives, and yet-to-be tested proposition of realizing high real rates of return from investments over a long period are some of the factors for the caution.[2] Moreover, there are doubts that a mandatory DC system could provide sufficient coverage to act as a universally accessible social safety net. It also lacks the social solidarity feature of the PAYG system.

The third option for financing social security involves private pension schemes, including occupational and personal plans, and contractual savings through financial institutions and life insurance companies. The practice of permitting individuals to set up tax-advantaged retirement accounts with financial institutions subject to certain regulations has become quite widespread in recent years.

Occupational pension plans could be of the DB or the DC type. A marked shift has occurred in recent years towards the DC type. As a result, investment risk borne by employees has grown significantly. Occupational pension plans are usually tax-advantaged and regulated. A regulatory framework for these plans is required to minimize loss of tax revenue, and to protect employees from imprudent behavior by asset managers. However, at the same time, a regulatory framework should minimize moral hazard, not stifle financial innovation and competition, or unduly constrain investment efficiency (Vittas, 1996).

Three conclusions may be drawn from the discussion of various options for financing social security. First, none of the broad options is by itself adequate to perform saving, redistribution, and insurance functions required of a social security system. A multi-option strategy, therefore, has strong justification (World Bank, 1995). Second, details concerning design, rules, and regulations, and administration associated with each option have a crucial bearing on economic and other effects and on the adequacy of social security provision. These, therefore, should not simply be inferred on the basis of the broad option adopted, but must be carefully analyzed. Third, the term 'privatization' of social security should be specified carefully. This is because in each broad option, government has a role to play, at least in regulation and tax policy. It also retains implicit moral responsibility to ensure adequate retirement protection for the population. The focus should, therefore, be on the appropriate balance among the three options, and on incentives generated by the detailed provisions.

There is no one blue-print of social security reform which is appropriate for all countries. Initial starting point, institutional capacities and arrangements, and the level of economic, financial, and social development do matter.

Social security arrangements in Southeast Asia

Elements of all three pillars discussed in the previous section may be found in the formal social security system of each of the five countries. There are, however, significant variations in the importance and the details concerning each pillar among the countries.

With the exception of the Philippines, the principle of social insurance, which permits pooling of the risk of variable returns to human as well as non-human capital across generations, has not been adopted for the general population in these countries. In the industrialized countries, this principle is operationalized through the PAYG method. The Philippines has a partially-funded PAYG system for the general population, modeled on the social security system of the United States.

Thailand's 1990 Social Security Act incorporates the social insurance principle of the provision of sickness, maternity, invalidity, and death benefits. Old age pensions, family allowances, and unemployment insurance were to be introduced in phases. However, even before the current economic crisis in Thailand, the authorities were moving away from social insurance, and towards the provident fund approach. So the expansion of the coverage to old-age pensions and others is unlikely to take place soon.

In all five countries, however, generous DB type of retirement protection, financed primarily by the PAYG method, is being provided to government employees, including military and civilian personnel.[3] The first pillar is, therefore, largely confined to the public sector, including the military in all countries except the Philippines. This is ironic as policy-makers in these countries, particularly in Singapore and Malaysia, have argued vehemently against the DB type PAYG arrangements as being inappropriate for their countries.

In the Philippines, the Government Service Insurance System (GSIS), created in 1936, administers pensions for all government employees and those in state enterprises. Armed forces and the judiciary have similar but separate pension plans. For the private sector employees in the Philippines, the Social Security System (SSS), created in 1954, administers DB type programs providing comprehensive retirement and work-injury related programs. The system is partially funded.

With the exception of the Philippines, the Southeast Asian countries have very heavily relied on the mandatory DC system, involving individualized accounts, to provide social security.

In Indonesia, the mandatory DC provident fund is designed to cover the entire private formal sector (roughly 40 million workers), except for the smallest firms (those below 10 employees) and the self-employed. This is called the Jamostek program and is administered by PT ASTEK. Those in the informal sector are excluded. In Malaysia, the employees' Provident Fund (EPF), set up in 1951, administers the mandatory savings scheme. Singapore's scheme, however, is not just for retirement, but it also encompasses housing, health care, education, and other areas. To a much lesser extent, this is also the case in Malaysia.

In Thailand, the role of provident funds for providing social security in the private sector and the state enterprise employees has been considerably expanded in recent years. In November 1996, the Thai cabinet required private companies who have been granted fiscal incentives, those listed on the stock exchange, financial institutions supervised by the country's central bank, and those receiving government contracts, to compulsorily set up provident funds for their employees within the next three years. The state enterprises were also mandated to set up provident funds by end of 1997.

The third pillar for financing social security involving occupational and personal pension plans is also found in Southeast Asian countries. However, its access is mainly confined to employees of large corporations, including state enterprises. Its role at present is not major.

Coverage

In analyzing the coverage of the social security system, a distinction between membership and active contributors must be kept in mind. The former includes not only those who are contributing during the current periods, but also those who may have contributed in the past and thus have an account with the relevant social security institution. The importance of this distinction is indicated by the fact that as at end-1996, membership in Singapore's Central Provident Fund (CPF) was 2.741 million, while contributors were only 1.194 million, or 43.6 per cent of the total members (CPF Board, 1997). Similarly, membership in Malaysia's EPF at the end of 1996 was 8.051 million, while contributors were 4.181 million, or 51.9 per cent of the total members (EPF Board, 1997).

The coverage of the social security system varies considerably among the five countries. In the affluent city-state of Singapore, two-thirds of the labor force contributed to the CPF in 1996; while the membership

(2.741 million as at end-1996) was equivalent to 90.0 per cent of the resident population[4] (CPF Board, 1997). Foreign workers amounting to about a fifth of the work-force,[5] most of the self-employed, certain category of contract workers, and unemployed, are among the non-contributors to the CPF. As pensionable government employees continue to contribute to the CPF, but at reduced rates, they are included among the contributors.

In Malaysia, contributors to labor force ratio has increased from 35.0 per cent in 1986 to 49.8 per cent in 1996 (EPF Board 1997). In Malaysia, a permanent government officer is eligible for non-contributory government pension provided his or her appointment is confirmed and he or she has completed not less than three years of recognized service. Those appointed on or after 12 April 1991 can opt to join the pension scheme or the EPF. In 1994, according to the official data, the total number of pensioners, including those receiving survivors' and dependants' pensions, was nearly 0.3 million.

In the Philippines, in 1993, the GSIS covered about 1.4 million government employees; and, in 1996, the SSS had a membership of 17.8 million. To put these numbers in perspective, in 1995 the labor force of the Philippines was 28 million, while its total population was 69 million (World Bank, 1997, Table 4, pp. 220–1). Thus, the combined membership of the GSIS and the SSS was equivalent to 27.8 per cent of the total population.

In Indonesia, the coverage is as follows. In the voluntary employer-sponsored pension plans, the membership in early 1996 was about 3.0 million. The civil servants and military pension systems had a membership of 4 million and 0.5 million respectively in 1995. The mandatory DC provident fund, while designed to cover the entire formal sector (except with less than 10 workers), had a membership of 11.0 million as at end 1996, or 41.8 per cent of those eligible (Indonesia, Employees Social Security System, 1996, Table 5, p. 18). Active contributors in each category are likely to be much smaller. At best, only around one-fifth of the labor force belongs to a provident or a pension fund.

The coverage data for Thailand are even more sparse. The only data available is that during the 1991–93 period, active contributors to the sickness, maternity, invalidity, and death benefits created under the Social Security Act of 1990 numbered 3.5 million, or 10 per cent of the total labor force (Hagemann *et al.*, 1993).

Investment guidelines, patterns and performance

In Indonesia, total assets of all the pension plans as at end 1994 were Rp. 21.1 trillion (5.6 per cent of GDP). The voluntary employer-sponsored pension plans had the largest share of the total assets (45 per cent), followed by the civil servants' pension program administered by PT Taspen (39 per cent); Jamostek program for the private sector employees administered by PT Astek (12 per cent); and the rest (4 per cent) by Asabri and others.

The aggregate asset allocation, as at end-1994, of all pensions combined was: stocks 8 per cent, bonds 11 per cent, bank deposits 41 per cent, short-term government paper 30 per cent, properties and others 10 per cent. There was little variation in asset allocation among different pension funds. All the investments are in Indonesian assets as foreign assets are excluded by law. So country risk-diversification is absent. Much of the investment is also short term, while pension liabilities are long term. Therefore, there is a mismatch between assets and liabilities.

While no detailed data on the rate of return are available, Leechor (1996) has estimated that during the 1988–95 period, the real rate of return on employer-sponsored plans was between 6 per cent and 8 per cent, a fairly attractive rate. Many of these plans are managed in-house, and only a small proportion of assets have been entrusted to professional investment companies (Koo, 1997). Tam (1997) reports that this situation may change as investment patterns of pension funds shift in favour of equities. But the ongoing economic crisis, which has exposed severe deficiencies in corporate governance and stock-market regulation in Indonesia, is likely to make such a shift, at best, a medium-term prospect. While many of the large companies, including state-owned firms, are moving towards funding pension plans in actuarially sound manner, many other firms whose plans are not approved by the regulators, have unfunded pension liabilities. In contrast to the employer-sponsored plans, in 1994, real investment return by PT Astek and PT Taspen was zero and 1.3 per cent respectively. This compares quite unfavorably with the real rate of return on time deposits of 9.4 per cent during the 1988–95 period.

Both PT Taspen and PT Astek incur extremely high administrative costs. In 1994, such costs as percentage of contributions amounted to 7.0 per cent for PT Taspen and 11.7 per cent for PT Astek. For Malaysia, the corresponding figure was 1.99 per cent (for 1989), and for Singapore 0.53 per cent (for 1990) (World Bank, 1994, Table 6.4, p. 224). As at end-1996, provident fund balances per member were Rp. 353 738 (US$41 at US$1 = Rp. 8600 prevailing on 1 April 1998).

In Malaysia, the total assets of all the provident and pension funds was M$ 135 944 million as at end-1996, equivalent to 54.5 per cent of the GDP (Bank Negara Malaysia, 1996, Table 3.16, p. 112). The EPF Board's investment portfolio has been considerably diversified in recent years, with clear evidence of a shift away from government securities, and towards equities, money market instruments, and loans and debentures. The 1996 composition of its investments totaling M$ 115 217.5 millions, equivalent to 46.2 per cent of GDP, with 1991 values in brackets was as follows: Malaysian Government securities, 33.6 per cent (73.6 per cent); debentures and loans, 20.8 per cent (11.0 per cent); equities, 15.6 per cent (2.1 per cent); money market, 29.7 per cent (13.3 per cent); property and other, 0.3 per cent (negligible).

The EPF undertakes the investment function in-house, with only a small proportion of its funds being managed by outside money managers (Koo, 1997). The SOCSO (with assets of M$ 5.2 billion as at end-1996), uses nine external fund managers to undertake the investment function (Koo, 1997). The EPF has been traditionally mandated to invest only within Malaysia. It has, however, secured permission to invest offshore, but has (as of April 1998) not undertaken any investments abroad. Between 1961 and 1996, there were only three years (1973, 1974, and 1981) when the real rate of return (nominal dividend rate less the inflation rate as measured by the Consumer Price Index) was negative (EPF Board, 1997). The real rate of return for the decade 1987–96, averaged 4.72 per cent.[6]

Valdes-Prieto (1998, p. 8) has argued that the EPF's returns are unsatisfactory when compared to the alternatives. Thus, he notes that the real rate of return credited to members over the 1971–91 period was 2.74 per cent per annum. However, the real rate of return obtainable from bank deposits, plus half of the spread between bank loans and bank deposits, was 4.26 per cent per year, while equities earned 5.61 per cent real per year. Thus, the implicit tax was at least 1.52 percentage points per year in real terms.

There are indications that the pension funds, particularly the EPF, are being used by the authorities to attain a variety of public policy objectives. As a result, administrative or non-market avenues are increasingly used to channel EPF savings into investment. In conjunction with the state management of provident funds, a monocentric power structure, and a lack of tradition of open public debate, lack of diversity in media, and centralized control over even basic socio-economic information, this has the potential to adversely affect the efficiency with which savings are translated into investment, and therefore, future growth and savings as well as allocation of resources (Tripathi, 1998; Lopez, 1998). They also indicate how political risk may arise in the national provident fund method, and how, inspite of the legal status, the pension fund bodies do not enjoy functional autonomy.

In the Philippines, as at end-1996, the total assets of the SSS and GSIS were P 143.2 billion and P 101.6 billion respectively.[7] The combined assets of the two were equivalent to 11.2 per cent of the 1996 GDP. Total investments of the SSS, as at end 1996, amounting to P 134.8 billion was distributed as follows: government securities[8] P 59.7 billion (44.3 per cent); loans to other government units (mainly National Home Mortgage Finance Corporation) and to members[9] P 50.8 billion (37.7 per cent); and private securities and loans: P 24.2 billion (18.0 per cent).

As the investment income in 1996 was 15.5 billion, the simple rate of return (15.5 divided by 134.8) was 11.5 per cent. This is lower than the treasury bill rate of 12.3 per cent, but moderately higher than the inflation rate of 8.4 per cent. The investment performance of the SSS has nevertheless improved since the People Power Revolution of 1986. Thus, during the 1987–95 period, the average annual real rate of return (nominal return less inflation as measured by the Consumer Price Index) was 5.58 per cent. In contrast, the corresponding rate for the 1976–86 period was a negative 0.7 per cent. According to unpublished World Bank calculations, the real rate of return on SSS investment was lower than the real return on the Philippine treasury bills by 0.59 per cent annually on the average during the 1976–95 period. However, the corresponding rate was higher by 0.38 per cent annually on the average during the 1987–95 period. Thus, there has been improvement in the investment performance of the SSS.

Since 1992, however, benefits paid plus operating expenses of the SSS have exceeded contributions. Thus, dependence by the SSS on investment income is becoming increasingly great. The Social Security Act of 1997 has liberalized the investment guidelines for the SSS. In particular, the limit for domestic and foreign mutual funds combined is 20 per cent of the investible balances, with a further stipulation that investment in foreign mutual funds cannot exceed 7.5 per cent of the balances. The SSS is, however, expected to proceed cautiously in investing in foreign mutual funds.

As at end-1996, the GSIS had total investments of P 96.6 billion. Their contribution was as follows: Current assets: P 33.0 billion (34.2 per cent), loans to members and to non-members: 34.9 billion (36.1 per cent), and other investments: P 28.7 billion (29.7 per cent). The annual Reports of the GSIS do not provide a breakdown of the above broad aggregates. The non-insurance income of the GSIS was P 9.3 billion. This implies a nominal rate of return of 9.6 per cent, much lower than the corresponding rate on treasury bills (12.3 per cent), but somewhat higher than the inflation rate (8.4 per cent). Loans and investments had much lower rate of return (9.2 per cent) than return on current assets (10.5 per cent).

For the GSIS, claims and benefits plus operating expenses amounted to P 10.7 billion in 1996, while net insurance income was P 17.6 billion. This partly reflects the fact that there is no salary ceiling on government's contribution to the GSIS as an employer. GSIS is unusual among the social security institutions in providing non-life insurance services. Indeed, it has targeted this area as the thrust area for the future.

Three separate pools of investible funds exist under Singapore's CPF system. The first and the largest is the members' balances with the CPF Board. As at end-1996, these amounted to S$ 73.8 billion (US $46.7 billion), equivalent to 55.6 per cent of GDP. According to the CPF Act, these funds must be invested in government bonds (and in advanced deposit with the Monetary Authority of Singapore, MAS, to be converted into government bonds at a later date). Thus, as at end-1996, investment in bonds amounted to S$ 51.6 billion and advanced deposit with the MAS S$20.4 billion. The bonds are floating rate bonds issued specifically to the CPF Board to meet interest and other obligations. They do not have quoted market values. What determines the floating rate? Since 1986, it is a simple average of the 12–month deposit and month-end savings rate of the four major local banks, subject to a minimum nominal rate of 2.5 per cent as spelled out in the CPF Act. This administrative arrangement for paying short-term interest rates for long-term funds, and further restricting the rate to what four relatively insulated local banks pay on local currency deposits, is rather curious. It is not, therefore, surprising that during the 1987–96 period, the real interest rate (defined as the difference between the nominal rate less inflation as measured by the GDP deflation) on these balances averaged a negative 0.33 per cent; with negative returns during half the number of years.

The Singapore government has been running rather large budgetary surpluses over many years. Yet, it has a large internal public debt amounting to S$ 94.5 billion (US $59.8 billion) as at end-1996, equivalent to 71.3 per cent of GDP. Thus, large budget surpluses and large public debt co-exist in Singapore. Since much of the debt is non-marketable, there is little activity in the secondary market for government bonds. Given the large budget surpluses over considerable period, the CPF funds have not been needed to finance infrastructure or other government expenditure. How are the CPF funds then ultimately deployed? Essentially, these funds are invested by the Singapore Government (through Singapore Government Investment Corporation, SGIF, and other government-controlled agencies). There is, however, no transparency or public accountability concerning where these funds are invested, and what has been the investment criteria and performance. These funds, however, are believed to be almost wholly invested abroad.

A statement in the parliament in March 1996 by the Finance Minister indicating that investment returns on Singapore's reserves have averaged over 5.0 per cent (no precise figure was given) in Singapore dollar terms over the last 10 years, could be used to estimate the implicit tax borne by the CPF members on their balances. Subtracting the nominal rate of 3.7 per cent in 1996 from the 5.0 per cent provides the difference of 1.3 per cent. Multiplying it by the average balances of members that year (calculated as the beginning balance plus one-half of the addition to the balances between the beginning and the end of 1996) of S$ 69.3 billion, gives the implicit tax on members of S$ 900.9 million, equivalent to 6.2 per cent of the contributions. It is important to recognize that as long as the nominal rate paid to members is less than what the government earns on members' balances, the implicit tax is paid by members each year, although the amount varies.

The discussion so far illustrates how political risks and non-transparency could arise even when there are individualized accounts.

The second pool of investible funds consists of insurance funds. These amounted to only S$ 1.5 billion (US $0.9 billion). These are invested in fixed deposits, negotiable certificates of deposit, equities, and bonds. Outsourcing of these funds for investment is believed to be much greater. In 1996, the implicit nominal rate of return on insurance funds (calculated as insurance premium plus net income and profit on sale of investment divided by the beginning balance plus one-half of the premium paid during the year) was 4.2 per cent. This compares favorably with 3.7 per cent rate paid on members' balances, but not with 5.0 per cent return earned by the government on country's reserves.

The third pool of investible funds consists of pre-retirement withdrawal by members under the investment schemes. These schemes do permit individuals to invest in the stock-markets through mutual funds (called unit trusts). As at end-June 1997, 411 235 CPF members (56.4 per cent of those eligible, but less than one-sixth of total members) had withdrawn S$ 10.82 billion (US $6.85 billion), 44 per cent of the potential amount of S$ 24.6 billion (US $15.6 billion) eligible for investment. Thus, the amount withdrawn for investment per participating member (S$ 10.82 billion divided by 411 235) amounted to S$ 26 311 (US $16 653). Only S$600 million of the above amount has been invested through CPF-approved unit-trusts (i.e. mutual funds). Thus, it is clear that individuals have chosen to primarily invest on their own.

Since 1 January 1998, CPF-approved unit-trusts have been allowed to invest up to 50 per cent of their funds in the following overseas markets: Malaysia, Thailand, Hong Kong, Taiwan, and South Korea, the US, the UK, and Japan. While the approved unit trusts and fund managers are well regulated, there are no performance standards to which they must adhere.

There are also no regulations concerning administrative charges. So transaction costs cannot be adequately ascertained. But, given that individuals are investing on their own and have low investment balances on the average, these costs must be substantial. This area needs to be researched further.

The expectation that such investments would permit higher returns was not realized even before the current currency and stock-market crisis in Southeast Asia. Thus, during each year during the 1994–97 period, less than 20 per cent of participating members realized returns above that which they would have made had they left the money with the CPF. In the aggregate, losses of those investing exceeded gains. Data on unrealized gains or losses are not available.

Available data on Thailand's social security pension and provident funds permit only some broad observations on their investments. Total pension-fund assets in Thailand in 1996 were only 6.0 to 8.0 per cent of GDP, although new provident funds being set up could increase this figure considerably over time.

As at end-1996, about 850 provident funds had investments of B 89.6 billion which were distributed as follows: cash and deposits B 44.1 billion (49.2 per cent); corporate debentures B 24.8 billion (27.7 per cent); debt instruments issues by banks B 9 billion (10 per cent); stocks B 7.2 billion (8.0 per cent); and others B 1.7 billion (1.9 per cent). Information on the rate of return obtained is not available. Revenue received by the state enterprises for pension liabilities is usually invested in bank or finance company deposits, stocks, and government securities. No financial details are, however, available.

The OPF had balances of B 69.8 billion as at 31 December 1997. The OPF is administered by a committee of 21 persons, with representation for members (8 out of 21), and for experts (3 out of 21). The accumulated funds may be contracted-out for management. As at end-1996, assets of the Social Security Fund (SSF) accumulated to B47.1 billion while the corresponding assets of the Workmen's Compensation Fund (WCF) were B9.3 billion (Thailand, Office of Social Security, 1997). It is not clear whether the accounts of the SSF and WCF are audited accounts. The two together were equivalent to 1.8 per cent of the 1996 GDP.

Under the current regulations pertaining to the SSF, at least 60 per cent of total investment must be in safe assets such as government, including state enterprise, bonds and treasury debentures, bills, and debt instruments of commercial banks. At least 30 per cent of investment must be in assets with little risk, such as debt instruments of a finance company or finance and securities company, and in projects generating indirect benefits for insured persons. Other instruments, such as housing projects, should not exceed 10 per cent of the total.

As at end-1996, 82.5 per cent of total assets were invested in fixed deposits, while bonds and debentures accounted for only 5.2 per cent of the total (Thailand, Office of Social Security, 1997, pp. 32–3). Thus, SSF's investment strategy is quite passive. The value of its investments is likely to be reduced by the closure of the 58 finance companies in late 1997, although its extent remains unclear. Its returns on investments was reported to be over 11 per cent in 1996, but no details of how this was estimated have been provided (Thailand, Office of Social Security, 1997, p. 29).

Conclusion: broad reform direction

To be sustainable, a social security system needs to provide a socially adequate level of retirement income protection, while simultaneously minimizing adverse effects on economic incentives and on a country's international competitiveness. Moreover, it needs to command broad political and social support.

Viewed in the above context, it is evident from the discussion in the previous section, that substantial reforms will be needed before the social security systems of Southeast Asia can be regarded as sustainable. A detailed discussion of the needed reforms is beyond the scope of this paper. The discussion below, however, highlights broad directions of reform.

First, it is essential that Southeast Asian countries view social security issues in a systemic rather than an *ad hoc* manner. The World Bank's multi-pillar framework, encompassing saving, insurance, and redistribution functions, could be used as a convenient starting point. A more balanced multi-pillar strategy could help move the systems towards greater sustainability. At present, there appears to be too much emphasis on the savings function, and an uncritical acceptance of the paternalistic, state-led economic development model, particularly in Indonesia, Malaysia, and Singapore.

Second, there is a strong need to improve investment performance and provide higher rate of returns under mandatory savings (DC) schemes. This, in turn, would require capital market and financial sector reforms with a view to increasing market-orientation and efficiency of the savings–investment process. It would also require explicit attention to the nature of political risk in mandatory savings schemes in various countries, and to the regulatory environment.

Third, the DB, PAYG systems for government employees in Indonesia and the Philippines are actuarially unsustainable. Urgent steps are needed, centering on the lowering of benefits, increased contributions, lowering of administrative costs and, in the case of the Philippines, better investment management, to make them actuarially sound. In the Philippines, similar reforms are needed for the SSS as well.

Fourth, in all Southeast Asian countries, contingent liabilities, whether *de facto* or *de jure*, of the governments' need to be made explicit. Such liabilities may arise not only from unfunded implicit pension liabilities of government employees, but also from guarantees provided to provident and pension-fund authorities for government-directed loans and investment.

Fifth, there appears to be a tendency in Southeast Asia to regard mandatory savings schemes as almost automatically increasing household, and therefore, national savings.[10] But, neither international experience (Mackenzie, *et al.*, 1997), nor econometric research on Singapore's CPF system (Husain, 1995), lends support to this proposition. This has led these countries to neglect innovative ways of combining savings-insurance-redistribution functions in an integrated social security system. Virtual absence of the tax-financed first pillar is particularly illustrative in this regard.

Sixth, it is evident that the Southeast Asian countries have not paid much attention to recent reforms, particularly in Latin America, centering on design, institutional, regulatory, and incentive issues concerning mandatory savings schemes. The previous sections indicated many such features, such as, extensive pre-retirement withdrawals in Singapore, creating perverse incentive effects; lack of development of annuity markets in all Southeast Asian countries; and lack of innovations in minimizing political risks of mandatory savings schemes. Greater transparency, and more open and participatory public debate are needed to increase awareness of the reforms being undertaken elsewhere. There is also a need to eschew using provident and pension funds as a tool for socio-political-economic control over its members.

Notes

1. According to the estimates by the investment bank Jardine Fleming, non-performing loans in the five Southeast Asian countries will peak at US$73 billion by end-1998, which is about 14 per cent of total loans outstanding, and equivalent to 13.3 per cent of the region's GDP. The magnitude of the bad loan problem facing the Southeast Asian banking crisis will require tough measures.
2. For a critique of the World Bank's pension reform strategy, see Minns (1996).
3. Singapore has, in recent years, limited such pensions to only the top civil servants, politicians, and military and security personnel. Both Malaysia and

Singapore have set up pension trust funds to ensure adequate financing for the eligible employees. In August 1993, Thailand required new government employees to compulsorily join a pension plan which is a blend of DB and DC types. Since March 1997, new government employees have been required to join the DC type Officials' Gratuity and Pension Fund (OPF). In Indonesia, the civil service pension program is administered by a public enterprise PT Taspen, while the pension fund for military and police personnel is administered by another organization, PT Asabri. In Indonesia, the government (since 1994) pays from the general budget 77.5 per cent of the pension benefits and all of the health-care benefits; while the lump sum and 22.5 per cent of pension benefits are from the contributions (Leechor, 1996).

4. As some of the expatriates continue to be members of the CPF, the proportion of resident population effectively covered is slightly lower.
5. Since August 1995, all foreign workers, including Malaysians, have been excluded from the CPF scheme. However, for those already employed at the time, the rules do not become fully effective till 1998. Therefore, some foreign workers may still be contributing as at end-1996. While Malaysians are excluded from the CPF, those from West Malaysia who have contributed in the past, cannot withdraw their CPF balances until age 55 unless they can demonstrate that they are leaving Singapore and Malaysia permanently. The current economic crisis has enhanced the importance of this issue as requests by the Malaysia government to alternate the present arrangements have not been accepted by Singapore to date i.e. April 1998.
6. The Consumer Price Index (CPI) is not the most appropriate price index as the market basket of the elderly is likely to vary considerably from the basket used to estimate the CPI. As the elderly consume more services, and as per unit cost of many services of interest to the elderly, e.g., health care, usually rise faster than prices of goods, the real return relevant for the elderly may be somewhat lower.
7. Unless otherwise noted, these and other investment data for the Philippines are from the Annual Reports of the SSS and the GSIS. It should be stressed that the financial data in these Reports are unaudited.
8. This includes saving and time deposits with the Philippines National Bank and with the Land Bank of the Philippines amounting to P 26.6 billion.
9. These are mainly salary, educational and calamity loans. According to the officials, availability of such loans is an important incentive to being a SSS member.
10. As an example, discussion of the possibility that mandatory saving may substitute for voluntary saving was almost entirely ignored in the public discussion of Thailand's recent moves toward mandatory setting up of provident funds.

References

Asian Development Bank, *Emerging Asia: Changes and Challenges* (Manila: Asian Development Bank, 1997).

Bank Negara Malaysia, *Annual Report*, Kuala Lumpur (1996).

Bos, E., M.T. Vu, E. Massiah and R. Bulatao, *World Population Projections 1994–95 Edition* (Baltimore: The Johns Hopkins University Press, 1994).
Claessens, S., and T. Glaesner, *Are Financial Sector Weaknesses Undermining the East Asian Miracle?* (Washington, DC, World Bank, 1997).
CPF Board, *Annual Report*, various issues.
Diamond, P.A., 'Government Provision and Regulation of Economic Support in Old Age,' *Annual World Bank Conference on Development Economics* (1996), 83–125.
Economist, London (27 January 1997).
EPF Board, *Annual Report*, various issues.
Hagemann, R., J. Amiera-Huerta and S. Ross '*Thailand: Developing the Social Security System*' (Washington, DC: International Monetary Fund, 1993).
Heller, P.S., 'Aging in the Asian "Tigers": Challenges for Fiscal Policy,' manuscript in progress.
Husain, A.M., 'Determinants of Private Saving in Singapore', in K. Bercuson, (ed.), *Singapore: A Case Study in Rapid Development*, Occasional paper No. 119 (Washington, DC: IMF, 1995) pp. 42–51.
Indonesia, Employees Social Security System, *JAMSOSTEK 1996 Factbook* (Jakarta: JAMSOSTEK, 1997).
James, E., 'New Systems for Old Age Security', *Policy Research Working Paper No. 1766* (Washington, D.C.: World Bank, 1997).
Koo, C., 'Waiting for the Dough', *Institutional Investor*, 22 (1997) 84–8.
Leechor, C., 'Reforming Indonesia's Pension System', *Policy Research Working Paper No. 1677* (Washington, DC: World Bank, 1996).
Lopez, L., 'Mahathir Pledges to use State Funds to Buoy Malaysia's Distressed Banks', *Asian Wall Street Journal*, (6–7 March 1998) pp. 1 and 5.
Mackenzie, G.A., P. Gerson and A. Cuevas 'Pension Regimes and Saving', *IMF Occassional Paper No. 53* (Washington, DC, 1997).
Minns, R. 'The Political Economy of Pensions', *New Political Economy* 1 (1996) 375–91.
Philippines, Social Security System, *Annual Report, 1996* (Manila, 1997).
Sato, M., 'The Workers of Asia Need Social Security Systems', *International Herald Tribune* (16 March 1998).
Tam, P.W., 'Asian Pension Funds Seek Outside Help', *Asian Wall Street Journal* (4 December 1997) 15.
Thailand, Office of Social Security, *Annual Report 1996* (Bangkok: Ministry of Labour and Social Welfare, 1997).
Tripathy, S. 'Savings At Risk', *Far Eastern Economic Review* (30April 1998) 60–2.
Valdes-Prieto, S., 'The Private Sector in Social Security: Latin American Lessons for APEC', *Paper presented at APEC Regional Forum on Pension Fund Reform*, organized by the Ministers of Finance of Mexico and Chile, Cancun (Mexico, 4–6 February, 1998).
Vittas, D., *Regulatory Controversies of Private Pension Funds* (Washington, DC: World Bank, Financial Sector Development Department, 1996).
World Bank, *Averting the Old Age Crisis: Policies to Protect the Old and Promote Growth*, (New York: Oxford University Press, 1995).
World Bank, *The World Development Report 1997* (New York: Oxford University Press, 1997).

12

Stable Expansion for the Chinese Economy: Lessons from International Experience*

Lawrence R. Klein

With some brief interruptions, economic development of China has proceeded on a remarkably steady path, ever since the time of reform, 1978. That makes the period just short of two decades, a long period of significant expansion on a world scale, yet one that has not yet come to a concluding phase of high living standards for the very large population. China is becoming an industrial nation at a high level on an international scale, but not yet in a class with the most advanced industrial nations and not yet in a *mature* phase of industrial development.

To place the state of the Chinese economy in historical perspective, it is instructive to point out that two 'miraculous' expansions appeared early in the immediate aftermath of the Second World War. The German Miracle and the Japanese Miracle started from war-torn destruction and recreated what were previously advanced industrial economies (Germany more so than Japan), but the periods of strong expansion did not last particularly long. Both economies performed superbly during the 1950s and 1960s, but succumbed to the unusual disturbances in food and fuel sectors during the 1970s, gradually slowing down to very modest growth rates, presently at real growth rates of just about 2 per cent annually. They are both having great trouble in recovering from their recessions of the 1990s.

Of course they are both powerful economies – Germany and Japan – and their present economic difficulties do not stain their older reputations as examples of 'economic miracles.' They fully deserved

* An earlier draft of the paper was presented at the CASS conference, Behai City, 2–4 September 1997.

that description and will, in the future, be able to deliver high living standards to their people.

The next group of 'economic miracles' occurred in East Asia, inspired to no small extent by the Japanese experience. The initial economic circumstances of this group did not encompass very much in the way of industrialization, but the participants went soon into some of the industrial pursuits that were important for the early steps in postwar Japanese growth. These Asian economies of the Pacific Basin, with some few exceptions, should be noted for holding inflation in check, in the presence of the oil shocks of the 1970s and accelerating their growth for a much longer time span than did Japan and Germany.

During the last year or two, some of the Asia-Pacific economies have encountered growth slowdowns, exchange depreciation, balance of payments deficits, and, in a few cases, financial crises. Nevertheless, expansion has not slowed to the 2 per cent trend levels that are now found in Germany or in Japan. The 'East Asian Miracle' is a deserving characterization because it has gone on for such a long time – for as long as three decades for some economies.

Other economic areas of the world system have watched, with envy, the East Asian performance but have not been able to duplicate the feat, in the sense of generating a *sustained* path of development, except possibly in one or two countries of limited size or scope. Some economies with extraordinary endowments, such as mineral fuels or other basic resources have done very well for many years running but have not generally established a truly industrial performance.

In trying to draw some judgment about China's economic performance since 1978, there are undoubtedly some lessons to be learned from the Asia-Pacific experience and, by implication, from German and Japanese experience.

An interpretation of China's economic expansion since 1978

Major ingredients of China's high rate of economic growth have been:

(i) Agricultural reform
(ii) Open door policy
(iii) Introduction of market pricing
(iv) Improvement of infrastructure (transportation, communication, energy, education)
(v) Demographics
(vi) Macroeconomic policy

It will be helpful to elaborate on each of these points in order to show how the expansion got underway and to judge its sustainability.

(i)

In an economy that must feed more than one billion people, agriculture is obviously of the greatest importance. Early economic visitors, in the late 1970s, could see that China would have to keep agricultural output on at least a minimal growth path of about 3 or 4 per cent per year. Most of the population was in rural areas, yet agricultural output was not outstanding. The disruption of the economy and agricultural involvement through the policies of the Cultural Revolution made the need for reform evident and urgently so. The commune system was quickly eradicated and farmers were given large measures of personal responsibility in dealing with land use. Under these circumstances, agricultural output expanded quickly at higher rates than were thought possible. The spurt in agricultural output was not sustainable at the high rates achieved in the early stages of reform, but the changes in agricultural policy enabled the sector to expand faster than was judged to be a subsistence minimum and has placed the food problem, in a relative sense, in the background for some time to come, if not indefinitely.

Also, it should be pointed out that land ownership was not strictly *privatized*. Decision-making was made personal and competitive in accordance with market socialism and not in accordance with capitalist land ownership. Furthermore, land reform in agriculture played an important role in the postwar expansion of Japan, South Korea, and Taiwan. This is a sense in which the Asia-Pacific experience is significant.

(ii)

Before 1978, China was almost a closed economy with very little foreign trade, having lost much of the small amount that previously existed in trade with the Soviet Union. The open door policy, which was implemented in step-wise fashion, made several contributions to Chinese economic activity. It gradually brought Chinese prices more into line with world prices. It is not being argued, in any sense, that the 'law-of-one-price' came into operation, either immediately or by the present time, but Chinese prices were so far out of line with international prices because they had barely changed for years. They started a process of moving more in step with world prices and have, basically, left a competitive margin.

At competitive prices, especially through lower labor market prices, China has been able to capture a significant place in world export markets, rising from a total turnover (exports and imports) of only a few to about 200 (US$) billion. Low prices alone do not account for this achievement of strong export-led growth, comparable to the experience of other prominent economies of East Asia; there had to be an associated improvement in the *quality* of Chinese export supply. This, too, was achieved through the open door policy. Foreign investment supplied a great deal of financial capital and, along with the financing, there has been a significant technology transfer. A further manifestation of openness has been the entrepreneurial transfer from the overseas Chinese community, particularly from Hong Kong.

In the sense of these comments there has been openness for market pricing, for trade flows, for capital flows, and for know-how (technological and entrepreneurial).

(iii)

At the international level, there has been market pricing, as explained in the above discussion, but there has also been domestic market pricing. *Relative* price movements contributed to more efficient resource allocation in markets for goods, services, labor, and financing. Financial markets have lagged behind other markets in an operational sense, because many of the institutional facilities or concepts are still being developed and put into place. Internal developments in Shanghai and Shenzen are moving forward, and there is an enormous asset in Hong Kong, which has already had important effects on the functioning of financial markets, but there is much more to come from that source.

Markets in agriculture, other primary activities, and in small-to-medium size industry have been functioning and continue to develop but, as will be shown below, there is a big gap, with respect to large state-owned enterprises, where economic efficiency appears to be lagging.

(iv)

Bottlenecks in transportation, communication, and energy continue to hamper overall economic development in an interrelated system. New modern roads are being built; new equipment is coming into service; software for scheduling transportation is being installed; new energy supplies are coming on stream. In short, work is taking place on a significant scale in avoiding the effects of bottlenecks. These domestic trouble spots will continue to work against modern economic progress, but the situation is improving.

In addition to physical facilities, there is a serious need for institution building – systems of business law, failure procedures for inefficient enterprises, and, above all, better educational facilities to build up *human* capital, at the possible expense of physical capital, is clearly called for.

After the Cultural Revolution, the educational system was in shambles. There were millions of adults without proper education – either general or technical – but that situation is steadily being replaced by an academic community that now has the capability of 'growing-their-own' scholars. This was not the situation in 1978, for institutions of higher learning. For example, at this stage there is a large community of Chinese economic scholars to train and develop fresh generations of scholars. That was not the case in 1978.

(v)

An enabling factor for keeping up a strong growth record after the 'take-off' during 1978–80 was the success in restraining population growth. New people did not wholly consume the increments to output.

There was no Malthusian problem in China because the population policy – one child per family, with some specific exceptions – held population growth near 1 per cent, *per annum*, thus allowing good results on a *per capita* basis of reckoning. While it is true that demographic policy served economic policy extremely well in this reform period, there can be future problems ahead, unless foresight and planning work well together to keep population growth on the side of good economic growth.

Consider the case of Japan, in a fresh light. After the Second World War, Japanese population developments took an unexpected turn. Without specific demographic policy, Japan's birth rate fell significantly below its traditional pattern and also held Japanese population growth to about 1 per cent *per annum*. The ultimate result, after 40 or 50 years is that Japan's population aged considerably. A combination of continuing low birth rate, together with a remarkable tendency towards longevity (good diet, good public health, enlightened medical care) has pushed Japan into the lead with population over the age of 60 years. Retirement has taken place at fairly young ages, and places an economic burden on a relatively limited labor force. The aging of Japan has worked towards lowering the saving rate, slowing the rate of productivity improvement, and contributing seriously to the previously mentioned sluggish growth performance of the Japanese economy in the 1990s. The low birth rate, maintained for several decades, eventually came to retard Japan's economic progress. Is China headed in the same direction? There will have to be some long-run demographic planning to prevent a development like that in Japan.

(vi)

Finally, let us consider overall macroeconomic policy. China was not in a position to fine-tune fiscal, monetary, and commercial policies, in the aggregate, as in Western industrial countries. This problem is particularly acute in the case of monetary policy, because the institutional environment is not in place.

Nevertheless, as China grew at a world record-setting pace for several years, (10 per cent or more annually) inflationary tendencies became apparent. Economic authorities used comparatively direct methods of credit restraint, applied in a trial-and-error fashion, together with aggressive industrial/commercial policy, and fairly steady fiscal policy to engineer a 'soft-landing,' that is, a slight lowering of the growth rate and a greater lowering of the inflation rate. Success did not come all at once or evenly but the 1996–97 performance results look very promising in terms of reaching the stated objectives of continuing high growth without inflation. Some degree of growth has been sacrificed, but China is presently faring much better than are other economies in East Asia.

The commercial policies are working well in the sense of building up comfortable positions of foreign exchange reserves, which, together with more direct controls on currency fluctuations, puts China in a better position than ASEAN economies to stave off the FOREX speculators who are causing so much concern for expanding Asian economies.[1]

This is not to say that large economic problems and issues are absent in China's case; they are simply not the purely macroeconomic problems that other transition economies or other Asian economies do face.

Economic issues facing the Chinese economy

In China, as in the United States, the United Kingdom, and a few other smaller economies (Canada, Norway, Ireland) there is, at the present time, good macroeconomic balance. Two important issues remain, namely microeconomic or distributional imbalances coexist with macroeconomic balance. Also, the good balance is fairly recent. There are still business-cycle fluctuations, and they have been present in most economies during the past decade; so the *sustainability* of the favorable macroeconomic conditions is at issue.

The United States and the United Kingdom are presently outstanding in that they have achieved good labor market conditions as part of their macroeconomic balance. In China, productive employment of the labor force, especially in attractive metropolitan areas is yet to be attained. There is disguised unemployment in agriculture and in the large state-owned-enterprises (SOEs), where people are kept at work in unproductive ways. Also, there is open unemployment in some large cities. For a more complete macroeconomic balance, China must improve labor market conditions.

As for distributional issues, China's economic development is quite uneven in a regional sense. Coastal areas are more prosperous than inland areas. Western China is in need of much stronger development. In small enterprises and in Town and Village Enterprises (TVEs) – some small; some not so small – productivity is more satisfactory and profits are better than in the large scale SOEs, where subsidies keep low productivity operations afloat.

As a socialist economy, China provides many humane social services for basic human needs. This is all to the good, but in the shift to market socialism, the distribution of income is reportedly becoming more unequal. This change is inevitable as direct central planning is phased out, but it is a matter of degree. A hallmark of the East Asian miracle has been a high degree of equality in the distributions of income and wealth, making for a high degree of economic democracy. Social and political stability are enhanced by the degree of equality, and these features are of fundamental importance in parlaying short-run achievements into longer-term performance that lends sustainability to economic development.

Features of the Mexican troubles of 1994–96 were political instability and deteriorating economic inequality. These are features to be avoided in China, to differentiate the economy from Mexican-type developments. Two important political events occurred in recent months, the death of Deng Xiaoping and the reunification with Hong Kong. At present, these changes are being favorably treated in smooth transition processes. They are, nevertheless, very important political issues that must be kept on steady paths.

Progress is definitely being made in connection with infrastructure enhancement. But the same bottlenecks – transportation, communication, energy, education – that were noted at the beginning of reform in 1978 are still bottleneck issues. It is not particularly surprising that 20 years later, the original bottlenecks are still bottlenecks. The issue is that these obstacles still exist.

Prospects for the Chinese economy

Can the strong performance of the Chinese economy during the past 20 years be extended for one, two, or three more decades? No one expects the economy to grow at 8–10 per cent annually for an indefinite period. As in the case of the more industrial countries, growth slowdowns will set in, but China has such a long distance to go, some more good decades of strong development are needed. This is the sense in which sustainability is being considered.

Extrapolations of Chinese econometric models, indicate a continuation of growth in the 8–10 per cent range, with single-digit inflation, and sound external balances. Also, some of the issues mentioned in the previous section will be improved upon, if not eliminated in some cases. But, apart from the econometric extrapolation, what can we say in a qualitative way about future prospects for the Chinese economy?

Agriculture has been growing at a steady rate, between 4 and 5 per cent annually, but its growth is much slower than that of industry and services. Agriculture will play a smaller role in the future economy of China but, in the near term, there should be no food crisis. In order to be on the safe side and feed the world's largest (and growing) population, there will have to be investment in agriculture and introduction of new technology. This will require expansion of both fixed and human capital in agriculture, together with substantial intermediate inputs (water, fertilizer, seed, feed, insecticide).

Inevitably, this expected shift towards more productive agriculture will require fewer people, and the excess labor force that will probably leave agriculture will have to be absorbed elsewhere in the economy; otherwise unemployment will be a serious matter. These are all thorny problems, but solutions are to be found.

To some extent, the institution of Town and Village Enterprise (TVE) has been important in providing highly productive work outside agriculture in rural areas. The TVEs are very productive and are expanding at a rapid rate. This is an excellent source for more manufacturing output and more jobs for the non-agricultural labor force.

On a limited basis the Special Economic Zones (SEZs) also represent an expansive force in the Chinese economy. The SEZs have proved themselves to be successful undertakings and will undoubtedly continue to do so. They solve many problems in their own right, but they also contribute to the solution of a different problem, namely, regional concentration. The first generation of SEZs are near harbors and contribute most to coastal areas, but economic development outside the main developed areas needs to be fostered. While there are advantages in having SEZs at ocean shipping locations because export trade is important for the zoned output, that aspect is not essential and Chinese planners should deliberately locate some new SEZs in more remote geographical areas. This will also require the upgrading of transportation and communication infrastructure. Infrastructure is also an integral component of China's sustainable development; therefore careful coordination of location of SEZs, together with extensive infrastructure development make an attractive package that deals with several problems all together. It also indicates how much needs to be done, which pushes the timetable for economic maturity further into the time horizon and makes for demand conditions that are favorable to sustained development.

In development planning, the recent Mexican crisis should be kept plainly in mind, as something to be avoided, at all costs. It is all the more important in light of some of the same problems, although on a much milder scale, appearing in other East Asian economies in 1997.

This issue brings to mind the international problems that were prevalent when China first embarked on economic reform in 1978. The delegation of US economists sent to China by the National Academy of Science, the American Council of Learned Societies, and the Social Science Research Council to establish economic contacts, had a meeting with Vice Premier Gu Mu, at which it was urged that China act prudently in the field of international finance and not be trapped into excessive debt build-up, as was occurring then in Poland. Eventually the process spread to many developing countries in the form of the World Debt Crisis. China was not dragged into that difficult financial situation and was able to pursue development policy on a healthier economic plane.

A similar situation is now present. China must avoid the problems of Mexico, South Korea, Thailand, and other ASEAN economies. This means careful borrowing, use of adequate collateral, emphasis on foreign direct investment, engaging in joint ventures with technologically superior partners, and de-emphasis on passive portfolio investment. These, too, are important steps for international policy that will lead to sound and healthy development that can be sustained.

It seems that China has diversified the inflow of foreign capital in such a way that the Mexican or ASEAN-type crises are less likely to build up to a critical point. Also, the FOREX reserve position has become large enough to impose a formidable barrier for speculators. Enough control over foreign investment flows, banking practices, and exchange rates exists for quick and decisive action. The '*savoir faire*' of international finance in Hong Kong can also be of great help to China. So far, the Hong Kong dollar has been little affected by the movements in ASEAN currencies.

Openness has done much for China already but, if openness becomes an oppressive burden, China would be well advised to look inward, temporarily, until foreign disturbances are settled. The domestic market is so large that there is much scope for economic activity at a high level, now that steps have already been taken to bring a great deal of Western technological skill into China. A barrier has already been broken.

Meanwhile China should not turn back, in a trend sense (only temporarily for short-run emergencies), from the path of financial market liberalization. As a major participant in world trade, world finance and world transport, the problem will be to build the infrastructure and know-how to make the open sides of the economy run smoothly. In the early stages it is a matter of warding off the difficulties of participating in the fast-moving activity of world trade and finance. Those are the realistic difficulties that are now affecting ASEAN economies and South Korea, too. The answer is to keep opening to the rest of the world in these new areas, step-by-step, mastering the obstacles at each stage, before moving on to the next stage. Ultimately, a very high degree of openness should be achieved, and this will enhance the sustainability aspect.

In the domestic market, one of the largest problems facing the Chinese economy in its quest for sustainability is the raising of the levels of productivity. The sorest point in this respect is the continuing subsidization of the large SOEs, where profitability and efficiency are lacking. Some feel that the key to success is privatization. There could be some gains in that respect, but a more important issue is competitiveness. The size factor should be reconsidered. Indefinitely large units often become unmanageable and are not the most efficient. Managerial analysis, marketing, and finance of large producing entities must be addressed systematically, in order to improve productive efficiency.

There will be worker displacement as productivity improves. On the plus side, this should release people to contribute elsewhere to economic performance, but it also puts pressure on the unemployment rolls, probably in urban areas. This requires careful planning for demand through fiscal, monetary, and commercial policy in order to absorb the displaced workers in productive activity. Both supply and demand management techniques are called for. It is probably the case that the process of streamlining the SOEs has gone too slowly. That does not mean that they must be completely overhauled, all at once. That could invite economic chaos. Nevertheless fresh, giant steps must be taken to turn the SOEs into efficient entities. The safety nets, training programs, and educational expansion should be put into place to absorb the released workers, while demand is being built up.

Problems of measurement

How large is the Chinese economy and at what rate is it developing? Difficult problems arise in giving a good answer to these questions. It is not purely a descriptive objective; it is an analytical matter that can have a great deal of influence on future developments.

A key member of our visiting delegation in 1979 was Irving Kravis. During the course of our visit, he collected many prices and commodity/service specifications. They were all too few for the job at hand – how to compare the Chinese economy with others in the world where the information flows and measurement techniques were more advanced. In spite of their sparseness, they were essential first steps to the objective measurement of China's GDP and associated accounts in a form that could be helpful in setting policy and appraising progress.

Generally speaking, when using Kravis's procedures, based on purchasing-power parity exchange rates (PPP) rather than market exchange rates (MER), developing countries' GDP estimates denominated in a *numéraire* currency (e.g. US$) are increased, while advanced industrial countries' GDP estimates are decreased, except of course for the GDP of a *numéraire* currency, which does not change. After our committee visit of 1979, we issued a trip report with Kravis's estimate for China which valued GDP *per capita* near the level for the Philippines and about 13 per cent of the corresponding US value.[2]

Economists inside and outside China considered the Kravis estimate as too large. I discussed the issues at stake with him many times and concluded that it would be possible to shave one or two percentage points (China as a percentage of USA) from his estimate, but that it was fundamentally correct. An abundance of inexpensive housing and many social services seemed to justify the high estimate.

International organizations continued to use MER-based estimates and treated China as a very poor developing country in official programs. When statistical services improved in China after 1978, as the economy opened to the world, and as many economic reforms were introduced, many economists, statisticians, and officials of the multinational organizations began to reconsider their views about the economy of China, both from the perspective of its *level* and its *rate-of-change*.

At more recent price levels, on a world scale, China was deemed to produce as much as $2000 GDP per head or more, and grow as fast as 10 per cent *per annum*, in total. About 1.25 percentage points could be subtracted for *per capita* valuations.

Kravis's estimates for China constituted a preliminary first step that aroused interest in China's economic potential. His associates, Robert Summers and Alan Heston, have made more intensive analysis of the China case and more extensive analysis for the PENN World Tables on a PPP basis.[3] For a period beginning with 1960, they estimate China's *per capita* GDP at only 5 to 7 per cent of the US figure until 1990. For a more recent period, they estimate a rapid increase, bringing China to about 10 per cent of the US *per capita* GDP, for 1995. Interesting enough, their figures for the Philippines in 1995 was $2622 *per capita*, close to their figure for China, at $2823 *per capita*. As quoted above, in 1980, Kravis characterized his China estimate, in relation to the US benchmark, as about the same as that of the Philippines.

In terms of real growth rates, Summers and Heston estimate values between 2 and 4 per cent for the 1960s, 1970s, and 1980s. The latter two decades are decidedly lower than most other estimates, but in order to bring their 1995 values up to 10 per cent of the US level, there had to be very strong growth after 1990.

To put matters in perspective, the Human Development Report (HDR) 1997 estimates that China's total GNP growth rate has been 9.6 per cent, 1980–93, and that the *per capita* rate has been 8.2 per cent. Although the preferred aggregate is GDP, the HDR statisticians prepared these particular figures in GNP terms. The same figures for industrial countries as a group are 2.5 per cent and 1.9 per cent.

Most China forecasts look for continuing real production growth (GDP or GNP) near 10 per cent in the aggregate and attribute about one percentage point of that to population growth. But industrial countries, serving as a target are also moving. Policy-makers in the US and Europe are quite satisfied with 2.5 per cent as their *potential* rate. Japanese and some other advanced country policy-makers might choose a rate as high as 3 per cent for *potential* growth. I, personally, think that the conservative figures for the advanced industrial countries are an underestimate. In any event, whether the rate is 2.0–2.5 per cent or 3.0–3.5 per cent, it is a *moving target*.

Suppose that China grows at 8 per cent *per capita* annually for 30 years – a very optimistic assumption. GDP *per capita* would expand tenfold, but for the US growing at 2 per cent annually for 30 years – a very pessimistic assumption – the GDP *per capita* would nearly double. If US GDP *per capita* is already at least 10 times as large as China GDP *per capita*, it is evident that 'catch-up' would not be achieved. It is likely that China's GDP *per capita* would not increase as much as tenfold because it grows more slowly when valued in international prices (PPP) than when valued in 'own' prices. For example, China's GDP value in 1987 (US$) grew by 5.3 per cent between 1960 and 1994, according to HDR (1997). But in real PPP units between the same two dates, the growth rate was only 3.8 per cent. That is why 30 years of growth, *per capita*, at 8 per cent is optimistic for the purposes of this comparative calculation.

It should be noted that the formation of a weighted average of 'own' price real growth rates across all countries of the world, with shares of World GDP at PPP prices as the weights, produces a *larger* world growth rate than when the weights are shares of constant-dollar World GDP (at MER). This is because the faster-growing developing countries get a larger share of World GDP at PPP than at MER conversion factors. However, for China alone, as an individual country, the growth rate of GDP at PPP valuation is less than the growth rate of GDP at MER valuation.

Let us assume that, for purposes of international comparison of *levels* of GDP among countries, PPP valuation is a preferred measurement. It is by no means clear whether comparative *growth rates* among countries should be estimated from 'own' price data (at constant prices) or from PPP data (at constant prices). Heston, Nuxoll, and Summers have found an interesting result in this respect.[4] From a 1991 data set (PENN World Tables) that, incidentally, does not include China, they estimate the cross-country regression (standard errors in parentheses)

$$r_3 - r_6 = \underset{(0.794)}{2.057} - \underset{(0.102)}{0.279} \text{ Log (DA)}$$

In this equation

r_3 = growth rate of *per capita* domestic absorption using national price weights

r_6 = growth rate of *per capita* domestic absorption using chained international price weights

DA = *per capita* domestic absorption in 1985 measured in 1985 international prices.

This result states that the more prosperous a country is (i.e. higher DA) the higher will be its growth rates based on international weights compared to its growth rate using national weights. In other words, the growth rates from the PENN World Tables will tend to be higher than growth rates using 'own'-price weights for richer countries and smaller for poorer countries. This would explain why a poor country (measured in 1985 international *per capita* absorption values) like China would be expected to show lower growth rates, as computed by Heston and Summers, from their tabulations than from domestic tabulations with domestic prices.

This is, in a sense, the opposite of what we find when estimating levels rather than rates of change.[5]

There is another issue to be considered when judging China's GDP figures, namely, an adjustment for quality. There is little doubt that the quality of the GDP basket of goods and services has vastly improved during the period of economic reform. Following in the footsteps of several advanced industrial economies, China should upgrade the level of growth or downgrade the level of price inflation. It is claimed that the basic price indexes of the United States, and also of some other industrial countries, overstate the rate of inflation; therefore real growth is actually higher than the figures show. The same is the case for China – only more so. Moreover, productivity increases are probably being understated because of the growing importance of services, where productivity is hard to measure. We would have a much better statistical picture of past, present, and future economic performances if these thorny issues were more properly examined.

Notes

1. It is interesting to note that China is now in a financial position to contribute a non-trivial amount to the support of Thailand's financial markets.
2. Kravis collected the price data in 1979 and possibly some supplementary material in 1980, but his original GDP estimate was for 1975. See *Report of the CSCPRC Economics Delegation to the People's Republic of China*, National Academy of Sciences, Washington, DC, 1980 (appendix by Irving B. Kravis, 'An Approximation of the Relative Real Per Capita GDP of the People's Republic of China,' pp. 64–86.
3. The data from the PENN World Tables are source information for the Human Development Report.
4. Alan Heston, Daniel A. Nuxoll, and Robert Summers, 'Comparative Country Performance at Own-Prices or Common International Prices', *Economics, Econometrics, and The LINK*, ed. by M. Dutta, *et. al.* (Amsterdam: Elsevier, 1995), 345–61.
5. In the above cited chapter by Heston, Nuxoll, and Summers, there is an editorial slip in stating the conclusion, verbally, rather than mathematically, as in the equation.

Part III

Cross-Border Networks

13
The Complexity of Self-Organizing East Asian Networks

*David F. Batten**

Predicting the future course of social and economic evolution is no simple task. Over fifty years ago, the noted economist, Joseph Schumpeter, delivered a cautionary message concerning the predictability of socio-economic development:

> The process of social life is a function of so many variables, many of which are not amenable to anything like measurement, that even mere diagnosis of a given state of things becomes a doubtful matter quite apart from the formidable sources of error that open up as soon as we attempt prognosis.
>
> (Schumpeter, 1942)

More recently, the astronomer, Carl Sagan, came to a similar conclusion:

> The pattern of evolutionary causality is a web of astonishing complexity; the incompleteness of our understanding humbles us.
>
> (Sagan, 1980)

* A crude outline of this paper was prepared while the author was visiting Italy and lecturing at the Politecnico di Torino in April 1996. Some of the material formed the basis of presentations at the Universities of Bologna and Venice, as well as at the Workshop on Sustainable Social and Economic Development in Northern Europe and East Asia in Macau (29 April–2 May 1996). The author is grateful for the helpful comments provided by the audiences at each presentation. He would also like to thank Jessie Poon for providing information on rank-size distributions and city hierarchies in Asia. Specific comments from Lata Chatterjee, Dimitrios Dendrinos, Fang FuKang, Britton Harris, Dino Martellato, Sylvia Occelli and Aura Reggiani are also acknowledged.

Causality remains a mystery whenever we attempt to ascertain the mix of factors generating social and economic development. As for most problems in evolutionary causality, the overriding difficulty is that too many variables are involved.

A good case in point is urban development. Much of the planning literature of the 1960s and 1970s was built on the belief that the growth and development of individual cities was sufficiently smooth to be predicted, controlled, indeed even optimized. Peering carefully through the sharper lens of non-linear dynamics, we can now see that periods of stasis or near-stasis are punctuated by periods of sudden and unexpected change. Because its future trajectory is contingent upon specific (and often seemingly minor) events in the past, an urban economy's path of development may, at times, be uneven and unpredictable. If its trajectory cannot be predicted under these conditions, its development can hardly be optimized.

The cities of East Asia are an interesting case study. Most of them have grown haphazardly, bit by bit in response to the needs and the opportunities of the moment. No single, compact, lawlike description of their evolution can be found. Some continue to grow, but so do their inherent problems. Others have already fallen from grace. The causes of one city's prosperity and another's demise are difficult to predict in advance and defy generalization. Sometimes the best we can do is simply stand back and watch the pageant unfold.

The pageant of East Asian urban development

Levels of urbanization

Seemingly rampant rates of population growth in some cities of East Asia have engendered an image of rapid urbanization throughout the region. But such a generalization is rather misleading. A different picture emerges if we divide the region into two subregions (following Yeung, 1990):

(1) East Asia, represented by countries north of, but including, Hong Kong; and
(2) Southeast Asia, consisting of those nations south of Hong Kong.

With the obvious exception of China, East Asia is characterized by a higher-than-world-average level of urbanization (see Table 13.1). Japan, Hong Kong and South Korea experienced greater than tenfold increases in *per capita* gross national product in the two decades prior to 1980. The doubling of South Korea's level of urbanization during this period went

Table 13.1 Levels of urbanization in Asia

Place	*1960*	*1970*	*1980*	*1994*	*2010*
China	18.7	21.7	25.7	38.8	43.0
Hong Kong	89.1	89.7	90.3	96.2	96.6
Japan	62.5	71.4	78.3	79.4	80.6
South Korea	27.7	40.7	54.8	89.4	91.4
Indonesia	14.6	17.1	20.2	45.2	49.7
Malaysia	25.2	27.0	29.4	61.1	64.4
Philippines	30.3	32.9	36.2	63.2	66.6
Singapore	77.6	75.3	74.1	100.0	100.0
Thailand	12.5	13.2	14.4	24.3	27.4
World	33.9	37.4	41.1	45.0	–

Sources: http://unescap.org/theme/poptab09.htm; Yeung 1990.

hand in hand with its extraordinary spurt of urban and economic growth after the Korean War.

By way of contrast, Southeast Asia can be viewed as one of the least urbanized regions of the world. Except for the city-state of Singapore, levels of urbanization are consistently below the developing world average. Nevertheless, substantial urban growth has occurred in all parts of Southeast Asia except Singapore since 1980. The urban populations have grown in tandem with the total populations, leaving levels of urbanization relatively unchanged.

Growth in the largest cities has been fueled by natural increase and migration. But growth has come at a price. Each of the great cities of Eastern Asia has inherited the usual litany of problems suffered by many Third World countries: housing shortages, traffic congestion, inadequate basic services, growing social inequality, widespread poverty, and limited employment opportunities. Several important questions arise. Can we manage or control these cities and their problems to any significant extent? Or is urban evolution beyond our own control? What do we really know about the evolutionary potential of an increasingly interdependent network of cities like those developing in East Asia?

Zipf's Law and city-size distributions

One thing we do know is that, in any system of settlements, small towns are far more common than large cities. The same is also true for earthquakes, storms, avalanches, wars and stock-market price gyrations (see Bak, 1996). In 1949, George Kingsley Zipf observed some striking regularities in systems of human origin (see Zipf, 1949). One of his observations linked city size to frequency of occurrence. Figure 13.1 shows

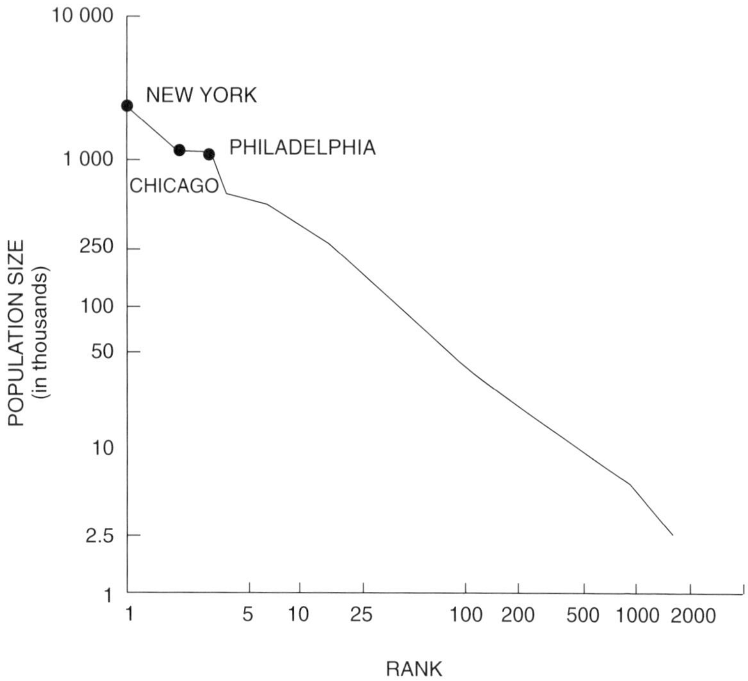

Figure 13.1 Rank-size distribution of urban centers in the United States, 1950

how the population of each American city in 1950 occupied a unique position in that nation's urban hierarchy. The size distribution of cities corresponded closely to a rank-size relationship. If we plot population size against rank for every urban centre in the United States, then the resulting downward-sloping curve is roughly a straight line on a logarithmic plot. This simply means that the size of each centre is inversely proportional to its population rank.

Zipf produced similar plots for many geographical regions in the 1920s and found the same kind of regularity. Subsequent research has confirmed that this rank-size rule relationship also seems to hold outside the United States. In a large comparative study of 38 countries at varying levels of economic development, Berry (1961) showed that 13 of these countries had city-size distributions that conformed to the rank-size rule (see Table 13.2). Later studies have also confirmed that rank-size distributions exist in some of the nations of Southeast Asia (e.g. Sendut, 1966). The regularity expressed by the straight lines in many of these logarithmic plots of size *versus* rank, with slope near unity, is known as Zipf's Law.

Table 13.2 City-size distributions in selected Asian countries

Countries with rank-size pattern	*Countries with primate pattern*	*Countries with intermediate pattern*
China	Japan	Malaysia
India	Sri Lanka	Pakistan
South Korea	Thailand	

Source: Adapted from Berry 1961.

But what about the 25 countries in Table 13.2 whose distributions did not follow the rank-size rule. A further fifteen seemed to exhibit a primate distribution, in which one or two very large cities dominated and there was an absence of medium-sized cities. The rest revealed patterns that could be seen as intermediate between rank-size and primate. In these cases, one or two cities were rather dominant but the overall pattern was generally closer to rank-size than to primate.

Is there a simple explanation for the differences shown in Table 13.2? The table itself does not suggest any obvious explanation. While many of the lesser developed nations (like Guatemala, Mexico, Peru and Thailand) do have primate patterns, others (like El Salvador and India) do not. Conversely, a number of advanced European nations (like Austria, Sweden and the Netherlands) seem to display a primate pattern rather than a rank-size distribution. On the basis of Berry's table alone, we feel obliged to conclude that numerous factors probably account for the differences – factors such as stage of economic development, changes in political status, length of time urbanized, and so on.

Before we accept such a conclusion, however, two observations warrant our attention. First, there is no convincing argument to support the arbitrary choice of national frontiers as the most appropriate way of defining a system of cities. Quite different results can be achieved after taking cultural and linguistic borders into account. More importantly, an historical analysis of flows and interaction patterns between all candidate cities is a more reliable way of defining a truly interactive system of cities. This method would suggest that the towns and cities of Malaysia and Singapore should be regarded as part of a single distribution of cities which, when treated in this way, is approximately rank-size (see Sendut, 1966). Furthermore, in Japan one finds a rank-size distribution of cities once Tokyo's chief rival is seen to be the multi-centred Kansai or Keihanshin conurbation (see Ginsburg, 1988; Batten, 1995).

Second, there is no reason to expect that very different systems of cities will converge to the same kind of city-size distribution at any single point in time. After all, we are comparing the outcomes of complex evolutionary processes which have commenced from different initial conditions and are evolving in different directions at different speeds. Some settlement systems are already well developed and strongly interactive. Others remain largely immature and only weakly interactive. The very fact that one system displays a rank-size distribution, while another remains primate, merely confirms that we are dealing with different classes of settlement systems. Some of these are dynamically stable. Others may be relatively unstable.

Self-organizing urban networks

Macro-stability and power laws

In some countries, the rank-size relationship has been remarkably stable over long periods of time. Take the case of the United States. Figure 13.2 shows that the slope of the rank-size relationship has remained more or less the same since 1790, depite the fact that the American urban system

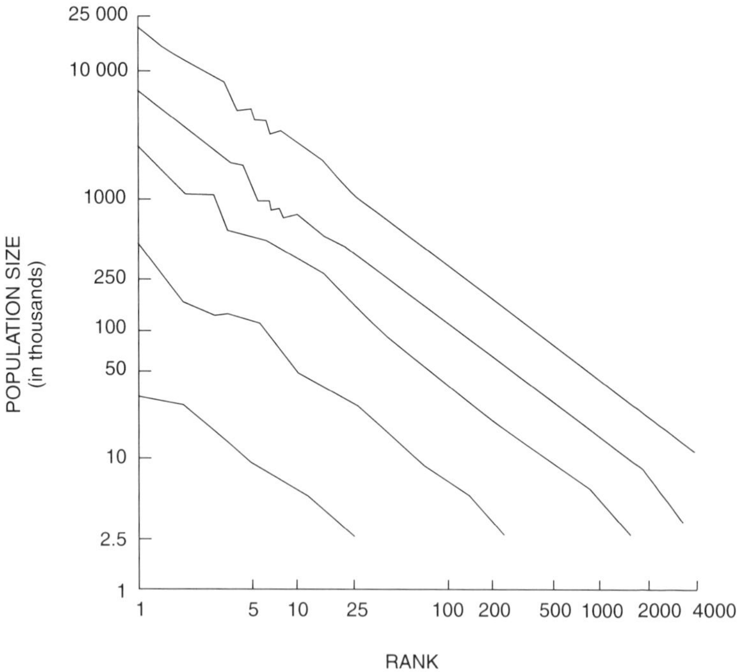

Figure 13.2 Stability of the rank-size distribution of urban centers in the United States, 1790–1950

has grown enormously since that time. The rank-size structure of the Malaysia–Singapore system of cities has also remained rather stable since the 1950s.

Why should the size distribution (or macrostructure) of some nation's system of cities display such stability over time? Zipf (1949) attributed this underlying regularity of city-size structures to the individual agent trying to minimize his or her effort. But he gave no clues about how to get from this individual level to his aggregate statistical observations. Berry (1961) suggested that, as the economic, political and social life of a country becomes more complex, its city-size distribution will tend to develop towards a rank-size pattern which represents the steady-state of an urban system.

Berry's suggestion raises two intriguing questions:

(1) Under what conditions can a nation's economic, political and social life be regarded as complex?
(2) Could the rank-size pattern be a sufficiently strong aggregative attractor (in the case of the United States) that the individual towns and cities self-organize in ways which ensure that the system as a whole preserves its rank-size structure over time?

Let us deal with the second question first. There is evidence to support the idea that the rank-size pattern is an attractor. Despite the high degree of macro-stability shown in Figure 13.2, the relative position of individual cities in the US urban system has varied considerably. Between 1870 and 1950, for example, Los Angeles leapt ahead 314 places to reach the top five. Among those cities with a population of more than 100 000 in 1950, 14 enjoyed a relatively stable ranking but another 10 experienced changes of more than 100 places. This is something like a forest whose contours never seem to change, but whose individual trees do. Perhaps the towns and cities self-organize into an equilibrium pattern or rank-size 'ecology'.

Similar macro-stability can also be found in several city-size distributions in East Asia. Indonesia, Japan, Malaysia–Singapore, South Korea and Taiwan have more or less preserved their rank-size distributions over the last fifty years, despite the fact that many individual towns and cities have changed their rankings markedly. Although Zipf's Law implies this stability in the number of cities within a given range of population sizes, it cannot tell us why a particular city has a certain number of inhabitants. All the observations are of a collective or statistical nature.

What is so magical about the rank-size distribution that it can command such rigid adherence? The rank-size distribution is emergent in the sense that it is not an obvious consequence of the underlying dynamical rules governing the behaviour of the individual elements (i.e. towns and cities). Mathematically speaking, however, Zipf's Law is nothing more than a specific kind of power law. Power laws express a quantity N as some power of another quantity s:

$$N(s) = s - t$$

By taking logarithms of both sides of the above equation, we find that

$$\log N(s) = -t \log s$$

The exponent t is the slope of the straight line formed when $\log N(s)$ is plotted against $\log s$. In Zipf's Law, the number N corresponds to the number of cities with more than s inhabitants, and is given by $N(s) = 1/s = s - 1$. It is simply a power law with exponent –1. Thus the problem of explaining the observed statistical features of complex systems such as rank-size distributions of cities can be seen as the problem of explaining the underlying power-law relationship.

Sandpiles and self-organized criticality

City-size distributions are not the only phenomena which can be expressed as straight lines on a double logarithmic plot. Various catastrophic events, fractals and low-frequency noise also exhibit this pattern (see Bak, 1996). Such coupled dissipative phenomena cannot be understood by studying them within a time frame which is short compared with the evolutionary process which created them. For example, the laws governing earthquakes cannot be understood just by studying earthquakes occurring in a single human lifetime.

A special feature of coupled dissipative systems is that they evolve naturally towards a self-organized critical state. To illustrate the basic idea of self-organized criticality in an interactive system, consider a simple 'pile of sand.' Suppose we start from scratch and build our pile by randomly adding sand, one grain at a time. The pile will grow and the slope will increase until eventually it reaches a critical value. If more sand is then added, it will slide off. Alternatively, if we had started off from a situation where the pile had been too steep, it would have collapsed until it reached the same critical state. By 'self-organized', we mean that the system evolves naturally to this critical state without detailed specification of the initial conditions. The critical state is an attractor for the dynamics. It is just barely stable with respect to further perturbations.

As the pile is built up, the characteristic size of the largest sandslide (or avalanche) grows, until at the critical point there are avalanches of all sizes up to the size of the whole system. Once this critical point is reached, the system stays there. This distribution of avalanches in a sandpile also happens to obey Zipf's Law. Perhaps we should be thinking of cities as being formed by avalanches of human migrations (see Fujita, 1996)? More importantly, we might ask whether certain nation's city-size distributions evolve spontaneously towards a critical state and later return to it even if perturbed at some later stage?

Self-organized systems start from disordered initial conditions and tend to move to more highly ordered behaviour. This highly ordered behaviour exhibits surprisingly simple regularities, such as rank-size distributions. One can imagine with city-size distributions that there might be many potential outcomes depending on initial conditions. But a handful of these potential outcomes – namely those self-organized ones in which city sizes roughly obey the rank-size rule – might be more or less independent of historical events in any one location. After all, a rank-size distribution does not depend on which particular cities belong to the various size classes. It simply defines the overall shape of the distribution. It might therefore be a favoured outcome under certain rather common conditions.

Lock-in, interactions and emergence

Lock-in and path dependence

Some urban networks persist for many centuries. In New York City, for example, the arrangement of many of the major streets dates back to the seventeenth century, the stock-exchange to the eighteenth century, the waterworks to the nineteenth, and the electrical power system to the twentieth. In the seventeenth century, you travelled between Brooklyn and Manhattan across the East River by ferry. In the nineteenth century, new technology allowed the construction of a suspension bridge across the river. It was built precisely at the site of the ferry terminal. When newer technology permitted the construction of a tunnel under the river, it too was built in exactly the same place. This reinforcement of existing interaction patterns by upgrading the technology of critical links is very much like the pattern of biological evolution. It also provides some insights into technological choices which permit the city to function more or less continuously over many centuries.

Given the vagaries of political decision-making and the tremendous costs of altering large infrastructure networks, it is rather easy for a city to 'lock-in' to a particular arterial system which was perceived to possess a socio-economic advantage at the time (see Arthur, 1994). Lock-in can occur as sequential decisions carve out self-reinforcing advantages for one location at the expense of others. Thailand suffers from an extreme case of urban lock-in. Bangkok's dominance over all other Thai settlements can be explained by the perceived advantages of its geographical location. The economic focus of the whole country towards the lower Menam Chao Phraya plain only serves to emphasize Bangkok's suitability as the chief export port for Thai rice. Because other towns lie in areas of agricultural subsistence and lack the vital ingredients for urban development (see Sendut, 1966), Bangkok's supremacy is continually reinforced. Thus Thailand's settlement distribution is strongly primate, with Bangkok-Thonburi being twenty-one times the size of Nakhon Ratchasima, the second largest city in Thailand.

Urban America provides another illustration of path dependence or lock-in. In the nineteenth century, Philadelphia was a more important port than New York. The opening of the Erie Canal then tipped the scales in favour of New York. Although the Erie has been more of a tourist attraction than a serious transportation route for more than a century, New York still dominates the USA's urban hierarchy. We shall never know whether Philadelphia might have achieved that status if the Erie Canal had never materialized. New York moved ahead and has never looked back. In cases such as these, history really matters.

The Thai and American examples highlight the importance of circulation and interaction patterns within and between cities. Circulation and interaction are the life-blood of human activity. Although urban infrastructure networks evolve relatively slowly, the patterns of human interaction which they facilitate can change quickly and unexpectedly (see Batten and Johansson, 1985). This is the signature of co-evolution. To identify the co-evolutionary potentials of systems of cities, we need a deeper understanding of what Karl Marx called their 'sphere of circulation.' In modern jargon, we must study the games of circulation and interaction which are played out on those logistical networks within and between cities.

Why are interaction patterns so important? The quick answer is because they provide important clues about the complexity of a city's behavioural relationships and thus its evolutionary potential. Here there are striking similarities between the functioning of a city and the workings of the brain. We know precious little about how nerve cells work and we lack rudimentary circuit diagrams for the brain. Even an expert electronic engineer would have trouble understanding how a circuit worked if he didn't know what its components did or how they were linked together (Cohen and Stewart, 1994). But this is precisely the situation in our cities.

Each person knows very little about what every other person or urban organization really does, and has limited knowledge of the circulatory patterns which a city generates. Yet the city somehow manages to survive despite all this uncertainty!

The sheer complexity of each system poses fundamental problems. For example, the brain has ten million neurons, each connected to (roughly) a hundred others. An accurate circuit diagram would feature one trillion connecting wires! This requires a very large computer system for its storage. Similar problems arise when we try to study the interactions between or within urban populations. Even when urban dwellers seem to be doing very simple things, their interactions can quickly add up to more complexity than we can handle. Once the ratio of interactions per inhabitant passes a critical threshold, then the qualitative impact of that population's interaction patterns can change unexpectedly. The following simple experiment helps to illustrate the unusual nature of these critical thresholds of interaction.

Buttons, threads and phase transitions

It is often helpful to look at a simpler toy problem first when trying to understand a more complex one. The toy problem to be discussed here was devised by Stuart Kauffman (1995) and involves random graphs. A random graph (or random network) consists of a set of nodes connected at random by a set of links. On paper it looks like a set of dots connected at random by a set of lines (see Figure 13.3). To visualize this particular toy problem in an everyday context, think of the dots as 'buttons' and the lines as 'threads.'

Imagine a hundred buttons scattered on a wooden floor. Now randomly choose two buttons and connect them with a thread. After putting this pair down, randomly choose two more buttons, pick them up, and connect them with a thread. As you continue to do this, at first you will almost certainly pick up buttons that you have not picked up before. Sooner or later, however, you are more likely to pick at random a pair of buttons and find that you have already chosen one of the pair. So when you tie a thread between these two buttons, you will find that you have linked together three buttons. As you go on choosing pairs of buttons randomly to link together with a thread, you will find that some of the buttons soon become interconnected into larger clusters. This is shown in Figure 13.3. Each connected cluster is known as a component in our random graph.

The thing to notice is that random graphs show very regular statistical behaviour as we increase the ratio of threads to buttons.

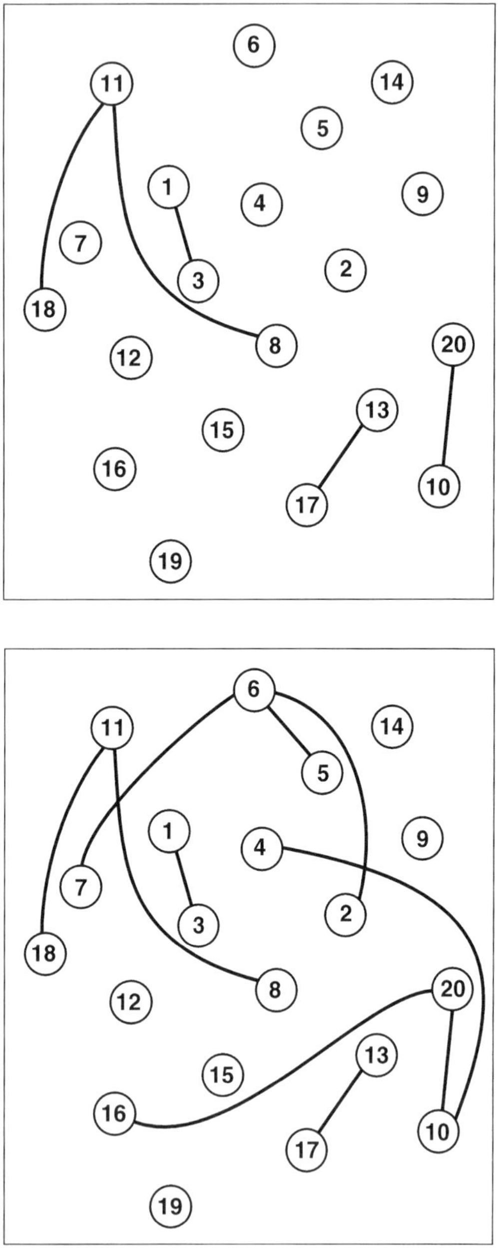

Figure 13.3 The crystallization of connected webs

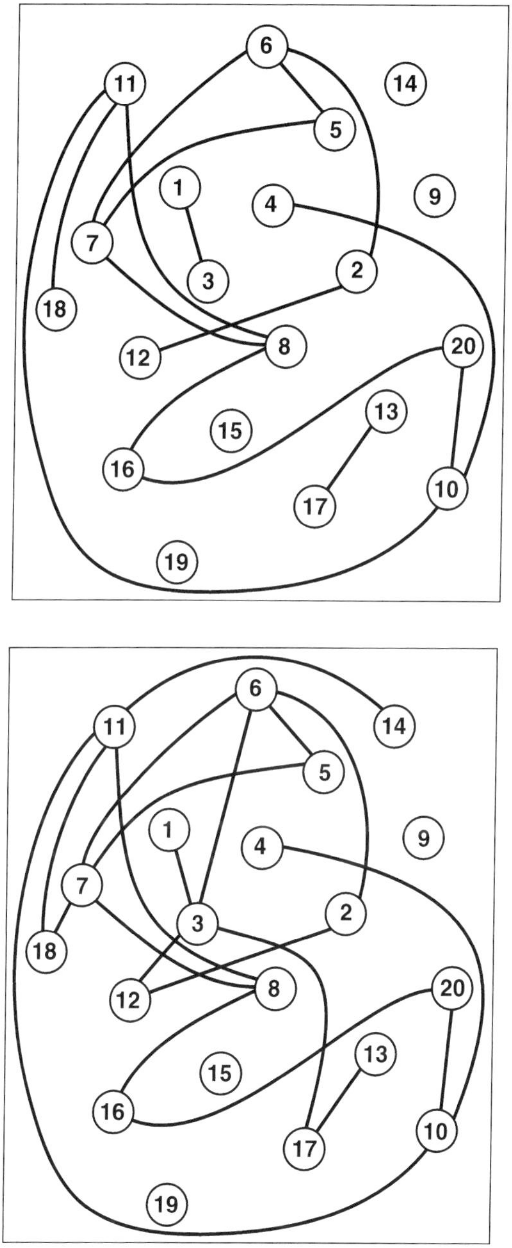

Figure 13.3 (continued)

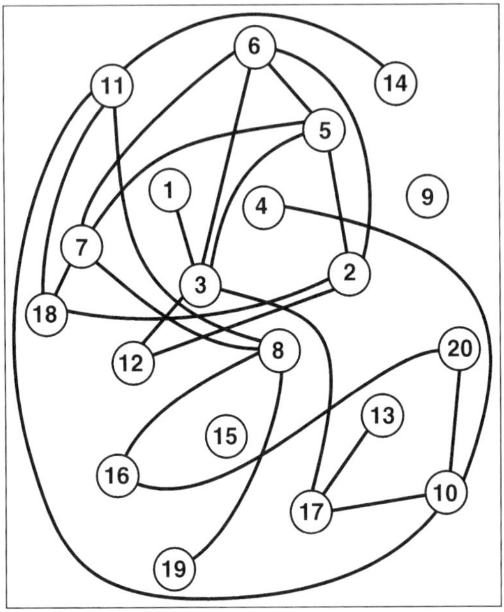

Figure 13.3 (*continued*)

Once the ratio of threads to buttons passes the 0.5 mark, something seemingly magical occurs. All of a sudden most of the clusters become cross-connected into one giant structure! When this giant component forms, most of the buttons are directly or indirectly connected. As the ratio of threads to buttons approaches one, virtually all of the remaining isolated buttons and small clusters become cross-connected into the giant component.

This rather sudden and unexpected change in the size of the largest cluster of buttons, as the ratio of threads to buttons passes 0.5, is the signature of something resembling a phase transition (see Figure 13.4). Note that the curve is S-shaped or sigmoidal. The size of the largest cluster of buttons increases slowly at first, then rapidly, then slows again as the ratio of threads to buttons increases further. Were there an infinite number of buttons, then, as the ratio of threads to buttons passed 0.5, the size of the largest component would jump discontinuously from tiny to enormous. The steep part of the curve would become more vertical than it is in Figure 13.1. This is typical of a phase transition, just like when separate water molecules freeze into a block of ice.

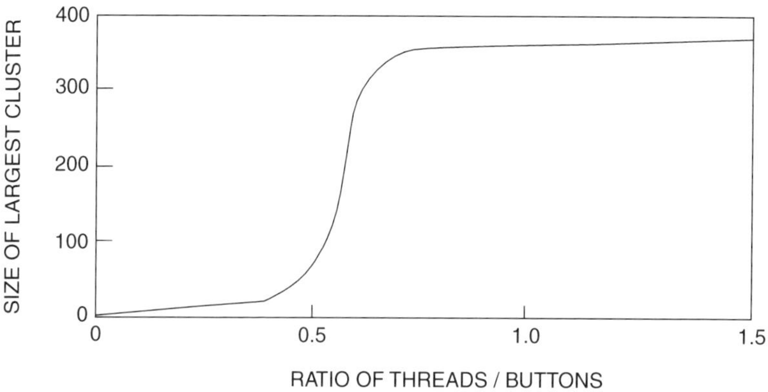

Figure 13.4 A phase transition

Emergence and urban complexity

Now let's return to our urban population. Consider what might happen if some residents start to interact more frequently with certain other residents. As the number of interactions increases, clusters of 'like-minded' residents begin to emerge spontaneously. Like-minded residents do not know in advance who their closest friends and allies may be. These kinships can only emerge after-the-fact. Furthermore, such like-minded clusters may do more than simply interact among themselves. In order to pursue their common interests more widely, eventually they may link up with other like-minded clusters, thereby creating even larger clusters. Sounds familiar, doesn't it? People behaving like buttons and threads!

In fact, the socialization process whereby common interest groups emerge and develop is analogous to the toy example discussed in the previous section. People form clusters (e.g. political parties, unions, clubs, teams) in order to pursue their common interests. These clusters represent decision-making units which can play a powerful role in the shaping of urban development. Because such clusters must take their decisions collectively (e.g. by preference voting), sometimes the outcomes can be quite different from those intended or expected by some of their members. We shall refer to these unpredictable outcomes as emergence.

For the purposes of urban research, it is helpful to think of a city as a complex social system which results from a large number of interactions between its inhabitants. The defining characteristic of this complex urban system is that some, perhaps even many, of its collective properties cannot be predicted simply from our individual knowledge of these underlying interactions. The whole urban system is greater than the sum of all its parts! Some collective outcomes can be predicted, others cannot. Many only emerge as by-products of the collective experience.

Complex systems breed emergence. For example, a car is a complex system because its ability to move cannot be predicted simply by knowing the individual rules which govern its parts (axles, gears, carburettors, etc.). A car's motion is an emergent property – a process that it can carry out only by virtue of its unique collective organization. Your mind appears to be an emergent property of your brain. Mind is a process, not a thing, and it emerges from the collective interactions of appropriately organized pieces of ordinary matter. Life itself seems to have emerged from chemistry by way of DNA.

In the urban context, voting outcomes at public meetings can be swayed spontaneously by the interactive debate and discussion of the key protagonists. Many meeting decisions are unpredictable in advance. As we shall see later, traffic jams on city highways emerge from the collective interactions of a critical density of drivers on a transportation network. Similar kinds of emergent phenomena can arise in many other social situations. Their common feature is that the population of interacting individuals can 'spontaneously' develop collective properties that may not have been intended or expected by each individual *a priori*. Each of these spontaneous outcomes is an example of emergence.

In this chapter, we have just begun to examine the role which emergence plays in urban evolution. We think of emergent phenomena as any large scale, group behaviour which does not seem to have any clear explanation in terms of the system's constituent parts (Darley, 1995). The rank-size urban distribution is a case in point. But only some of the collective phenomena observed among/within cities will be emergent. This is because urban systems may exhibit non-emergent behaviour under some conditions but generate emergent behaviour under others. Emergence may simply be the result of a phase change in the amount of computation necessary for the optimal prediction of certain phenomena (Darley, 1995). As the size and rule complexity of a city increases, more and more of the useful predictive knowledge about it will be contained in the accumulation of interactions.

Concluding remarks

A city's development certainly has some features in common with the evolution of the human brain. The brain's neurochemistry is astonishingly busy, its circuitry being more incredible than any machine devised by humans. It develops from a small centre, grows slowly and changes discontinuously. Innovative replacement can only be selective since the system must continue to function during any renovation. The functions of many old parts are too vital for them to be replaced altogether. They possess vintage properties, in the sense that some bits are older and less reliable than others. Nevertheless these parts struggle on, mostly out of date and sometimes even counter-productive, an inevitable consequence of evolution.

I have hinted at the idea that cities and human brains may have a great deal more in common. Both are living organisms whose patterns of development display the traits of complex dynamic systems. Perhaps the most important feature they have in common is that cities and brains are co-evolving complex systems. Cities co-evolve with other cities, with other living organisms (including brains) and with an ever-changing environment. This kind of co-evolution can produce surprising macroscopic outcomes, such as the rank-size distribution of cities discussed in this paper. Such collective outcomes are sometimes referred to as emergent behaviour.

Although we can never predict the exact branchings of cities (or brains), we can hope to uncover laws that govern their general behaviour. We must seek explanation rather than prediction. To further our understanding of urban change in the Asian region, we must strive to understand various processes of self-organization and their emergent properties. This paper has focused on these processes because they offer the urban analyst a powerful new lens for the recognition of certain comparative aspects of urban development.

References

Arthur, B., *Increasing Returns and Path Dependence in the Economy* (Ann Arbor: University of Michigan Press, 1994).

Bak, P., *How Nature Works: The Science of Self-Organized Criticality* (New York: Springer-Verlag, 1996).

Batten, D.F., 'Network Cities: Creative Urban Agglomerations for the 21st Century', *Urban Studies*, 32 (1995) 313–27.

Batten, D., *Discovering Artificial Economics: How Agents Learn and Economies Evolve* (Bowder: Westview Press 2000).

Batten, D.F. and B. Johansson, 'The Dynamics of Metropolitan Change', *Geographical Analysis*, 19 (1985) 189–99.

Berry, B.J.L., 'City Size Distributions and Economic Development', *Economic Development and Cultural Change*, 9 (1961) 573–88.

Cohen, J. and I. Stewart, *The Collapse of Chaos: Discovering Simplicity in a Complex World* (New York: Penguin Books, 1994).

Darley, V., 'Emergent Phenomena and Complexity', *Artificial Life IV Proceedings*, (1995) 411–16.
Fujita, M., 'On the Self-organization and Evolution of Economic Geography', *The Japanese Economic Review*, 47 (1996) 34–61.
Ginsburg, N., 'Reflections on Primacy: Cases from Asia,' in W. Tietze, (ed.), *Asian Urbanization: Problems and Processes* (Berlin: Gebrueder Borntraeger, 1988).
Kauffman, S., *At Home in the Universe: The Search for Laws of Complexity* (London: Penguin, 1995).
Sagan, C., *Cosmos* (New York: Ballantine Books, 1980).
Schumpeter, J., *Capitalism, Socialism and Democracy* (Cambridge, Mass.: Harvard University Press, 1942).
Sendut, H., 'City-Size Distributions of Southeast Asia', *Asian Studies*, 4 (1966) 165–72.
Vining, R., 'A Description of Certain Spatial Aspects of an Economic System', *Economic Development and Cultural Change*, 3 (1955) 147–95.
Yeung, Y.M. *Changing Cities of Pacific Asia: A Scholarly Interpretation* (Hong Kong: The Chinese University Press, 1990).
Zipf, G.K., *Human Behaviour and the Principle of Least Effort* (Reading, Mass.: Addison-Wesley, 1949).

14

Asia Pacific and European Patterns of Intra- and Extra-Regional Trade Compared

Jessie P.H. Poon and Edmund R. Thompson

International trade is presently subject to paradoxical and potentially conflicting phenomena. On one hand, is the explosion of regional trade agreements in the wake of the European Union's 1992 single market initiative, like NAFTA, MERCOSUR and AFTA (Baldwin, 1993). On the other, is the increasing relevance of multi- and bilateral trade arrangements, as evidenced by China's eagerness to become a World Trade Organization member and the strong advocacy of export-led development by emerging economies.

Debate surrounding the trade impact of these ostensibly opposing trends has been and continues to be fierce and inconclusive. The emergence of formal regional trade agreements has long been accompanied by fears that they engender trade diversion rather than creation, thereby directly reducing world trade and welfare (Viner, 1953). Indeed, the spectre of closed regional trade blocs has been seen as a potential threat to an open, welfare-maximizing, multilateral trading system (Bhagwati, 1992; Perroni and Whalley, 1996).

Others have argued that regional trade blocs can actually enhance welfare, despite trade diversion (Lipsey, 1957), and that trade regionalization is a 'natural' result of transaction cost efficiencies derived from geographic, cultural and historical links between proximate countries (Krugman, 1991; Frankel, Stein and Wei, 1995). Additional efficiencies are also said to derive from the exploitation of scale economies as production is concentrated to serve sizeable, compact rather than dispersed, markets (Baldwin, 1994). Hence, politically agreed *de jure* regionalism is argued simply to be the formalization of economically driven, *de facto* trade regionalization.

Moreover, and adding to the controversy, formalized regional trade areas have been argued to act as building rather than stumbling blocks for multilateral trade agreement because of negotiational efficiencies afforded by the reduction of national negotiants and the effectiveness of *en bloc* policing (Lawrence, 1991). By analyzing the internal and external trade patterns between 1965 and 1995 of two very different, broadly defined regions, Europe and the Asia Pacific, this chapter aims to shed light on this debate.

Few would disagree that Europe represents the world's oldest and most highly developed, formally integrated trading region. At its core, the European Union, in theory if not always in practice (*The Economist*, 15 March 1997), has already become a single market in which production factor mobility and trade are free, and arrangements are already in hand for economic and monetary union (Tsoukalis, 1993). Those few non former Soviet bloc countries which have so far eschewed membership, are formally linked to the Union through the European Economic Area agreement of 1992 (Swann, 1996). Nearly all ex-Soviet bloc East and Central European countries already have trade agreements with the Union and, without exception, they, along with Cyprus, Turkey and tiny Malta, are queuing up to become members. Free trade within the Union is policed not only jealously by individual members, but also by a supranational civil service, the European Commission, and disputes are adjudicated by the supranational European Court of Justice (Dinan, 1994). The deep, clearly defined and increasingly extensive formal integration of Europe has led to speculation that it is a closed 'fortress' designed to keep world trade out as much as to encourage free trade within (Aho, 1994; Bruce, 1988; Tigner, 1988).

In sharp contrast, the Asia Pacific is characterized by a series of newer, less formal and overlapping free trade agreements which, it has been argued, preserve the region's greater trading 'openness'. Indeed, the loosely defined region's most encompassing organization, APEC, was started in 1989 with a central aim of countering potentially protectionist blocs in Europe and North America (Cave and Crawford, 1996). Members of APEC have sought to emphasize extra-regional trading links and have pursued a vague notion of intra-regional cooperation rather than any definite integration (Blomqvist, 1993). Only with the 1994 Bogor declaration did APEC's members commit to the achievement of free trade amongst themselves – by 2010 for developed countries and by 2020 for less developed ones – although the mechanics of how this is to be achieved have yet to emerge. Like the ASEAN's Free Trade Area (AFTA) and NAFTA, APEC deliberately has no supranational bodies to police its agreements or adjudicate in trade disputes (Cuyvers and Pupphavesa,

1996; Theobald, 1995). Such institutional arrangements are anathema to the national-sovereignty guarding Southeast Asians and the United States (Langhammer, 1995). The deep economic integration being pursued in the European Union has even been cited by a former Singaporean minister as 'the surest way of fragmenting ASEAN into politically and economically unstable contending States' (*Straits Times*, 14 January 1989). Hence, an adamantly consensual style of informal, open regionalism has been pursued in the Asia Pacific, and it remains the case that 'only in Western Europe is there massive evidence of the process of international rationalization of nation-states into supranational institutions' (Haas, 1993 p. 507).

The tight, formal, 'closed' regionalism of Europe might be expected to manifest itself in patterns of higher intra-regional trade intensity, possibly at the expense of extra-regional trade. Whereas, the opposite might be anticipated in the Asia Pacific because of its looser, 'open' regionalism. Moreover, it could be speculated that such traits may be exacerbated by other differences between the two regions which are likely to affect 'natural' trade patterns. Whereas Europe comprises mostly contiguous states within roughly 40 degrees of both latitude and longitude, the Asia Pacific includes several archipelago and island states and straddles the world's widest ocean and both northern and southern hemispheres. Indeed, the Asia Pacific region has been described as multi-regional (Poon and Pandit, 1996a), and the very existence of a meaningful region has been questioned, despite frequent reference to it in both academic literature and common parlance (Yahuda, 1988; Montgomery, 1993; Manning and Stern, 1994). Certainly, transaction cost enforcement of 'natural' intra-regional trade as a result of cheaper transportation would be far more likely to occur in Europe than the Asia Pacific for geographical reasons. European countries also have a longer history of cultural commonality than the relatively new Asia-Pacific states with their highly diverse ethnic and cultural traditions. Undoubtedly, the Asia Pacific lacks any history of regional consciousness compared with Europe (Drysdale, 1988), and, insofar as such considerations do in fact facilitate ease of trade, Europe might again be expected to show greater signs of being the more 'natural' trading region of the two.

Intra-regional trade patterns

Methodology

Mapping the intensity of trade interlinkages between countries can be done using a number of aggregation techniques (Masser and Scheurwater,

1980). However, the work of Fischer, Essletzbichler *et al.* (1993) suggests that the Intramax approach tends to be superior in terms of establishing regional patterns, and is used here. In the Intramax method, an objective function is defined such that:

$$\text{Max } (I_{ij} - I'_{ij}) + (I_{ji} - I'_{ji}) \qquad i, j = 1, \ldots, n$$

where,

I_{ij} = the observed value of (i, j) in the trade intersection matrix, and

I'_{ij} = $(\Sigma_j \, I_{ij} \, \Sigma_i \, I_{ij})/\Sigma_{ij} \, I_{ij} \quad i, j = 1, .., n$

By applying the above objective function, a transformed matrix can be derived which measures the largest total interactions between pairs of countries in excess of the total of the expected values derived from row and column totals. This transformed matrix can then be used to cluster trade flows by incrementally grouping countries with high levels of interactions, building up from small to large clusters.[1]

The data consist of 1965–95 country exports in US dollars from the International Monetary Fund's trade tape. These data are also published annually in the *Direction of Trade Statistics* (DOT). Because of ambiguity surrounding the extent and shape of the Asia Pacific (Kojima, 1981; Kahler, 1988), the definition provided by UNCTAD (1993) is used. This includes East Asia, South Asia, Southeast Asia and the Pacific Islands. North America, Australia and New Zealand have also been included as they are APEC members and have been seen to have become more economically oriented towards Asia (Poon and Pandit, 1996b). In the case of Europe, the countries comprise western, central and eastern European countries.

Using the Intramax procedure, dendrograms for 1965 and 1995 for both Europe and the Asia Pacific can be derived (Figures 14.1–14.4). Dendrograms are tree diagrams where every 'branch' of the tree is associated with a cluster of countries. Each branch, in effect, delimits the area of trade influence based on the strength of relative trade intensities calculated from the Intramax algorithm. Because the Intramax method involves an iterative process, two countries, or groups of already joined countries, are married together at each step or iteration. With every fusion, the interaction between the countries becomes intrazonal or intergroup for the new resulting spatial unit (see horizontal axis of Figures 14.1–14.4). When all countries have become fused together, all interactions are intra-regional at this point (that is, 100 per cent).

Results

The Intramax analysis indicates that regionalization tendencies in the Asia Pacific are indeed comparatively weaker than in Europe, as suggested by the historical, geographical and economic factors discussed. Intra-bloc export shares of most countries in the Asia Pacific are less than half their total exports, while the European countries conduct at least two-thirds of their trade with one another. However, it would be wrong to assume that Europe represents a unified and homogeneous 'natural' trading bloc, just as it would be incorrect to view the Asia Pacific as displaying no signs of 'natural' trade patterns. Both regions have clearly defined subregional clusters of countries with relatively high intensities of trade.

Figures 14.1 and 14.2 reveal two major subregions in Europe centered on a north–south delineation.[2] In both years, the northern cluster is predominantly made up of the old EFTA countries including UK and Ireland, while the southern cluster comprises the rest of Europe. The only major change in the two subregions over the period is that Portugal left the northern region, where it had been attached essentially to the UK, its oldest ally by several centuries, and became a part of the southern subregion in 1995. However, on the whole, the two subregions display observable stability in terms of membership over the period examined.

However, by moving down the tree to about 52 cumulative per cent (1965) and 42 per cent (1995) level of intrazonal interactions, it is immediately apparent that the southern cluster may be further split into two subregions. In 1965, a cluster composed mainly of Eastern European countries (Greece, Italy and Austria) is evident. The other cluster is made

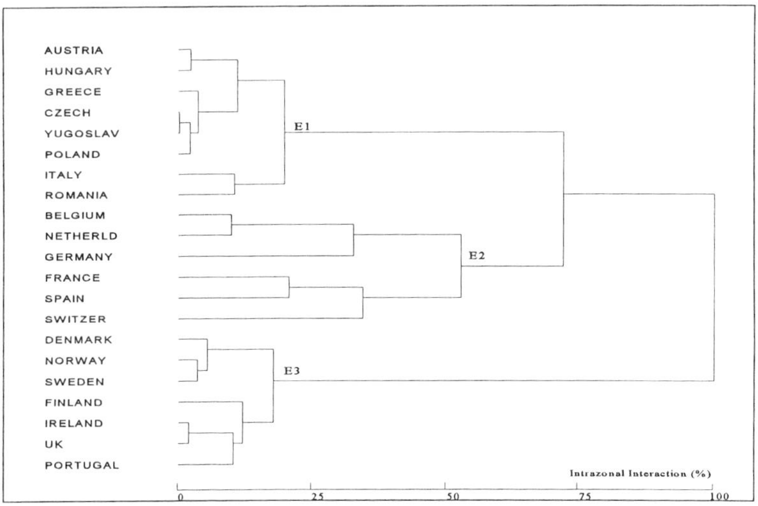

Figure 14.1 Subregional clustering in Europe, 1965

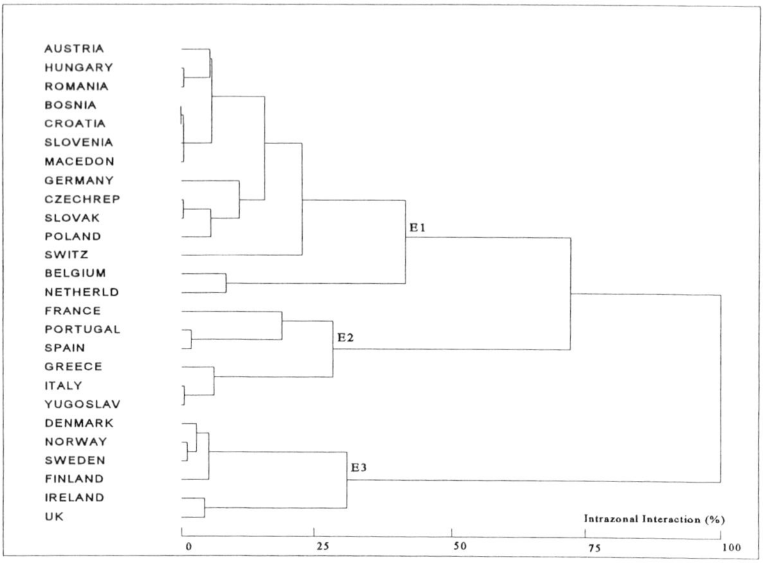

Figure 14.2 Subregional clustering in Europe, 1995

up of mostly the original EC-6 countries as well as Spain and Switzerland. This pattern had changed by 1995. While Eastern Europe remains tightly connected, Germany has also merged with the region. On the other hand, France has become more connected to the countries of Southern Europe and the newly-formed Federal Republic of Yugoslavia. The 1995 Intramax analysis suggests that within the European economic space, the large economies of France, Germany and UK act as subregional cores,[3] when their relative trade intensities with other European countries are taken into consideration.

Unlike 1965, the three subregions in 1995 (labeled E1, E2, E3) demonstrate strong core–periphery patterns. Germany acts as a magnet for East–West trade linking Eastern Europe with the Western European countries of Austria, Belgium, the Netherlands and Switzerland. Similarly, Southern Europe pivots around France, and, Scandinavia and Ireland around UK. Such spatial differentiation is reinforced by the fact that the France and Germany clusters failed to merge until further down the tree, that is, after roughly 72 per cent of intrazonal interaction has been accounted for. Hence Europe is actually rather loosely connected as a whole. The reality of Europe is three discrete and relatively internally tightly-connected trade clusters. Within each cluster there are sub-clusters exhibiting high levels of intra-regional bias, such as Eastern Europe, where, by 1995, the countries had become merged by the 15th cumulative per cent intrazonal interaction level.

Turning to the regional structure of the Asia Pacific, three clusters may also be delineated in 1965 (Figure 14.3). But the shape of each subregion displays comparatively less geographical coherence than those of Europe. The first cluster (A1) consists of Oceania countries as well as South Asia (Afghanistan, Pakistan, Sri Lanka), Southeast Asia (Myanmar) and East Asia (China, Hong Kong). The second cluster (A2) is made up of mostly Southeast Asia (ASEAN-7), and East Asian countries (Japan, Taiwan and South Korea). The final cluster (A3) comprises North America, India and Nepal.

Regional trade intensities had changed considerably by 1995 (Figure 14.4). The number of clusters increased to four as China, Hong Kong and Taiwan separated from East and Southeast Asia to become a distinct subregion (labeled A3). While the A1 cluster retains its Oceanian membership, it is now joined by Japan and South Korea, as well as Indonesia and the Philippines. In the A2 cluster, the remaining Southeast Asian countries of Brunei, Cambodia, Lao PDR, Malaysia, Myanmar, Singapore, Thailand and Vietnam became fused with South Asia. The last cluster, A4, retains the members of Canada and the US, but lost India and Nepal as they became more integrated with Southeast Asia.

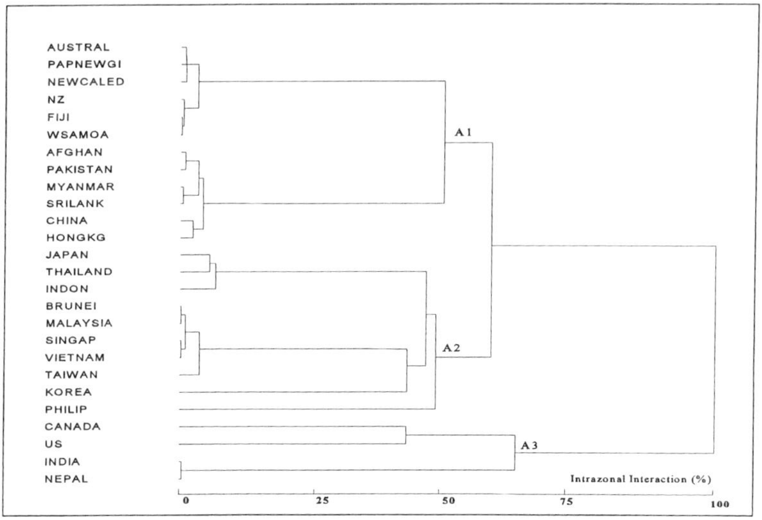

Figure 14.3 Subregional clustering in the Asia Pacific, 1965

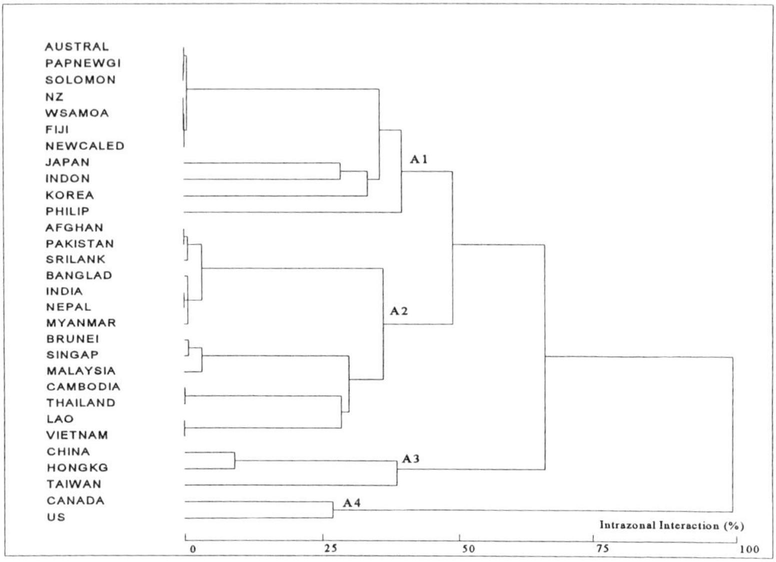

Figure 14.4 Subregional clustering in the Asia Pacific, 1995

Despite an increase in intra-Asia-Pacific trade from 32 to about 50 per cent over the 31–year period, the analysis suggests that intra-regional bias remains relatively weak confirming the observation of Frankel (1993). For example, Indonesia and the Philippines had become more integrated with the Japan group than the other ASEAN countries in 1995. This contrasts somewhat with Europe. Despite the existence of three economic clusters, Europe's subregions are far more geographically-oriented. Subregional cores may also be found in the Asia Pacific, but it is apparent that the two clusters of China, Taiwan and Hong Kong (A3) as well as the US and Canada (A4) contain rather too few countries for the term to be meaningful. The largest clusters are centered on the poles of Japan for A1, and Singapore for A2. These two cores' pole countries are significant in terms of their shares in subregional export shares: 43.0 and 49.2 per cent respectively for Japan and Singapore.

Comparing the two areas, regionalization in the Asia Pacific points to a lower degree of economic interdependencies and is less geographically circumscribed than in Europe. The Intramax results confirm the literature's observation of Asia Pacific's greater territorial and spatial fragmentation. North America appears to be even less integrated with the Asian countries in 1995 than in 1965. Research elsewhere suggests that

North America is still more integrated with Latin America despite the increase in trans-Pacific trade levels in the past three decades (Poon and Pandit, 1996b). In the case of Europe in 1995, four clusters or subregions are already discernible by the 30th percentile of intrazonal interaction. In contrast, the Asia Pacific is marked by seven clusters or subregions at the same level for the same year, and South Korea, the Philippines and Taiwan are not joined to any country at this point. The Asia-Pacific area's patterns are not surprising as the Intramax results confirm the importance of global rather than regional markets to many of its countries when compared with Europe.

Similarities and differences in regional structure between Europe and Asia Pacific are further explored by mapping the 1995 trade flows between the various subregions identified in Figures 14.2 and 14.4. In Figure 14.5, it can be seen that the UK-subregion (E3) has a trade surplus with the other two subregions, while the cluster based on the pole of France (E2) has an overall deficit. The France-based subregion (E1) has a deficit with the UK subregion, but a surplus with the Germany subregion. The North American (A4) and Japan (A1) based clusters display similar patterns to Germany and UK subregions: North America, particularly the US, acts as a major market and conduit for the exports of Asia Pacific, experiencing trade deficits with all the other subregions, while the Japan cluster registers positive flows (Figure 14.6). Unlike the UK cluster, however, North America's trade deficits with the region are high. For example, its exports

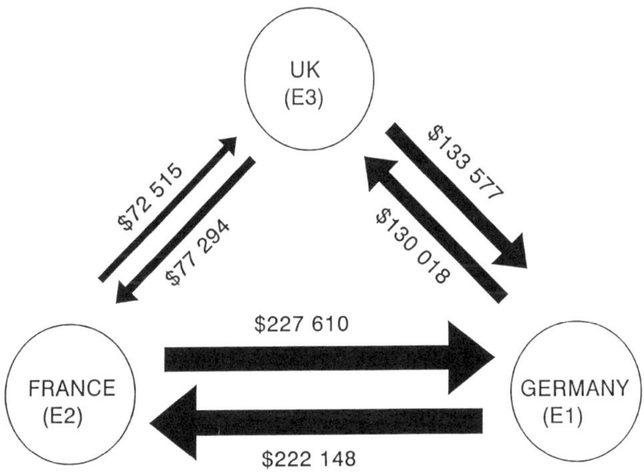

Figure 14.5 1995 trade flows between the subregions of Europe

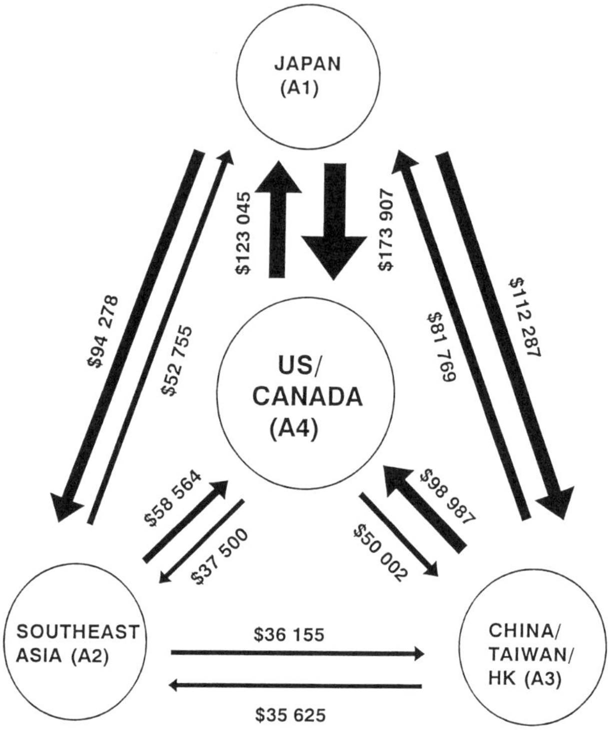

Figure 14.6 1995 trade flows between the subregions of Asia Pacific

to China, Hong Kong and Taiwan (A3) are half the latter's exports to its markets. Comparably, the largest deficit registered in Europe, that is between the UK and France clusters, is only less than one-tenth. Trade flows between the various subregions are relatively more balanced in Europe than in the Asia Pacific.

The above is interesting given that North America is far more integrated to Latin America than Asia. The role of the United States in the region's trade thus cannot be under-emphasized. Figure 14.7 clearly demonstrates this point. Here, the direction of the largest export flows is mapped for the various subregions. It is apparent that both regions are characterized by a regional hierarchy with the German and North American clusters dominating the intersections of trade flows within their respective regions.

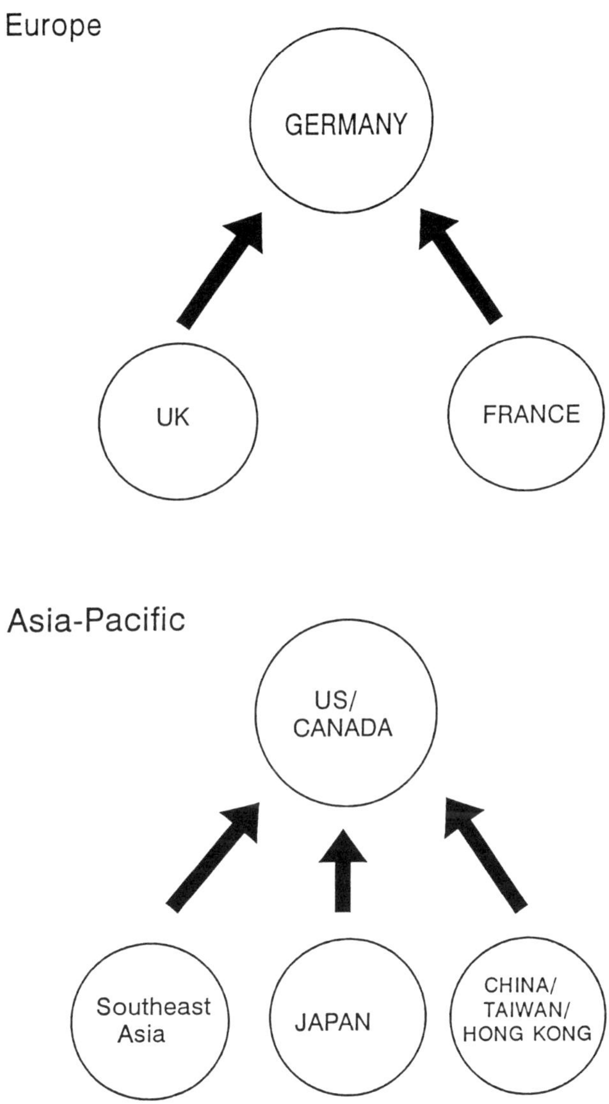

Figure 14.7 Direction of largest export flows between subregions in 1995

Extra-regional trends

It would seem then that the regional patterns revealed by the Intramax are explained partly by the fact that European countries trade comparatively more intensively with one another than the Asia-Pacific countries. But high intra-regional shares in exports do not necessarily reflect the openness of a region's trade. Even though the share of Europe's extra-regional trade fell from about 44 to 30 per cent over the 31 years, this does not mean that Europe has decreased its propensity to trade extra-regionally because of the increase in its GDP share that is traded extra-regionally (Anderson and Norheim, 1993).

A propensity to trade index may be defined which takes into consideration both regional bias as well as openness to trade. P_{ij}, the propensity of *i* to trade with *j*, is expressed as:

$$P_{ij} = X_{ij}/G_i \div [G_j/G_W(I_j/G_j \div I_W/G_W)] \tag{14.1}$$

where,

X_{ij} = exports of *i* to *j*,
I_j, I_W = imports of *j*, world, and
G_i, G_j, G_W = GDP of *i*, *j*, world.

This index is a modification of the trade intensity index, (I_{ij}), reviewed extensively by Kunimoto (1977) and Drysdale and Garnaut (1982). The interpretation of I_{ij} is that when I_{ij} is greater than 1, we expect above-average trade intensity between *i* and *j*. I_{ij} is also similar to P_{ij} except that G_i is replaced by total exports of *i*. A detailed comparison of the usefulness of I_{ij} and P_{ij} in examining trading propensities may be found in Anderson and Norheim (1993). One important difference between the two indices is that, unlike I_{ij}, P_{ij} is only useful for comparisons across time rather than across regions. Both the I_{ij} and P_{ij} of intra and extra-regionalization were calculated for both Europe and the Asia Pacific from 1965 to 1995 on a five-yearly basis.

In Figure 14.8, the I_{ij} values for intra-regionalization register 1 and above in the case of Europe, and less than 1 for the Asia Pacific. Over the period examined, Europe also exhibits greater fluctuations, plunging to a low of about 1.0 in 1985 from highs of 1.26 (1970 and 1990). This contrasts with the Asia Pacific which shows a steady increase. On the other hand, Asia-Pacific's I_{ij}s are consistently below 1, unlike Europe's. Hence, despite the latter's fluctuating trend, the evidence here suggests that intra-regionalization tendencies may have increased in the Asia Pacific, but they still remain much stronger in Europe. This is further

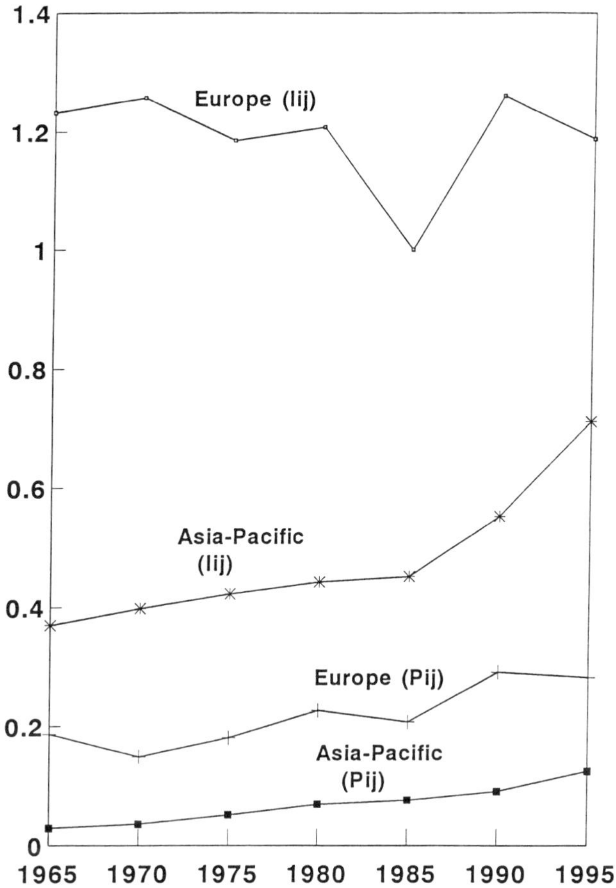

Figure 14.8 Intra-regionalization trends for Europe and the Asia Pacific, 1965–90

reinforced by the propensity to trade (P_{ij}) time trends. Both regions register increases between 1965 to 1995 generally. Europe's P_{ij} also exhibits less fluctuations than its I_{ij}s. The P_{ij} trends indicate that, on the whole, both regions' propensity to trade intra-regionally was generally strong over the 31 years, although dips in 1985 and 1995 were present for Europe. The sharp decline in Europe's 1985 I_{ij} and P_{ij} may speculatively be explained by the recession in the early 1980s. The region's exports contracted by 1.5 per cent over 1980, and its total exports, by 6 per cent. In contrast, exports from the Asia Pacific remained buoyant during this

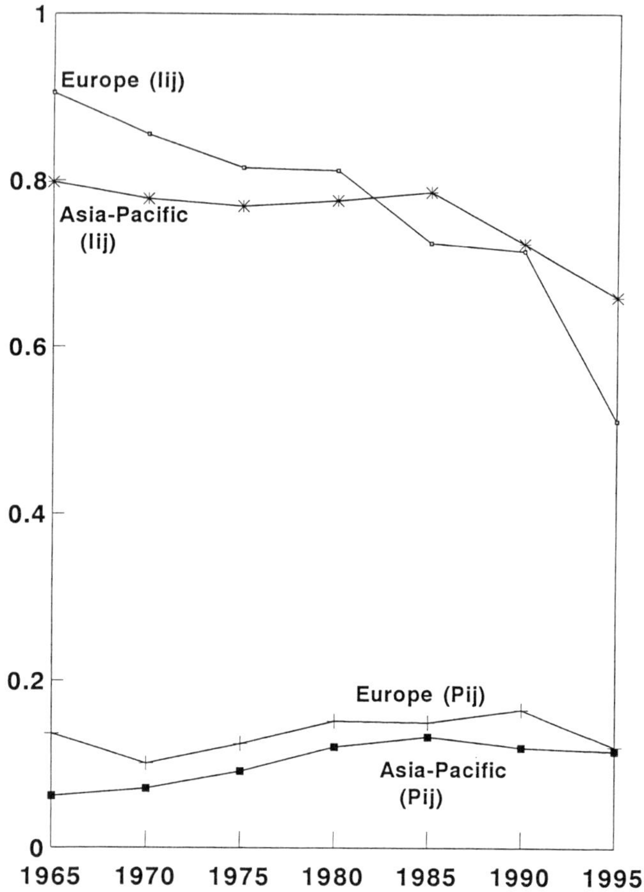

Figure 14.9 Extra-regionalization trends for Europe and the Asia Pacific, 1965–90

period: they rose by nearly 30 per cent both intra-regionally and in total terms from 1980 to 1985.

Turning to extra-regional patterns in Figure 14.9, Europe's I_{ij} shows a general decline over the period except between 1975 to 1980. Asia Pacific's registers stable to increasing values from 1965 to 1985, and a decline thereafter. Bearing in mind that the higher the I_{ij}, the stronger the extra-regionalization tendencies, we note that since 1985, Asia Pacific's I_{ij}s have exceeded Europe's, whereas it was the reverse before. The fall in

European I_{ij} is especially sharp in the 1990s, reflecting, perhaps, recessionary conditions which began at the very end of the 1980s.

The I_{ij} analysis also indicates that between the two regions, the extra-regional dimension is more important for the Asia Pacific since almost all of its extra-regionalization figures of I_{ij} are greater than its intra-regionalization figures. This is the opposite for Europe. Intra-regionalization index, I_{ij}, is well above 1 for most years and below 1 for extra-regionalization. This may reflect the relative wealth and buying power of proximate markets. Whereas European countries represent reasonably attractive and affluent markets to each other, many Asia-Pacific countries, as developing economies, do not represent such lucrative markets to one another as do those outside the region.

The P_{ij} index, on the other hand, reveals a more optimistic trend for both regions. In both cases, it shows a generally stable to increasing trend, although it displays a downward trend for Europe since 1990. The P_{ij} time-trends are particularly interesting when aligned against those of intra-regionalization in Figure 14.8. Clearly, they hint at the fact that increased extra-regionalization is not necessarily matched by decreased intra-regionalization. That is to say, increased intra-regional linkages may be achieved alongside increased extra-regional linkages. This in turn suggests that when extra-regional tendencies decrease, as in 1985 and 1995 for Europe, it is not necessarily a consequence of an increase in intra-regionalization tendencies. Hence, while Europe is clearly more oriented to its own internal markets from the I_{ij} analysis, the P_{ij} results, however, imply that Europe also compares favourably with the Asia Pacific in its extra-regional orientation over most periods in the time analyzed.

Conclusion

The premise that the European and Asia Pacific 'regions' demonstrate institutional, geographical, historical and cultural differences which are likely to be evidenced in differing intra- and extra-regional trade intensities and propensities would seem to be born out by analysis of available data. Europe, as a geographically contiguous and compact area with strong historical and cultural affinities now reinforced by increasingly extensive and deep formal political and economic integration, does indeed, as predicted, display considerably greater internal trade intensity than the Asia Pacific. Likewise, the more loosely and less formally politically integrated Asia Pacific region, with its greater geographical, historical and cultural disparateness, is revealed to have a higher degree of extra-regional trade intensity.

Whether or not these different patterns can be attributed directly either to the conditions facilitating 'natural' trading regions, or the extent of formal political and economic integration, is impossible to tell from the analysis. However, the patterns of subregional clusters of high trade intensity, particularly within Europe, would seem to lend support to proponents of 'natural' trade areas. Distinct subregional clusters in both regions generally consist of geographically proximate and, usually, contiguous countries which, moreover, could be loosely classified as culturally and historically linked, especially in the case of Europe. The existence of such relatively discrete clusters within Europe would seem to indicate that a high degree of formal regional integration does not necessarily create even intra-regional trade and that 'natural', economically driven, 'mini trading blocs' will continue to exist regardless of and alongside broader political initiatives.

The notion that greater formal regionalization necessarily results in greater, 'fortress-like' traits is not supported by the analysis, nor is the obverse idea that an externally oriented trade outlook will diminish intra-regional trade. While Europe has seen its intra-regional trade increase, its propensity to trade extra-regionally has not been reduced, although there is no telling whether or not it may be less than it might otherwise have been. On the other hand, the Asia Pacific, while deliberately pursuing extra-regional trade opportunities, has, nevertheless, increased its propensity to greater intra-regional trade. Time and further research will clearly be needed to see if the embryonic subregional, informal, 'natural mini clusters' in the Asia Pacific become still more greatly integrated through trade and whether or not this subsequently results in greater formal steps towards deeper political and economic integration.

Notes

1. This consists of an iterative process where at each stage the objective function is applied to the matrix which is reduced as pairs of spatial units or countries become fused together. Such a process of transformation and comparison is repeated at subsequent stages in order to take into account the effects of previous fusions, the total number of iterations being $n - 1$ (Masser and Brown, 1975).
2. Subregions are defined when the incremental intrazonal interactions display large increases. In this case, the increment was about 25 per cent for 1965 and 30 per cent for 1995.
3. Germany, France and UK had the highest shares of subregional exports at 40.8, 36.4 and 26.8 per cent respectively.

References

Aho, C.M.. 'Fortress Europe: Will the EU Isolate Itself from North America and Asia?', *Columbia Journal of World Business,* 29 (1994) 34–9.

Anderson, K. and M.H. Norheim, 'From Imperial to Regional Trade Preferences: Its Effect on Europe's Intra- and Extra-Regional Trade', *Weltwirtschaftliches Archiv,* 129 (1993) 78–102.

Baldwin, E., *Towards an Integrated Europe* (Washington, DC: Center for Economic Policy Research, 1994).

Baldwin, R., 'A Domino Theory of Regionalism', *NBER Working Paper No. 4465* (Cambridge, Massachusetts, 1993).

Bhagwati, J., 'The Threats to the World Trading System', *World Economy,* 15 (1992) 443–56.

Blomqvist, H.C., 'ASEAN as a Model for Third World Regional Economic Cupertino?' *ASEAN Economic Bulletin,* 10 (1993) 52–67.

Bruce, L., '1992: The Bad News', *International Management*, September (1988) 22–6.

Cave, M. and D. Crawford, 'APEC: Breaking Down Barriers', *Asia, Inc.* (November, 1996).

Cuyvers, L. and W. Pupphavesa, 'From ASEAN to AFTA', *Discussion paper No. 6 Centre for Asian Studies* (Antwerp: University of Antwerp, 1996).

Dinan, D., *Ever Closer Union: An Introduction to the European Community* (Basingstoke: Macmillan, 1994).

Drysdale, P., *International Economic Pluralism: Economic Policy in East Asia and the Pacific* (Winchester, Mass.: Allen and Unwin, 1988).

Drysdale, P. and R. Garnaut, 'Trade Intensities and the Analysis of Bilateral Trade Flows in a Many-Country World: A Survey', *Hitotsubashi Journal of Economics* 22 (1982) 62–84.

Fischer, M., J. Essletzbichler, H. Gassler and G. Trichtl, 'Telephone Communication Patterns in Austria: A Comparison of the IPFP-Based Graph-Theoretic and the Intramax Approaches', *Geographical Analysis,* 25 (1993) 224–33.

Frankel, J.A., 'Is Japan Creating a Yen Bloc?', in J.A. Frankel and M. Kahler, (eds), *Regionalism and Rivalry: Japan and the United States in Pacific Asia* (Chicago: University of Chicago Press, 1993).

Frankel, J., E. Stein and S.J. Wei, 'Trading Blocs and the Americas: the Natural, the Unnatural and the Super-Natural', *Journal of Development Economics,* 47 (1995) 61–95.

Haas, E., 'Nationalism: An Instrumental Social Construction', *Millennium V,* 22 (1993) 505–45.

Kahler, M., 'Organising the Pacific', in R.A. Scalapino, S. Sato, J. Wanandi and S.J. Han (eds), *Pacific-Asia Economic Policies and Regional Interdependence* (Berkeley: University of California, 1988).

Kojima, K., 'Economic Cooperation in a Pacific Community', *Asia Pacific Community* 12 (1981) 1–10.

Krugman, P., 'Is Bilateralism Bad?' In E. Helpman and A. Razin, (eds), *International Trade and Trade Policy* (Cambridge, Mass.: MIT Press, 1991).

Kunimoto, K., 'Typology of Trade Intensity Indices', *Hitotsubashi Journal of Economics,* 17 (1977) 15–32.

Langhammer, R.J., 'Regional Integration in East Asia: from Market-Driven Regionalization to Institutional Regionalism?' *Weltwirtschaftliches Archiv,* 131 (1995) 167–201.

Lawrence, P.R., 'Emerging Regional Arrangements: Building Blocks or Stumbling Blocks?', *Finance and the International Economy* (Oxford: Amex Bank Review. Oxford University Press, 1991).
Lipsey, R., 'The Theory of Customs Unions: Trade Diversion and Welfare', *Economica,* 24 (1957) 40–6.
Manning, R.A. and P. Stern., 'The Myth of the Pacific Community', *Foreign Affairs,* 73 (1994) 79–93.
Masser, I. and P.J. Brown, 'Hierarchical Aggregation Procedures for Interaction Data', *Environment and Planning A,* 7 (1975) 609–23.
Masser, I. and J. Sheurwater, J., 'Functional Regionalization of Spatial Interaction Data: An Evaluation of Some Suggested Strategies', *Environment and Planning A,* 1 (1980) 1357–82.
Montgomery, J.D., 'The Asia-Pacific as an Environment Region', *Journal of Developing Areas,* 28 (1993) 3–12.
Perroni, C. and J. Whalley, 'How Severe is Global Retaliation Risk Under Increasing Regionalism?' *American Economic Review,* 86 (1996) 57–61.
Poon, J.P.H. and K. Pandit, 'Pacific Trade and Regionalization, 1965–1990', *International Trade Journal,* 10 (1996a) 199–221.
Poon, J.P.H. and K. Pandit, 'The Geographic Structure of Cross-National Trade Flows and Region-States', *Regional Studies,* 3 (1996b) 273–85.
Swann, D., *European Economic Integration: the Common Market, European Union and Beyond* (Edward Elgar: Cheltenham 1996).
Theobald, D.M., 'The North American Free Trade Agreement', *Harvard Business School Case* 9–592–039 (1995).
Tigner, B., 'Fortress Europe', *International Management,* December (1988) 24–30.
Tsoukalis, L., *The New European Economy* (Oxford: Oxford University Press, 1993).
UNCTAD, *Handbook of International Trade and Development Statistics* (New York, 1993).
Viner, J., *The Customs Union Issue* (New York: Carnegie Endowment for International Peace, 1953).
Yahuda, B., 'The Pacific Community: Not Yet', *Pacific Review* 1 (1988) 119–27.

15

Japanese Exports and Foreign Direct Investment*

Pontus Åberg

International investment flows have grown dramatically in the last few years. The total foreign direct investment (FDI) was $225 billion in 1994, up from $50 billion per year on average in the early 1980s. A major agent of FDI is the multinational corporation (MNC) which, until the last ten years or so, have been dominated by firms from North America and Europe. More recently, however, Asian MNCs, particularly those of Japan, South Korea and Taiwan, have also become important FDI sources.[1] In Japan, the increase in FDI outflows may be traced to the 1985 Plaza Agreement where the yen was forced to appreciate *vis-à-vis* the currencies of its major trading partners. East and Southeast Asian countries were more or less tied to the dollar, so that the Japanese yen rose *vis-à-vis* the currencies of Japan's neighbour countries. Japan's total FDI increased rapidly after 1986. In the period between 1986 to 1989, FDI grew at an average annual rate of more than 50 per cent.

The increase in Japanese FDI has promoted intra-regional trade in Asia, the latter rising from 31 per cent in terms of total exports in 1986 to 43 per cent in 1992.[2] Intra-firm trade is also increasing which is a direct effect of foreign investments. The inflow of foreign investments has become a major factor determining economic growth in Asia. Among the ASEAN countries, the average economic growth rate has closely followed the trends in FDI inflow from Japan.[3]

* I prepared this paper during my stay as a visiting researcher at Tottori University, Japan. Financial support from the Foundation for Japanese Studies at the Swedish Institute and the Institute for Futures Studies, Stockholm is gratefully acknowledged. I am also grateful to Professor Kiyoshi Kobayashi who directed me into the subject. I would also like to acknowledge Börje Johansson and an anonymous referee for valuable comments. A first draft was presented at a scientific workshop in Macau, 29 April to 1 May, 1996.

An important factor associated with a firm's decision to invest abroad relates to the amount of information and knowledge about 'new' markets. Since investments demand more engagement by the source firm compared with exports, FDI is therefore more information intensive. It has been demonstrated in gravity-like trade models that exports are negatively correlated with distance.[4] Information tends to decrease with distance, which implies that FDI is also negatively affected by distance.

Increased activities of multinational companies and their foreign investments, raise questions about their impact on the host country economy. As noted by some scholars, 'The effect of foreign production by a country's firms on the home country's exports continues to be a puzzle after many years of controversy and a considerable amount of empirical research'.[5]

This chapter has two purposes. First, I will examine the impact of Japanese FDI on trade, and the relationship between FDI and trade from 1990 to 1993. The theories underlying FDI, as well as the practice of investments, do not provide a clear answer. The second purpose is to study the spatial distribution of Japanese FDI; in particular, the relationship between the distance of host countries and FDI inflows.

FDI and trade theory

FDI theory

Why a firm invests abroad depends on its objective function. The firm could either maximize its profit or maximize its sales capacity. The literature in this field is vast[6] and a broad survey of FDI theory is elaborated below. First, a distinction should be made between home and host country variables, that is, push as opposed to pull factors (Andersson, 1993). Push factors explain why firms invest abroad, while pull factors explain why firms choose specific countries. Examples of push factors are financial deregulation, integration of markets, current account surpluses, integration with other countries or regions, increasing domestic cost of production factors, and currency alignment. Pull factors on the other hand include political stability in the host country, undervalued currencies, favourable macroeconomic conditions, including high growth and moderate inflation, straight economic policies (such as open trade regimes) and low taxes, institutional and cultural conditions, and low cost of production factors. It is also important to mention trade policies. This refers to both tariffs and non-tariff barriers in the receiving country, and trade policies from a third country. To circumvent trade restrictions, firms tend to move their facilities to a third country, exporting back to the original country.

Second, FDI motivation depends on whether it is market-seeking, efficiency-seeking, or resource-seeking (Brewer, 1993). If investments take place as a result of a market-seeking strategy, the size of the host country is of principal concern. If the strategy is efficiency-seeking, then variables such as inflation, exchange rates, wage rates, savings rates and domestic investments are of greater interest. If the investor's strategy is resource-seeking, then the most valuable feature of the host country would be its natural resources. Kojima (1978) has taken the FDI type argument further by suggesting that US and Japanese FDI differ in motivation, and this creates different impacts on host economies. US outward FDI is associated with investment in which the US has a comparative advantage, while Japanese FDI tends to be in those industries where firms have a comparative disadvantage.

The above suggests that FDI may be explained by several motivations so that one way of identifying pertinent explanatory variables is to divide them into microeconomic–macroeconomic, and, micropolitical–macropolitical determinants. Microeconomic explanations tend to focus on industry structure and transaction costs (Williamson, 1979). Firms in an oligopolistic position have economies of scale that give them market power, and this helps them overcome the disadvantages of being foreign, thereby allowing them to compete with local competitors in host countries. Firms invest abroad because transaction costs associated with trade and licensing provide inefficient alternatives compared with FDI. In this case, FDI represents an internalization of transactions within the firm such that international transactions within the firm replace market-based transactions.

Finally, firms are motivated to engage in FDI in order to establish specific links between agents. This explanation focuses on the establishment of economic networks reinforced by language and cultural similarities, personal relations, historical bounds, and so on, all of which affect transaction costs and thereby investment patterns (Johansson, 1995).

FDI and trade

In this section, I will show how investments abroad affect trade between two countries. For explanation purposes, the presence of a third country is ignored and, instead, the effect of FDI on trade between the investing and receiving country is highlighted. Assume two countries, I and II, and furthermore three types of investments: (i) services, (ii) intermediate goods and (iii) final goods. The investments are outward oriented from country I to country II. In the first case, country I invests in country II to establish a trading company, a banking business, a retail or wholesale store, or, a consulting firm. These businesses facilitate the interaction between actors in country I and II. Trade between country I and country II is therefore expected to expand, including both exports and imports. In the second case, country I invests in the other country to produce intermediate goods. Trade in materials to produce intermediates may increase from I to II. Exports of intermediates from II to I may also rise. The outcome in this example should be positive. Finally, a third case exists where country I invests in country II to produce final goods. First, exports of investment goods needed for the branch, such as industrial equipment and elements for plant installation, and the material for processing, would increase. Furthermore, country I's import of final goods produced in country II may expand. At the same time, country II's import of final goods from I may decline. The total effect of an investment for producing final goods is hence uncertain.

The discussion above suggests that the effect of an investment abroad on foreign trade could be positive or negative depending on the final purpose. Although it would appear from the examples above that the dominant effect would be positive, the outcome is unclear.

The above may be further illustrated by dividing the effects of an investment on trade into four different stages. Assume a special case, say a Japanese firm building a car factory in Thailand. Four possible outcomes exist:

(i) *Import-expansion* effect. This refers to the increase in imports to support production in the new factory. At the initial stage, when the plant is under construction, this involves a considerable increase in imports of capital goods and construction materials. At the later stage, when the plant is completed, the imports shift to intermediate goods, for the construction of a car.
(ii) *Export-substitution* effect, which refers to the decline in Thai exports of intermediate products, since it is now used as inputs in the domestic production. In the two following effects, we assume the building of the factory is completed and the production has come on-line.
(iii) *Import-substitution* effect, which occurs when there is a fall in Thai imports of Japanese cars with the expansion of domestic production.
(iv) *Export-expansion* effect where there is an increase in exports when part of the output of the plant is exported.

These four effects together create a J-curve pattern of trade balance over time (Figure 15.1)

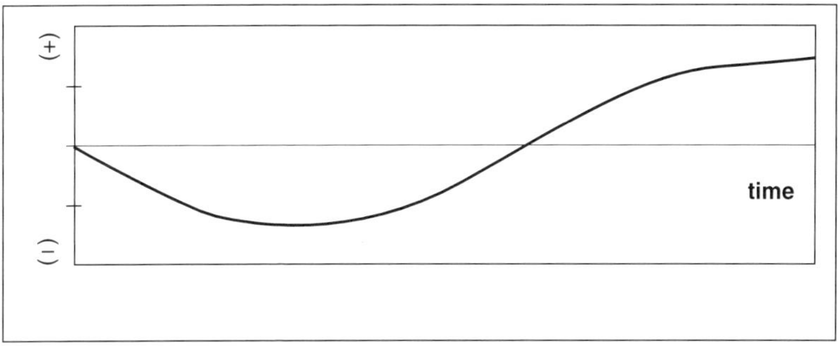

Figure 15.1 The J-curve effect of FDI on goods trade

Most Japanese investments tend to be in the service sector. In 1984, this sector alone accounted for 68 per cent of the total amount invested in foreign countries. Although this fell to 65 per cent in 1993, the decline was marginal. Finance, insurance and business services are the dominant industries in this sector.[7] This type of investment is not trade replacing, under the Kojima thesis, but trade creating, given that Japan invests mostly in trade creating facilities; FDI in this case is expected to be positive. Hence, we may establish that:

$$X_{jr} = f(FDI_{jr}, TSI_{jr}) \tag{15.1}$$

The predicted signs of the partial derivatives are

$$f_{FDI} > 0 \qquad \text{and} \qquad f_{TSI} > 0 \tag{15.2}$$

TSI is the total stock of investment and should measure the long-term engagement that stems from an investment. Building a plant in a foreign country will range over a number of years. This variable takes into account the transportation of all kinds of goods, material or final goods resulting from all past FDI (Lin, 1995).

FDI and trade: overall patterns

In this section, the distribution and sectoral breakdown of Japanese outward FDI is explored. In 1990, Japanese outward investments totalled US$57 billion. Over the 1990–93 period, North America was the most attractive place for Japanese outward investments (Table 15.1). In 1990, it accounted for 48 per cent. Europe[8] attracted 25 per cent while Anzcerta[9]

Table 15.1 Japanese outward FDI by regions (million US$, current prices)

	1990	*1991*	*1992*	*1993*
Europe	14 183	9 110	6 924	7 687
North America	27 192	18 823	14 572	15 287
Anzcerta	3 900	2 786	2 217	1 938
South and East Asia	7 053	5 936	6 425	6 637
Total	56 915	41 586	34 138	36 025

Source: OECD reviews of Foreign Direct Investment, 1994.

hosted 7 per cent, and, South and East Asia[10] 12 per cent. In Anzcerta, Australia received more than 95 per cent of the investments. China is the fastest growing country in receiving investments from Japan among the nations in South and East Asia. Other countries of importance are Hong Kong, Indonesia, and Malaysia. In Europe, Britain has been the dominant destination of Japanese investments. In 1990, it received nearly 50 per cent of the total Japanese investments in Europe. Although the importance of the UK market for Japanese FDI has since declined, it continues to be the largest host country in Europe, followed by the Netherlands.

On the whole, Europe shows a decline in Japanese FDI inflows from 25 per cent in 1990 to 21 per cent in 1993. Similar declines may also be found for North America and Anzcerta at 6 per cent and 2 per cent respectively. On the other hand, the Asian share of FDI increased from 12 per cent to 18 per cent. Japanese investments clearly switched from Europe and North America to Asia.

When market size is considered, that is, when investments are 'normalized', Table 15.2 shows that Anzcerta is the biggest market for outward Japanese investments. While it may have attracted only between 5–7 per cent of total Japanese investments over 1990–93, its market size is

Table 15.2 Japanese outward FDI by regions in relation to the receiving market size

	1990	*1991*	*1992*	*1993*
Europe	2.05	1.27	0.89	1.09
North America	4.49	3.02	2.24	2.24
Anzcerta	11.49	8.18	6.66	5.89
South and East Asia	4.72	3.53	3.47	3.42

Note: million investments/billion GNP.
Source: See Table 15.1 and World Bank Atlas, various issues.

Table 15.3 Japanese outflow FDI by selected sectors (million US$, current prices)

	1990	*1991*	*1992*	*1993*
Chemical products	2292	1602	2015	1742
Electric, electronic	5684	2296	1817	2762
Wholesale, retail trade	6158	5247	3705	5096
Transport, storage	2169	2489	1725	2157
Finance, insurance	8047	4972	4579	6401

Source: See Table 15.1.

also very small. South and East Asia are the next most important market, followed by North America.

Table 15.3 reviews some of the more important sectors where Japanese outward investments have occurred. As noted earlier, finance, insurance and business services constitute the largest sector. Japan also invested 11 per cent in wholesale and retail trade, and 10 per cent in electrical and electronics industries. Transport and storage, as well as chemical products attracted similar amounts of investments, that is, about 4–6 per cent. In the period between 1985 and 1988, Japan invested approximately 30 per cent in finance and insurance businesses, but in 1989 and 1990 this fell to 23 per cent and 14 per cent respectively. This was due to the recession in the OECD countries.[11]

Turning to trade, North America was the biggest export market for Japanese products in 1990 (Table 15.4). Exports to South and East Asia were about $87 billion while the corresponding value for Europe was $60 billion. But, by 1993, South and East Asia had overtaken North America as Japan's largest export destination. Further, when exports are expressed in terms of market size, the importance of South and East Asia becomes even more marked (Table 15.5). Europe, on the other hand, is the least important, while Anzcerta has moved up to second place.

The tables analyzed in this section clearly indicate that South and East Asia have an absolute advantage as an export market for Japanese goods

Table 15.4 Japanese exports to selected regions (million US$, current prices)

	1990	*1991*	*1992*	*1993*
Europe	60 599	66 403	69 679	62 336
North America	97 858	99 458	103 792	113 226
Anzcerta	8 136	7 586	8 170	9 013
South and East Asia	86 992	102 272	113 797	132 496

Source: IMF Direction of Trade Statistics Yearbook 1994.

Table 15.5 Japanese exports in relation to the receiving market size

	1990	*1991*	*1992*	*1993*
Europe	8.78	9.29	8.99	8.88
North America	16.15	15.94	15.93	16.57
Anzcerta	23.97	22.28	24.53	27.39
South and East Asia	58.22	60.75	61.41	68.28

Note: million export/billion GNP.

compared with Europe and North America. On the other hand, Anzcerta captures the largest share of Japanese FDI when market size is taken into consideration.

Econometric analyses

In this section, two models testing the relationship between trade and FDI will be presented. First, a simple chi-square statistic is obtained which tests the hypothesis that the pattern of Japanese trade flows correlates with that of its FDI flows, such that:

$$\text{Reject } H_0 \text{ if} \sum_{n=1}^{K} \frac{(O_i - E_i)^2}{E_i} > X^2_{K-1,\alpha} \tag{15.3}$$

The critical value of χ^2 with $\alpha = 0.05$ and $K = 144$ is 171.907. We run this procedure on shares instead of absolute values and obtain the following results:

$$\sum_{n=1}^{144} \frac{(X_{jr} - FDI_{jr})^2}{FDI_{jr}} = 7.19 \quad \text{and} \tag{15.4}$$

$$\sum_{n=1}^{144} \frac{(FDI_{jr} - X_{jr})^2}{X_{jr}} = 2.25 \tag{15.5}$$

The above show that a correlation between FDI and export pattern exists. Such a relationship is further confirmed in Figure 15.2 which graphs exports on the y-axis against FDI on the x-axis.

Econometric model 1

In the first model, exports are treated as the dependent variable, and various investment proxies, the explanatory variables. The model uses time-series data (1990–93) and cross-country data (36 different countries) in a pooled regression equation. This is a panel data set since it includes a

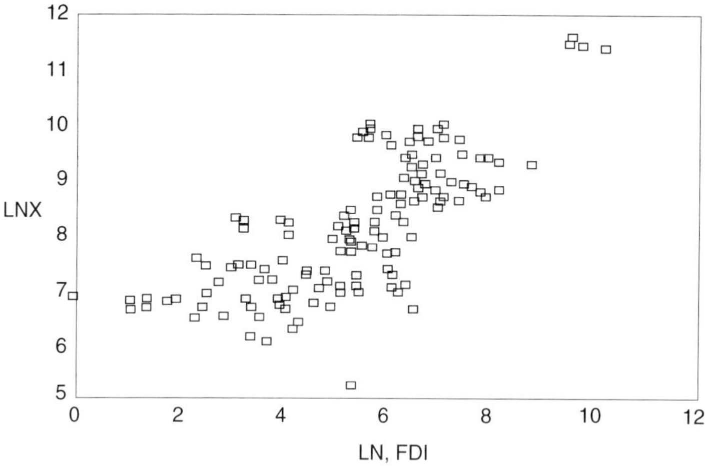

Figure 15.2 FDI and exports

large number of cross-sectional units and only a few periods. A typical panel data set is more oriented toward cross-sectional analyses. They are wide but short.

$$X_{jr,t} = \alpha FDI_{jr,t}^{\beta_2} TSI_{jr,t-1}^{\beta 2} e^{\varepsilon_{it}} \tag{15.6}$$

where

$X_{jr,t}$ = the export from Japan to country r at time t (1990, ..., 1993)
$FDI_{jr,t}$ = Foreign Direct Investments from Japan to country r in 1990, 1991, 1992 and 1993, respectively.
$TSI_{jr,t-1}$ = total stock of investment up to time $t-i$
α, β = parameters to be estimated
ε = an error term

Transformed to a log-linear form, equation (15.6) becomes

$$\ln X_{jr,t} = \alpha_0 + \beta_1 \ln FDI_{jr,t} + \beta_2 \ln TSI_{jr,t-1} + \varepsilon_{i,t} \tag{15.7}$$

According to the theoretical discussion above, one would expect a positive correlation between exports and foreign direct investments as well as a positive correlation between exports and total stock of investments. This last variable is lagged one year owing to time lags in production. Overall, investments tend to 'live' over a number of years which will have effects on production and trade.

Econometric model 2

One of the variables that impacts on FDI is the size of the host country. Gross national product or economic growth rates are common proxies. It is also a proxy for market orientation. Another variable of interest is distance (*D*) since gravity-like formulations of trade models suggest that distance often increases transaction costs, and therefore depresses trade between geographically distant countries. The model may be specified as:

$$\ln FDI_{jr,t} = \alpha_0 + \beta_1 \ln GNP_{r,t} + \beta_2 \ln D_{jr} + \varepsilon_i \tag{15.8}$$

GNP is expected to be positively correlated to FDI, while the expected outcome between the distance and FDI would be negative. The *a priori* explanation for this expectation depends on the following consideration: microeconomic determinants on FDI deal with transaction costs and internalization theory. Instead of using the market mechanism, firms establish their own partner and supplier in another country. Hierarchically administrated international transactions within the firm replace market-based transactions, for several reasons. First, the market mechanism may not be able to provide the firm with acceptable solutions since transaction costs are too high. Second, to achieve more certainty about quality and delivery, it might be best for the firms to have their own facility. This is particularly important for markets that are far away from the parent company. Finally, the further the market, the less perfect is the information resulting in a higher probability of establishing a subsidiary in order to overcome spatial barriers. In the latter case, distance could be expected to have a positive impact on FDI motivation.

Estimation results

The results of the above two models (equations 15.7 and 15.8) are reported in this section.

FDI and exports

The data set consists of 36 cross-sectional units, observed at each of 4 time periods which gives a total of 144 observations. Since the regression equation is logged, observations with zero values were deleted. The observations were pooled and estimated using OLS (Table 15.6).[12] The OLS estimation shows that there is a positive and significant relationship between Japanese exports and current foreign direct investment (FDI) as

Table 15.6 OLS estimation

Variable	*Coefficient*	*Standard error*	*t-value*
Intercept	4.487	0.31	13.40
FDI	0.176	0.075	2.43
TSI	0.365	0.079	4.25

$R^2 = 0.609$, Adjusted $R^2 = 0.603$, $F(2139) = 108.22$, DW-statistic = 0.473
Note: Estimation uses White's heteroskedasticity-consistent covariance matrix estimator.

well as between exports and total stock of investments (TSI). The statistical result reveals that an increase of current investments by 10 per cent in a particular country would raise the exports to that country by 1.8 per cent. Similarly, an increase in investments by 10 per cent will lead to a 3.6 per cent increase in exports. The results are consistent with expectations. It would appear that historical investments have a greater impact on trade when compared with current investments. This could be explained by the fact that the dominant part of investments is in the service sector. It can also be explained by intra-firm trade or intra-cultural trade, that is, Japanese facilities abroad tend to import material and production factors from mother companies or companies from Japan. Parent–subsidiary relationships are also very strong under the Japanese business system.

Fixed effects

The econometric technique used above is a combination of cross-section and time-series data in a pooled regression. If we take the αs to be the same across units, as we did above, OLS provides consistent and efficient estimates of α and β. A common formulation of the model above assumes that differences across units can be captured in differences in the constant term, the intercept α. Thus, in (15.7), each α is an unknown parameter to be estimated. This is usually referred to as the least square dummy variable (LSDV) model or the fixed-effect model. The fixed effects could be either on different destinations (36) or on different times (4). The fixed-effect value could be interpreted as the mean of X_{jr} where each of the other explanatory variables is equal to zero. In other words, the dummy variable coefficients would measure the change in the cross-section or time-series intercepts respectively. There are, however, some problems in the fixed-effect model. First, the use of dummy variables is an attempt to adjust for important missing information in the model. The reasoning underlying the fixed-effect model is that in specifying the regression model we have failed to include relevant explanatory variables that do not change over time but explain the differences in destination.[13] The second problem relates to the loss of the number of degrees of freedom. In this model, the degree of freedom decreases from 139 (OLS) to 104 (destination fixed effect). This loss may decrease the statistical power of the model.

In equation (15.9) below, least square estimation with individual destination effects is considered, while estimation based on individual time effects is presented in equation (15.10). Since we are interested in whether differences across groups or different years exist, we can test the hypothesis that the constant terms are all equal with an F-test.[14] The results from this test are presented below.

(1) Destination fixed effects

$$\ln X_{jr} = -0.131 \ln FDI_{jr} + 0.342 \ln TSI_{jr} \qquad (15.9)$$
$$(-0.364) \qquad (3.008)$$

$R^2 = 0.98$, adj. $R^2 = 0.973$, F-value = 138.10, DW-statistic = 1.982, *t*-values in brackets.

From equation (15.9), the high R^2 and adjusted R^2 may be explained by the significant number of dummy variables (35) describing the individual effect. The loss of information ($R^2 = 0.609$) and the sizes of the residuals are now captured in each dummy variable. However, we have not added any substantial information into the model. We have only transferred the unknown explanatory factors to the different intercepts.[15]

The variable measuring past investments, *TSI*, is approximately the same as that for the OLS estimation. On the other hand, the *FDI* variable is now negative and statistically insignificant. This is probably due to its correlation with *TSI*. There are 36 different dummies describing individual destination effects. The values range from 7.563 (USA) down to 4.147 (Argentina) (see Table 15.7).

The ranking partly supports the empirical survey earlier in the text that showed that Asia is becoming a more important market for Japan. Countries in Asia, together with important countries such as the US and Germany, have the highest 'productivity' in terms of exports. The higher figures of the dummy variables reveal that exports to these countries are higher than expected. Higher values of the individual constant terms imply a greater lack of explanatory variables. The lack of information could be the distance to the destination; further, it would appear from the results that Japanese exports are regionally concentrated. The market size of the importing country is another factor that has an effect on trade. This

Table 15.7 Destination fixed-effect constants

	Coefficient		Coefficient
USA	7.56	Australia	5.63
Taiwan	7.21	Philippines	5.63
Korea	7.04	Mexico	5.52
Germany	7.04	Indonesia	5.50
Hong Kong	6.73	Denmark	5.48
China	6.56	Belgium	5.36
Singapore	6.54	Spain	5.36
Thailand	6.44	Switzerland	5.31
Malaysia	6.22	Greece	5.26
Sweden	6.07	Turkey	5.07
UK	6.07	Norway	4.90
Canada	5.95	Portugal	4.85
France	5.93	Ireland	4.83
Italy	5.88	New Zealand	4.77
Saudi Arabia	5.83	Chile	4.59
Netherlands	5.73	Liberia	4.28
India	5.69	Brazil	4.23
Austria	5.68	Argentina	4.15

explains why the US and Germany hold top positions in the ranking above. Affinities in terms of language, culture, religion or trading agreements are additional variables that are important to trade. Finally, the effect of different networks on trade could also be hidden in the dummy variable figures. These networks might be a knowledge network between Japan and the US, or a neo-colonial network between Japan and Asian countries. Today, many scholars in Japan have spent at least one year of their academic careers in the US and this creates special bonds between them and their colleagues. We could call it investment in personal relations. These relations are useful in the contacts with foreign countries, whether one works as a scholar or as a professional.

In recent years, Japan has become more interested in Asia in many ways. Production, exports and imports, education and political and economic cooperation are concentrated towards countries in Asia. The dynamics of the economies, the increasing level of purchasing power, and efforts to strengthen the political systems around the area are factors that make the region attractive. We may regard the movement towards an Asian focus as a neo-colonial network between Asian countries and Japan.

(2) Time-fixed effects

$$\ln X_{rj} = \underset{(2.63)}{0.20 \ln FDI} + \underset{(3.83)}{0.339 \ln TSI} \qquad (15.10)$$

$R^2 = 0.611$, adj. $R^2 = 0.596$, F-value = 42.73, DW-statistic = 0.477, *t*-values in brackets.

For time-fixed effects captured in equation (15.10), the results indicate a higher level of consistency with the OLS estimations. The parameters and the *t*-test (in brackets) show similar figures. This regression also includes four different time effects, the individual year effects being:

4.466 (1990) 4.543 (1991) 4.621 (1992) 4.599 (1993)

This illustrates a rather stable time trend. The individual dummies also show an increase from 1990 to 1993. This is obvious since the creation of links between countries for trade and investments is expensive. This is also supported by the F-test. The test between this estimation and the pooled OLS estimation above gives a value of 0.209. The one per cent critical value is 1.63 so the hypothesis that the time effect is the same is not rejected at the one per cent significance level.

Distance and FDI

Finally, we performed OLS regression on distance and FDI. This is consistent with the literature which has identified distance as having an impeding effect on trade and investment. Further, the distance effect has been shown to be larger for trade than for FDI (Eaton and Tamura, 1996). Table 15.8 shows that the market size and the volume of direct outward investments are positively and significantly related. Hence, if the size of a foreign market increases by 10 per cent, we could expect that Japanese investments to that market would increase by approximately 8 per cent. Distance is found to have a negative effect on FDI as expected. The results

Table 15.8 OLS estimation on distance, GNP and FDI

Variable	*Coefficient*	*Standard error*	*t-value*
Intercept	4.192	2.443	2.031
Distance	–0.942	0.235	–4.805
GNP	0.792	0.113	7.592

$R^2 = 0.32$, Adj. $R^2 = 0.31$, $F(2135) = 31.15$, DW-statistic = 0.869
Note: Estimation uses White's heteroskedasticity-consistent covariance matrix estimator.

also suggest that Japanese investments are located mostly in the Asian region because of the distance effect (see also Eaton and Tamura 1996).

Conclusion

This chapter has shown that Japanese outward investments create Japanese exports. Past investments are more important to exports compared with current foreign direct investments. Accumulated investments create an economic link between two agents which imply new investments and exports. The results support Kojima's (1978) thesis that Japanese outward investments are trade creating. South and East Asia has an absolute advantage as an export market for Japanese goods compared with Europe and North America. It also has a relative advantage in receiving outward investments from Japan in comparison with Europe and North America, but is outcompeted by Anzcerta. The econometric analyses also show that Taiwan, Korea, Hong Kong, China, Singapore and Thailand are the most important and 'productive' markets for Japan, together with the US and Germany. Both investments and exports seem to be regionally concentrated. There is a large variation between countries of the fixed-effect destination variable, and this reveals a lack of information for some of the countries. Finally, estimation of different years yields no time effect. Rather, time dummies are only marginally different from one other.

Notes

1. Japanese multinational corporations or transnational corporations such as Matsushita Electric (electronics), Sony (electronics), Mitsubishi (trading) and Mitsui (trading) are all high-ranking MNCs among the largest corporations in the world; *World Investment Report 1993*.
2. Hellvin (1994).
3. See for example Kwan (1994) p. 5.
4. See Strömquist and Åberg (1997).
5. Blomström *et al.* (1987).
6. Lizondo (1991) gives a good overview on the subject.
7. The data is reported with an anonymous group of services including real estate. This group has become the largest in the whole service sector.
8. EU-12 and EFTA-6.
9. Australia New Zealand Closer Economic Relations Trade Agreement.
10. South and East Asia includes Hong Kong, Korea, Malaysia, Singapore, Taiwan, Thailand, China, India, Indonesia and the Philippines.
11. In 1991, the USA experienced a negative real GDP growth.
12. To test for homoskedasticity, the White test will be examined. We regress the squared OLS residual on a constant, $\ln FDI$, $\ln TSI$, $\ln FDI^2$, $\ln TSI^2$ and $\ln TDI \times$

ln*TSI*. The R^2 in this regression is 0.059, so the chi-squared statistic is $(rT)R^2 = 8.378$, with five degrees of freedom. The null hypothesis, $\delta_1^2 = \delta_2^2 = \delta_r^2$ is rejected if $(rT)R_w^2 > X_{5,\alpha}^2$. The one per cent critical value is 15.086 and the 5 per cent critical value is 11.070. Therefore, we cannot reject the hypothesis of homoskedasticity on the basis of this test. When the null hypothesis is true, the estimated variances should, in large samples, differ only because of sampling fluctuations. Even though this does not indicate the importance of further investigation, we have corrected all the estimations with White's consistent covariance matrix. An estimation without White's covariance matrix gives the following results.

Variable	*Coefficient*	*Standard error*	*t-value*
Intercept	4.4872	0.335	14.47
ln *FDI*	0.176	0.0723	2.34
ln *TSI*	0.365	0.0861	4.60

This result differs marginally compared to the result in Table 15.7, which may prove the homoskedasticity.

13. Kmenta [1990] p. 633.
14. The F-ratio used for the test is,

$$F(n-1, nT-n-K) = \frac{(R_u^2 - R_p^2)\,/\,(n-1)}{(1-R_u^2)\,/\,(nT-n-K)},$$

where n is observation at each T time period and K = regressors, u indicates the model with fixed effects and p the pooled least square estimation.

15. *Johansson and Westin (1993)* use the same technique (a fixed-effect model on individual nodes) on a sample with 10 trade relations over seven years. They reach adjusted R^2 between 0.95 and 0.98.

References

Andersson, T., 'The Role of Japanese Foreign Direct Investment' in L. Oxelheim (ed.), *The Global Race for Foreign Direct Investment – Prospects for the Future* (New York: Springer-Verlag, 1993).

Blomström, M., R.E. Lipsey and K. Kulchucky, *U.S. and Swedish Direct Investments and Exports* NBER Working paper No. 2390 (1987).

Brewer, T.L., 'Foreign Direct Investment in Emerging Market Countries', in L. Oxelheim, *op. cit.*

Eaton, J. and A. Tamura, 'Japanese and U.S. Exports and Investments as Conduits of Growth' in T. Ito, and A.O. Krueger (eds), *Financial Deregulation and Integration in East Asia* (Chicago: University of Chicago Press, 1996).

Hellvin, L., 'Trade and Specialisation in Asia', *Lund Economic Studies No. 56* (1994).

IMF, *Direction of Trade Statistics Yearbook* (International Monetary Fund, Washington D.C. 1994).

Johansson, B., 'The Dynamics of Economic Networks' in D. Batten, J. Casti and R. Thord, (eds), *Networks in Action* (New York: Springer-Verlag, 1995).

Johansson, B. and Westin, L. *Affinities and Network Attributes in Sweden's Trade with Europe* (Royal Institute of Technology, Stockholm 1993).

Kmenta, J., *Elements of Econometrics* 2nd edition (London: Macmillan, 1990).

Kojima, K., *Direct Foreign Investment: a Japanese Model of Multinational Business Operation* (London: Croom Helm, 1978).

Kwan, C.H. *Economic Interdependence in the Asia-Pacific Region* (Routledge, London 1994).

Lin, A.L., 'Trade Effects of Foreign Direct Investments: Evidence for Taiwan with Four ASEAN Countries', *Weltwirtschaftliches Archiv* 131 (1995).

Lizondo, J.S., 'Foreign Direct Investment', *Determinants and Systematic Consequences of International Capital Flows*, IMF Occasional paper 77, March (1991).

Strömquist, U. and Åberg, P., *Trade and Modal Change in the Baltic Region (*Hamburg/Stockholm: Transnord Temaplan, 1997).

Williamson, O.E., 'Transaction-Cost Economies: The Governance of Contractual Relations', *Journal of Law and Economies* 22 (1979).

World Bank, *The World Bank Atlas*, various issues (The World Bank, Washington).

World Investment Report 1993 (New York: United Nations).

16

Business Integration across the Hong Kong–Chinese Border: Patterns and Explanations in the Garment Industry

Edmund R. Thompson

The service sector of the Hong Kong Special Administrative Region now generates over 85 per cent of its gross domestic product (GDP), while manufacturing generates less than 10 per cent (Hong Kong Government, Census and Statistics Department). This is the highest ratio of services to manufacturing in any advanced economy in the world, with the next most service-intensive major economy being the United States, whose GDP comprises 75 per cent services and 20 per cent manufacturing. Singapore, in some respects a reasonably comparable economy to Hong Kong, has a GDP made up of just 63 per cent services with still nearly 30 per cent manufacturing (*Economist* 1998). Between 1991 and 1995 alone, the proportion of manufacturing in Hong Kong's economy dropped by over 40 per cent (Hong Kong Government, Census and Statistics Department).

Unsurprisingly, Hong Kong's largest manufacturing sector, the clothing industry, has contracted drastically. In terms of both numbers of establishments and people engaged in the sector, the clothing industry has shrunk to less than one third what it was during its peak in the mid-1980s. Nevertheless, despite this rapid decline, Hong Kong, with a population of just 6.3 million, remains the world's second largest exporter of garments and the value of domestic exports was still higher during 1997 than a decade earlier, and actually increased by 12 per cent in the first six months of 1998 alone (Hong Kong Government, Census and Statistics Department).[1]

This paradox is not easily explained solely by the general factor cost rationale behind the often observed sequence of clothing-industry growth and decline concomitant with GDP expansion (Toyne *et al.* 1984; Dicken 1992). This would predict that production and exports should diminish broadly in line with employment and production-unit decline, with, of course, a time-lag due to the substitution of labor- with capital-intensive manufacturing. Equally unsatisfactory as explanations are those revolving around the particular political economy of Hong Kong and its 'China connection', which, in essence, rests primarily on opportunities to exploit comparative advantages (Woo and Sung, 1995). Combined, such approaches could readily explain why Hong Kong's garment industry might now either have shifted lock, stock and barrel to, or begun massively to import from, mainland China caused by exploitation of shifting comparative advantages. But they cannot explain why much of the industry has not in fact done this and has, instead, vertically integrated across the Chinese border. To explain this, we need to look at firm-level competitive advantage. This chapter attempts to do so through an examination of data gathered directly from over a hundred Hong Kong garment firms.[2]

Patterns of production and putative explanations

In 1960, Hong Kong's clothing industry employed about 50 000 people and comprised less than 1000 firms. From a peak of employing around 300 000 people in more than 10 000 garment-industry establishments in 1987, the sector had shed well over 200 000 jobs and dwindled to fewer than 3000 firms by 1997 (Hong Kong Government, Census and Statistics Department). This cycle of growth and decline approximately accords with the general, sequential development of the clothing industry noted by Toyne *et al.* (1984; 20–1). However, the decline phase, which took over a century in the United Kingdom, is remarkably rapid, even by contrast to other contemporary producing countries, such as South Korea and Taiwan.[3] Moreover, there has not been a particularly pronounced but lagged decline in exports as the number of firms and employment have dropped in the way Toyne's sequential model anticipates in its later stages (see Figure 16.1).

There can be little doubt that high factor cost growth in Hong Kong has underlain the sharp reduction in employment and number of factories, as pointed out by numerous authors (Enright, Scott and Dodwell 1997, 133; Berger and Lester 1997, 139–85). Hong Kong land and rental costs are some of the highest in the world, and average annual GDP growth of around 6.5 per cent between 1980 and 1995 has ensured that, with *per capita* GDP around $25 000 in 1999, Hong Kong labor is some of the

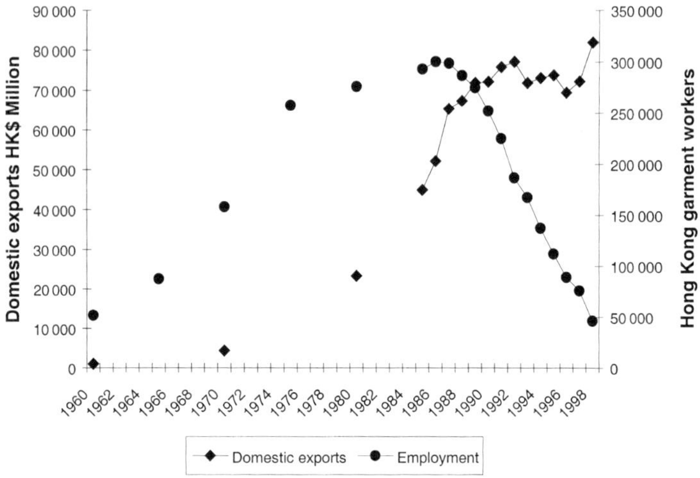

Figure 16.1 Hong Kong garment industry exports and employment
Source: Hong Kong Government Census and Statistics Department, various years.

most costly on earth (World Development Indicators 1997; *Asia Week* 1998). Increases in factor costs, particularly labor, might have resulted in an intensification of capital employed in the garment industry. However, there is scant evidence that the Hong Kong industry has consequently been supplanting space- and labor-intensive manufacturing with the high levels of capital investment required to reduce, in a decade, the number of facilities and employees in the sector by roughly two-thirds, and still maintain relatively high export levels. Such capital investment would imply a productivity increase of nearly 300 per cent, not the 38 per cent which has occurred in the sector; this is itself, in fact, a lower improvement than the 64 per cent increase in labor productivity for all manufacturing industries in Hong Kong (Hong Kong Government 1996).[4]

Existing data suggest that a better explanation is the shift of labor-intensive activities across the border to mainland China. Since Deng's 1979 'open door' policy, it has become increasingly easy for Hong Kong firms to locate manufacturing plant in neighboring China. This 'China factor'[5] has been argued to have allowed Hong Kong's clothing makers to mitigate rising local factor costs by moving low value-added production to the lower factor cost special economic zones of Guangdong and other Chinese provinces (Woo and Sung 1995). At the beginning of the 1990s, some 26 per cent of Hong Kong garment firms were reported to have investments in mainland China (Federation of Hong Kong Industries 1992). By 1993 this had increased to 51 per cent (Federation of Hong Kong Industries 1993). Research for this chapter shows that, by the end of 1997, this had increased to 87 per cent of firms.

Such mainland investments, with an average employment of around 700 people, would seem almost overwhelmingly to relate to labor-intensive activities. The activities which the highest proportion of Hong Kong firms carry out in mainland China are relatively low value-adding as well as highly labor-intensive, such as packaging, manufacturing, assembly and sample making, or space-intensive, like warehousing. Other activities are still overwhelmingly conducted in Hong Kong. Order processing and distribution are still centered in Hong Kong; so, too, are product and process development and higher value-added activities relating to finance, strategy and information technology (see Figure 16.2).

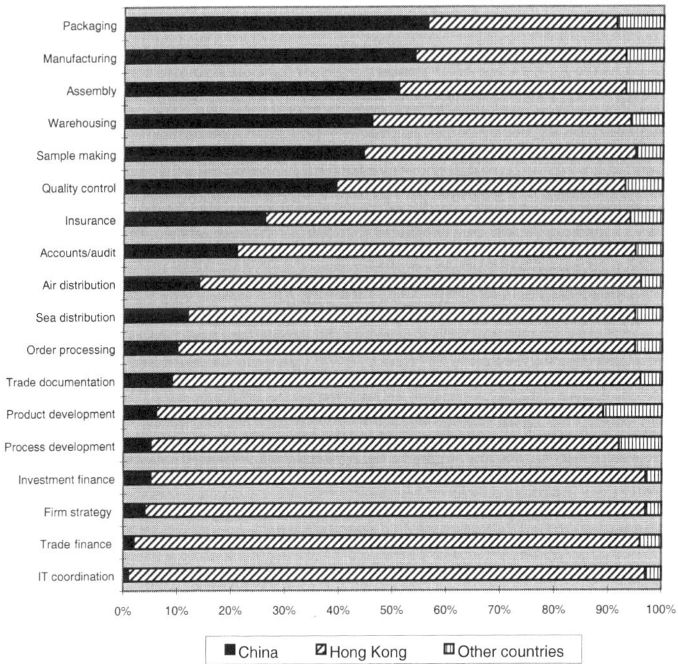

Figure 16.2. Location of value-adding activities (%)
Source: author's survey.

This pattern of firms shifting labor- and land-intensive activities to mainland China concurs with the most commonly stated reasons for setting up mainland operations; that is labor costs, cited in 67 per cent of instances, followed by escalating Hong Kong land and rental prices, cited in 24 per cent of cases (Federation of Hong Kong Industries 1992). Labor costs in mainland China are less than three per cent of Hong Kong's on average (*Asia Week* 1998) and, even in neighboring Guangdong, where labor prices are typically up to three times higher than elsewhere in China, human capital is still less than one-tenth of Hong Kong prices (Sung *et al.* 1995; 109–32).

Growth in the percentage of firms with operations in mainland China almost precisely mirrors the decline in the number of operations in Hong Kong, suggesting that there is certainly some correlation between the rise in factor costs in Hong Kong and the rise in operations being set up in China (see Figure 16.3). However, just because there appears to be a close connection between differential factor costs and the number of Hong Kong owned garment manufacturing establishments in both Hong Kong and mainland China, that correlation should not imply any causality. Clearly, it would be reasonable to assume that Hong Kong firms would *not* set up mainland China establishments if factor costs were not actually lower there (unless, of course, they set up in China in order to sell into its market; but, as will be shown, this is not the case). This simply means, however, that factor costs can be regarded as necessary, though not sufficient, conditions in determining the pattern of Hong Kong firms'

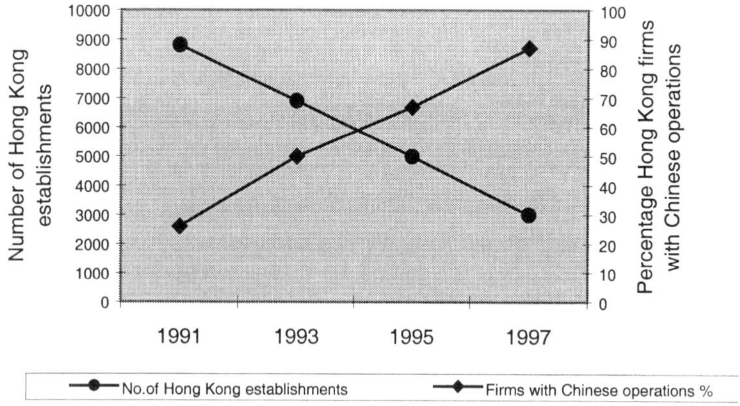

Figure 16.3 Rise of China, fall of Hong Kong
Source: Hong Kong Government Census and Statistics Department, various years.

trans-border production investments. This is because Hong Kong firms could conceivably do one of two things to take advantage of lower mainland factor costs without incurring the added expenses and difficulties of coordinating transnationally configured, vertically integrated structures.

First, they could move all operations to the mainland. However, this option is ruled out by the existence of multi- and bilateral quota agreements affecting both Hong Kong and China's garment industries. Second, Hong Kong firms could simply purchase intermediate products from independent producers across the border and then assemble them in the Special Administrative Region. The various protectionist clothing-sector agreements, with their complex rules-of-origin limitations, to which Hong Kong and China have been obliged to be a party, do not distinguish between whether or not intermediate products are acquired through intra- or extra-firm trade. Hence, there can be no advantage in internalizing intermediate product transactions to 'evade trade restrictions', as suggested by some commentators (Woo and Sung 1995; 2). Thus, on their own, neither political economy nor comparative advantage approaches appear to provide a satisfactory explanation of why Hong Kong garment firms are vertically integrated across what is supposed to remain, until 2047, effectively an international border. For a fuller explanation, a firm-specific, competitive advantage approach may prove more useful.

The competitive advantage of transnational structure

Explanatory theories of cross-border businesses are founded on the question of why firms choose to internalize certain activities rather than transact them in the market (Coase 1937). The various, essentially cost-related benefits suggested by Coase for maintaining value-adding activities under common control have been substantially elaborated through transaction cost economics (Williamson 1985) and the development of vertical integration theory (Perry 1989). To the literature on cost minimization has been added competitiveness maximization analysis (Hymer 1976 (1960); Kindleberger 1969; Caves 1971). This approach focuses not so much on cost but on revenue and takes, as its starting point, the competitive activities of firms operating in oligopolistic markets. The logic rests on the fact that, in achieving competitive advantage for products in the market place, companies develop firm-specific assets which cannot easily or quickly be replicated by rivals. Such assets either enable the firm to produce more cheaply than competitors or to produce advantageously differentiated goods or services capable of commanding a premium price in the market place, or both. Such assets may be proprietorially helped by way of patents, or may consist in branding, reputation, knowledge and expertise. Exploiting these latter firm-specific assets or advantages in overseas markets, without their being appropriated by local or other foreign rivals, often obliges companies to internalize them within the hierarchy of the firm through transnational horizontal integration (Hymer 1976 (1960)).

Clearly Hong Kong garment firms are not following a pattern of horizontal transnational integration in any classical sense. The pattern of value chain activities is very much one of vertical rather than horizontal integration. Moreover, China represents just two per cent of the total market for the firms surveyed. These firms are not attempting to access the China market and they are not there to sell. However, the competitive advantage logic underpinning horizontal transnational integration might still help in explaining why Hong Kong firms are vertically transnationally integrated. Dunning's 'eclectic theory of foreign investment' attempts to marry both comparative and competitive advantage analyses (1981). His 'theory' suggests that firms transnationalize when the 'ownership' of firm-specific (competitive) advantages and the exploitation of 'location' (comparative) advantages cannot successfully be maximized without internalization. Does this model of transnationalization apply to Hong Kong garment firms?

The answer is, partially, yes. There can be little doubt that garment firms seek to exploit the low cost 'location' advantages of China: but this should not be taken to imply that they are in the business of competing on low cost alone. For Dunning's theory to apply, Hong Kong garment firms would need also to internalize some kind of non-cost, firm-specific assets – even if those assets, in fact, result primarily in lower costs. On the face of it, the markets where Hong Kong firms compete would suggest that they might. Of the firms surveyed, some three per cent of their sales are in Hong Kong itself, with over 90 per cent in Europe, the Americas, Japan and Australasia (see Table 16.1). Arguably, each of these oligopolistic markets is sophisticated and competitive, and it is unlikely that any garment firm could expect to succeed in them simply by keeping costs down alone.

Garment firms' competitive strategies

To find out precisely how Hong Kong firms create competitive advantage, surveyed firms were asked a scale of questions based on previously

Table 16.1 Global markets

Destination of sales	*Average percentages reported by sample*
Europe	40
North America	35
Japan/Australasia	20
Hong Kong	3
China	2

Source: author's survey.

developed constructs (see Table 16.2). Over 90 per cent of the firms make garments to-order for a mixture of wholesale and retail customers. The majority of these customers are certainly not looking for a cheap and cheerful service. Most are looking for premium quality products suitable for high-priced market segments, and over 70 per cent of firms claim to be delivering precisely such products. This is reinforced by over 86 per cent of firms claiming that their quality has improved over recent years, with more than 72 per cent saying that they spend more on quality control than previously. The delivery of high quality products for high-priced market segments is not normally associated with firms that compete on price. Unsurprisingly then, less than 15 per cent of firms claimed that their prices were lower than competitors, indicating that few are essentially concerned with price as a predominant competitive advantage.

For Hong Kong firms to attempt to follow competitive strategies of cost leadership would be very difficult. Their existing customer base (which demands quality and specific features rather than just low cost), and the prevalence of myriad low-cost producers not just in China itself, but around the world, rule out competing solely on price. Effectively denied, and evidently not following, the option of cost-leadership strategies, Hong Kong firms have the option of pursuing competitive strategies of differentiation comprising either of real or perceived differences from their competitors (Porter 1980). Differentiation based on perceived rather than real product qualities, generally boils down to branding, which is indicated as a strategy by variables relating to advertising and marketing. However, the development of brands is not normally associated with made-to-order, original equipment manufacturing (OEM). And, certainly, the questions designed to establish whether or not Hong Kong garment firms may be following branding strategies, indicate that they are no different from most OEM producers in this respect. The majority of respondents do not advertise heavily and only eight per cent believe they

Table 16.2 What firms say about their customers, products and competitiveness[6]

Please indicate the degree to which you agree or disagree with the following questions using the scale, 1 for strongly agree and 5 for strongly disagree

	Strongly agree	*Agree*	*Neutral*	*Disagree*	*Strongly disagree*	*N*	*Mean*
1. Your main customers are wholesalers	20	52	2	12	15	102	2.5
2. Your main customers are retailers	17	44	0	20	20	101	2.8
3. Your main customers are consumers	10	17	2	16	56	102	3.9
4. Your products are mainly made to order	59	33	0	1	7	102	1.6
5. Your products are mainly own label	12	18	1	14	56	102	3.8
6. Your products/services are mainly aimed at high-priced market segments	11	39	13	34	4	101	2.8
7. Your products/services are mainly heavily advertised	2	23	31	13	31	102	3.5
8. Your products/services are mainly of a premium quality	30	40	22	6	2	102	2.1
9. Your products/services are mainly well branded	7	41	13	9	30	102	3.1
10. Your products mainly incorporate uniqueness of design	3	21	22	27	28	101	3.6
11. Your products mainly incorporate uniqueness of materials	3	39	22	29	7	102	3
12. Your products compete mainly on the basis of features not offered by competitors	4	28	7	52	9	102	3.3
13. Your products are mainly priced below those of competitors	1	13	6	67	14	102	3.8
14. Your products are mainly competitive because they meet special market segment needs	8	48	24	20	1	102	2.6
15. Your products are mainly competitive because of the close attention paid to efficient manufacturing	35	56	6	3	0	102	1.8
16. Your products are mainly competitive because of strict cost control	44	48	1	7	0	102	1.7
17. Your products are mainly competitive because they are strongly customized for buyers	4	53	31	12	0	102	2.6
18. You are competitive because of rapid production and fast delivery	43	36	11	10	0	102	1.9

Table 16.2 (continued)

	Strongly agree	*Agree*	*Neutral*	*Disagree*	*Strongly disagree*	*N*	*Mean*
19. Compared to recent years, your product range is getting narrower	10	7	7	60	16	101	3.7
20. Compared to recent years, your product range is targeted at fewer market segments	8	12	8	58	15	102	3.6
21. Compared to recent years, your product range is of better quality	35	51	4	7	3	102	1.9
22. Compared to recent years, your product range differs more greatly from those of competitors	1	23	31	40	6	101	3.3
23. Compared to recent years, you spend more on product research and design	10	27	25	15	23	102	3.2
24. You spend more on product research than competitors	2	13	52	24	9	98	3.2
25. Compared to recent years, you spend more on market research	2	11	43	19	25	102	3.5
26. Compared to recent years, you spend more on advertising and marketing promotion	5	12	40	14	29	100	3.5
27. You spend more on all market, advertising and promotional activities than competitors	2	6	67	12	12	97	3.3
28. Compared to recent years, you spend more on quality control	33	39	16	11	1	102	2.1

Source: author's survey.

spend more than competitors on promotional activities, suggesting that perceptual differentiation is not a prevalent competitive strategy.

Given that Hong Kong garment firms do not pursue cost leadership or branding strategies, they could either blindly compete without any strategy – which seems improbable given the healthy 15 per cent average gross margin on sales reported – or they must follow differentiation strategies comprising real product differences. Such differences do not consist in the actual garments produced. These are not thought particularly to incorporate either uniqueness of design or materials compared with those produced by competitors. This is precisely as would be expected when customers specify their own requirements. The 'product' of Hong Kong's garment firms consists in the service they offer to buyers wanting to have clothes produced. Where firms believe they are distinctive at this service, is in their ability to take and deliver on orders quickly and flexibly, with 80 per cent citing rapid production and fast delivery as key to their competitiveness. Hence, Hong Kong garment firms compete by offering not just a high quality, but a speedy and flexible service to buyers.

A competitive approach of this kind is very much in tune with the sort of buyers found in advanced industrial economies. These buyers cater to highly fragmented distributional channels and to highly segmented, relatively sophisticated consumer markets where fashions change rapidly, and often unpredictably, both seasonally and otherwise.[7] Unable in advance to know for sure which product lines will 'take off' with sometimes capricious consumers, such buyers minimize risk by keeping inventories low and operating as nearly as possible 'just-in-time' stock control. They do this by passing on the burden of rapid, flexible production of generally small and variable batches of particular garment specifications to OEM producers. For Hong Kong firms to be competitive in these circumstances, they need to be extremely efficient at managing their manufacturing activities. They cannot obtain much in the way of scale economies through large production runs and must constantly ensure that capacity is utilized in a cost-effective manner. This is reflected in over 90 per cent of firms claiming that they are competitive because of close attention paid to efficient manufacturing and strict cost control.

Internalizing competitive strategy and advantages

Once the way in which Hong Kong garment firms compete has been identified, the question becomes one of whether or not they could successfully pursue their general competitive strategy without vertically integrating across the border with the mainland. The question here is partly one of value chain configuration, but mostly one of value chain coordination.[8] In answer to the question of configuration, it is doubtful that firms could hope to compete cost-wise without exploiting comparative advantages in labor that exist in China – human capital in Hong Kong is just too expensive. Hence, the more interesting and important question is: can the competitive strategy of extremely flexible, very rapid and high quality production be implemented other than by internalizing the coordination of value chain elements across the mainland China border?

The answer is no, for a combination of cost and competitiveness reasons. First, the flexibility needed to cater to buyers' requirements for relatively small production runs would be nearly impossible to obtain at a reasonable price through market transactions. External suppliers would charge a premium for the process downtime and retooling necessary for the production of numerous short runs. They would also charge premiums for very urgent jobs and for last minute rescheduling of process activity. Transactions in the market would also attract considerable costs in terms of gaining knowledge of supplier competencies, availability and prices, together with the expense of negotiating and drawing up contracts with different suppliers. The only way to overcome these difficulties without actually internalizing production would be through special, probably long-term contractual relations with suppliers, a form of quasi vertical integration. However, such supplier relationships might well reduce the benefits of market transactions along with their costs, and would not necessarily facilitate the competitive necessities of speed and quality.

Supposing, even if market transactions could provide sufficient flexibility, there is no guarantee that they could consistently ensure speed at a reasonable cost. Just arranging market transactions takes time. However, more detrimental to speed of production is the potential for bottlenecks when supplier capacity is fully committed. Even when supplier capacity is nearing full utilization, firms would find themselves beginning to pay higher prices or, worse, being forced to accept lower quality. Attempting to get and ensure through the market the consistently high quality demanded by Hong Kong garment firms' buyers, while at the same time ensuring flexibility and speed, would be very difficult. To a great extent, flexibility and speed of manufacturing are antithetical to uniform high quality, especially when very strict cost control is required. Consequently, the only way that firms can combine the elements of flexibility, speed and quality, and thereby achieve their competitive strategy, is by controlling their manufacturing processes themselves.

Such an analysis of Hong Kong garment firms' internalized, transnational, vertically integrated structures would seem not to indicate that any particular 'ownership' advantages are being protected. Consequently, Dunning's eclectic paradigm is not obviously or neatly illustrated. However, this could be due to the misleadingly vague specification of his paradigm rather than anything else. If 'ownership' advantages are taken solely to refer to replicable advantages that could be appropriated by rivals, then Hong Kong firms do not fit the paradigm. In China itself, they are exploiting comparative advantages, not competitive advantages. However, by exploiting those comparative advantages through internalization, Hong Kong firms are preserving their competitive advantage in their more global market place, and, simultaneously, building up the kind of managerial, value chain coordination expertise that winds up as a firm-specific and firm-owned asset – which is generally associated with the rationale for vertical integration. Such an ownership advantage could not be preserved without internalization. Hence, the ownership advantages of Dunning's eclectic paradigm appear dangerously to collapse into vertical integration advantages by another name.

Notes

1. After mainland China, Hong Kong is the world's second largest garment exporter, when both domestic and re-exports are taken into account. In 1997 the value of domestic garment exports stood at HK$72 228 million, re-exports of garments totaled HK$106 669 million in the same year (Hong Kong Government, Census and Statistics Department).
2. The research on which this chapter is based was conducted by the author during the second half of 1997, with the support of the University of Hong Kong School of Business. To make the findings comparable with the most detailed and extensive pre-existing data available, that from the Federation of Hong Kong Industries' occasional research conducted among its members, it was decided that the same universe used by them – their members categorized as garment manufacturers – would be used. An original list of around 300 firms, was reduced to 289 extant companies traceable by telephone and facsimile. All were faxed a letter in both Cantonese and English saying that they would be telephoned in the next few weeks either by the author or a bilingual research assistant. A total of 114 firms were surveyed using a closed ended questionnaire, yielding a response rate of 39.5 per cent. This rate is in line with the gradually declining response rates achieved by the Federation itself and represented a reasonable cross-section of the population. No control variables had been asked in any of the Federation of Hong Kong Industries' surveys, so none could be asked to test directly the comparability of the final results. However, the average number of employees in mainland China per respondent, which has been variously between 640 and 773 in Federation surveys, was 722, suggesting that the final sample was at least broadly similar and comparable to those from which prior data is used.

3. Toyne elaborates a six-stage sequence of clothing and textile industry growth. He suggests that by 1984 Hong Kong had, along with Taiwan and South Korea, reached the fourth stage, in which production and trade are extensive. Hong Kong would seem clearly to have joined, along with the UK, Germany, France Belgium and the Netherlands, the sixth and final stage in which substantial reductions in employment and production units are observed.
4. This figure is derived by taking nominal value added per employee in the sector between 1984 and 1994 and accounting for inflation at the conservative rate of 7.5 per cent during the period (Hong Kong Government, Census and Statistics Department, various years).
5. Hong Kong's 'China factor' collapses down to a facilitation of foreign direct investment by Hong Kong firms through geographical proximity and socio-cultural affinities and links which foster the development of '*guanxi*' – the connections and relationships which are sometimes deemed to be indispensable to doing business in mainland China where market, legal and judicial institutions for the conduct of contractual commercial transactions are underdeveloped or non existent (Guthrie, 1998; Leung, 1993; Smart and Smart, 1991).
6. The scale is based on constructs used by Nayyar (1993) to assess competitive strategies.
7. Of course such markets are large consumers of less fashion-sensitive clothing items, like jeans and T-shirts, which can be sourced more on the basis of cost combined with reasonable but not particularly high quality over time periods negating the need for great flexibility or speed. Hong Kong's garment industry has had to exit this part of the industry and concentrate on low volume, high quality and speed production.
8. For discussion of value chain configuration and coordination see Porter (1985). His device of the value chain broadly separates and relates firms' various value-adding activities in a logical sequence, running from inbound logistics, through processing to marketing and delivery to buyers.

References

Asia Week, Hong Kong, January (1998) p. 51.

Berger, S. and R.K. Lester, *Made by Hong Kong* (Hong Kong: Oxford University Press, 1997).

Caves, R.E. 'International Corporations: the Industrial Economics of Foreign Investment', *Economica,* 38 February (1971) 1–17.

Coase, R.H. 'The Nature of the Firm', *Economica,* 4 November (1937) 386–405.

Dicken, P., *Global Shift: The Internationalization of Economic Activity,* 2nd edn (New York: Guilford Press, 1992).

Dunning, J.H. *International Production and the Multinational Enterprise* (London: Allen & Unwin, 1981).

Economist 1997 Pocket World in Figures (London Economist Newspapers Ltd., 1998 edn).

Enright, M.J., E.E. Scott and D. Dodwell, *The Hong Kong Advantage* (Hong Kong; Oxford University Press, 1997).

Federation of Hong Kong Industries, *Hong Kong's Industrial Investment in the Pearl River Delta: 1991 Survey Among Members of the Federation of Hong Kong Industries*

(Hong Kong: Industry & Research Division, Federation of Hong Kong Industries, 1992).
Federation of Hong Kong Industries, *Investment in China: 1993 Survey of Members of the Federation of Hong Kong Industries* (Hong Kong: Industry & Research Division, Federation of Hong Kong Industries, 1993).
Federation of Hong Kong Industries, *Investment in China: 1994 Survey of Members of the Federation of Hong Kong Industries* (Hong Kong: Federation of Hong Kong Industries, 1995).
Federation of Hong Kong Industries, 'Industry Focus: Garment industry', *Hong Kong Industrialist* June (1997) p. 54.
Guthrie, D. 'The Declining Significance of Guanxi in China's Economic Transition', *China Quarterly,* 154 (1998) 254–82.
Hong Kong Government Census and Statistics Department. Various years.
Hong Kong Government, *Hong Kong's Manufacturing Industries* (Industry Department, 1996).
Hymer, S.H., *The International Operations of National Firms: a Study of Direct Foreign Investment,* Ph.D. dissertation MIT 1960 (published by MIT Press 1976).
Kindleberger, C.P., *American Business Abroad. Six Lectures on Direct Investment* (New Haven: Yale University Press, 1969).
Leung, C.K., 'Personal Contacts, Subcontracting Linkages, and Development in the Hong Kong – Zhujiang Delta region', *Annals of the Association of American Geographers,* 83 (1993) 272–302.
Nayyar, P.R., 'On the Measurement of Competitive Strategy: Evidence from a Large Multiproduct US firm', *Academy of Management Journal* 36 (1993) pp. 1652–69.
Perry, M.K, 'Vertical Integration: Determinants and Effects', in R. Schmalensee and R.D Willig, *Handbook of Industrial Organization Vol 1* (Amsterdam: North-Holland, 1989) 183–255.
Porter, M.E., *Competitive Strategy: Techniques for Analyzing Industries and Competitors* (New York: Free Press, 1980).
Porter, M.E., *Competitive Advantage: Creating and Sustaining Superior Performance* (New York: Free Press, 1985).
Smart, J. and A. Smart, 'Personal Relations and Divergent Economies: a Case Study of Hong Kong Investment in South China', *International Journal of Urban and Regional Research,* 15 (1991) 216–33.
Sung, Y.W., P.W. Liu, and Y.C.R. Wong, *The Fifth Dragon: The Emergence of the Pearl River Delta* (Hong Kong: Addison Wesley, 1995).
Toyne, B., J.S. Arpan, D.A. Ricks, T.A. Shimp and A. Barnett, *The Global Textile Industry* (London: Allen & Unwin, 1984).
Williamson, O.E., *The Economic Institutions of Capitalism: Firms, Markets, Relational Contracting* (New York: The Free Press, 1985).
Woo, T.O. and Y.W. Sung, 'The Hong Kong/China connection: trade and the wool industry', *Economics Division Working Paper 95/4* (Research School of Asia and Pacific Studies: Australia National University, 1995).
World Bank, *World Development Indicators* (Washington, 1997).

17

Illiberal and Successful? In Search of Sustainable Regional Growth in Authoritarian States

Janerik Gidlund

This chapter is a comparative study of two industrial parks: one in Batam in Indonesia and one in Suzhou, China. Both parks have been created by Singapore in cooperation with the host governments. Above all, they are political efforts to solve important institutional problems common in authoritarian states in East Asia, such as the unpredictability of administrative procedures, the instability in the rules of the market, and the corruption associated with involuntary joint ventures. These parks are interesting in that they represent a possible approach for authoritarian states to the problem of how to combine a rather closed society with institutions that are favorable for the development of an open economy. The industrial parks can thus be viewed as a way of coping with the challenges posed by an internationalizing economy.

One method in the field known as 'futures studies' is to analyze a new phenomenon as the expression of an emerging pattern of development. Here I try to apply that methodology to the regionalization of East Asia in a globalizing economy. The chapter is partly based on secondary sources and public documents, including a systematic inquiry of news items in the *Straits Times* during the 1993 to 1997 period. Unfortunately, it has been impossible to check the accuracy of every piece of information. Therefore, there is a risk that cheerful official news reporting is over-represented at the expense of problematic aspects of the projects. This chapter is also based on interviews conducted in Batam (April 1996), and in Suzhou (October 1996).

Theory of success

In presenting itself as a regional model, Singapore's economic success may be explained in terms of factors that can, at least partly, be reproduced in other locations.

Economic success can be measured in different ways. It is often noted that Singapore's GDP growth rate averaged 8.4 per cent between 1964 and 1994. *Per capita* GDP is now almost on a par with the United States. Another indication of success is that Singapore has been able to develop a world-class infrastructure for business, having attracted more than 3000 multinational corporations (MNCs) with regional headquarters or production facilities.

As an expression of their pride in Singapore's development, those in power share a conviction that Singapore's success is the result of advanced and far-sighted economic and social policies. When the city-state gained independence in 1965 there were some quite obvious reasons for pessimism. Singapore had a typical entrepot economy with an under-developed industrial structure. Other problems included massive unemployment, widespread poverty, and ethnic tensions. Singapore's only inherent advantage was its perfect geo-economic location. Thus, Singapore had to rely on its citizens' skills and its ability to attract foreign investment. True, Singapore shared this predicament with several of the successful postwar economies, for example Japan, South Korea, Germany, and Hong Kong. Still, Singapore faced a unique combination of political and economic challenges.

The economic success of Singapore is explained by Somjee and Somjee (1995) in the following way:

> Apart from stable government and geographic location, Singapore also possessed the 'ingredients' whereby business could flourish. These were: (i) a developed infrastructure; (ii) an industrious, disciplined and well-trained workforce; (iii) well established international trading links; and (iv) relatively cheap labor. But these factors by themselves were not going to produce results, they had to be put to effective development use. And Singapore did precisely that. Very early in its development strategy, it moved away from the short-sighted industrialization which went with import substitution. Instead it aimed at export-led growth and threw open its economy to various multinationals for investment. This no doubt increased its dependency both on foreign capital as well as on the transfer of technology. But as long as these could produce results, the external interest in developing

> Singapore's economy continued. In 1979, it entered another phase of development to 'supplant' labor-intensive, low-skill, low value added economic activities, with capital-intensive high technology and high value added ventures. [...] Added to this were its effort to become a center of finance, travel, and of all the high-tech developments in the region.

The modernistic development policy was carried out by reinforcing the role of the state in economic development. The economy was provided with new Government-linked Corporations (GLC), which together with the MNCs dominated production. Simultaneously, ambitious state-controlled construction programs were conducted. Government-built housing soon came to dominate the housing market, which had the effect that the citizens'/tenants' dependence on the state increased markedly.

In analyzing the possibility of exporting Singapore's successes, it is useful to concentrate on the following seven factors:

(1) Illiberal democracy

The distinction between state and society is blurred in Singapore. The limited opportunities for voluntary political participation reflect the fear of those in power for disruptive ethnic tensions and political competition. Even though Singapore displays formal democratic procedures and elections, it has become increasingly evident that the political opposition faces enormous difficulties in mobilizing electoral support and in financing electoral campaigns. In the parliamentary election of January 1997 these difficulties became obvious when an opposition candidate was accused by the PAP leadership of being 'an Antichrist and a Chinese chauvinist' which he, not surprisingly, denied. As a result he was sued in court for having accused the leadership of lying and subsequently had to flee the country.

This kind of authoritarian, but formally democratic political system is often called illiberal democracy (see Chapter 6). A contradiction is thus created between the economic freedoms enjoyed by the MNCs and the limited economic and political freedoms enjoyed by Singapore's citizens. The result has been a closed society with an open market economy.

(2) 'One-stop' and non-corrupt management of fast economic growth

For three decades, Singapore has demonstrated its capacity for achieving rapid economic development. An important precondition has been efficient, professional and seemingly non-corrupt political leadership and public administration. It was an integral part of Singapore's strategy to involve experts from universities and businesses in its development endeavors, on the condition that they toed the government line. For example, when Singapore experienced an economic recession in 1985, a special high-level economic committee was formed to examine the causes of the recession and to recommend policy changes. The result was a long series of thorough policy recommendations, of which the majority seems to have been implemented. The long-term goals were: (i) that a high savings rate should be maintained; (ii) Singapore should create a conducive business environment including competitive costs, low taxes, friendly regulations, and good work attitudes; (iii) that the economy should depend on private sector enterprises. Both MNCs and national companies (including the GLCs) were to be nurtured.[1]

A growing economic and political problem is that Singapore's model of development is dominated by centralized land-use planning and development strategies as well as an over-reliance on large-scale investments. The long-term consequences are limited adaptability to new and possibly unanticipated comparative advantages, market under-performance of land-use, and increasing risks of large-scale consequences of industry-specific downturns or firm-specific mismanagement.

(3) Excellent physical infrastructure

The transportation and communication infrastructure, as well as the quality and accessibility of business facilities, are generally regarded as being of very high quality on any measure.

(4) An industrious, disciplined and well-trained workforce

Singapore's multi-ethnic population is currently experiencing economic progress as a manifestation of the nation-building process. There can be no doubt about the work ethic and professionalism of Singapore's work force, although these traits are partly maintained by strong social institutions and heavy-handed political control.

(5) Well established global trading and financial links

The presence of global production and financial capital shows that Singapore has excellent linkages to the networks of the global economy. Moreover, Singapore's political leaders certainly cannot be at the helm of the MNCs to the same extent as they are of their own citizens and the GLCs. Singapore must thus attract global capital, which requires a sufficient ability to adapt to external conditions and a significant degree of pragmatism.

(6) Relatively cheap labor

Next to Japan and perhaps Hong Kong, Singapore has achieved the highest living standards in Asia. This implies that the cost of labor has increased rapidly from the 1960s onwards. But relatively low productivity gains in the least advanced sectors of the economy have necessitated an expanding work-force. A significant proportion of Singapore's unskilled labor has for this reason come to consist of foreign workers with time-limited work permits of between one and three years. In total there were as many as 450 000 foreign workers out of a total work-force of 1.7 million in Singapore in 1996.

(7) Excellent geo-economic location

The geographical location of Singapore at the heart of Southeast Asia, with a total population of 300 million people, is of strategic importance. Originally, of course, Singapore was first and foremost an important junction for shipping.

The growth triangle[2]

Even in 1979, the idea of establishing a linkage between Singapore and the nearby Indonesian Riau archipelago was raised by the Indonesian politician B.J. Habibie in a discussion with the former prime minister of Singapore, Lee Kuan Yew. The discussion was evidently inspired by the Benelux countries, which early on dismantled intra-regional barriers to the free flow of capital, labor, goods, and services. Southeast Asian efforts at regional integration, whether ASEAN-wide or sub-regional, have however been a matter of negative integration (i.e., the removal of different obstacles to economic interaction), which make these efforts qualitatively different from European integration policies.

It was, however, not until December 1989 that Singapore's Goh Chok Tong, in accordance with the Strategic Economic Plan which was formulated as a response to the recession of 1985, officially proposed the creation of a growth zone encompassing Singapore, Batam in Indonesia, and Johor in Malaysia. In terms of official treaties, the Triangle has primarily resulted in a number of bilateral agreements between Singapore and Indonesia; for example, allowing foreign investors initially to own 100 per cent of the plants they set up in Batam as well as investment guaranties by the Indonesian government. In contrast to the European Union, there is no freedom of movement for citizens of the three countries.

In defense of the Triangle, it was pointed out that it offered regional complementarity. Singapore was to provide capital, business services, management capability, an advanced infrastructure and its experience of export trading. Conversely, Johor and Batam were to provide water, land and cheap labor. By creating an investment zone, Singapore's expansion could spill over into its surrounding regions, and simultaneously attract investment from abroad. None of the involved states, least of all Singapore, was interested in heavy migration. By generating investments on location, the movement of people between the countries could instead be restrained. However, the investments in Johor and Riau have already resulted in a shortage of labor, causing many Indonesians to move to the archipelago, as well as causing Malaysians to move to Johor. Partly as a result of the Growth Triangle project, Johor has established itself as the second-most important industrial area in Malaysia.

The primary political task is considered to be negative integration. There is no common organization or transnational secretariat. The basic idea is expressed in terms of 'open regionalism,' which aims to attract foreign investors to profitable projects on favorable terms. And the investments have been impressive. Major investments have been made in the physical infrastructure; for example, in roads, sea links, and industrial parks. Furthermore, passport controls have been facilitated through the use of smartcards. On Batam island, an industrial park has been established which has attracted total investments of US$3 billion by investors from Singapore and Indonesia. On another Indonesian island, Bintan, a similar industrial project has been initiated, at a total cost of US$4 billion. Total investments in Johor and Riau amounted to approximately US$7 billion for the initial five-year period. Still, the 'Triangle'-concept lacks efficient linkages between Johor and Riau. In effect it is more akin to a growth corridor centered on Singapore than a tripartite triangle.

The Batam Model

In East Asia, the perceived early success of the Triangle has aroused admiration and interest. Of course, an accurate assessment of its economic performance requires more rigorous criteria. In several regions in East Asia, new triangle projects have been initiated, and there is an ongoing discussion on triangles as a new way of integrating an international region. There is also a discussion on the indirect security role of the triangles, especially when they are established across sensitive territorial conflict zones. It can be argued that the Singapore–Johor–Riau (SJR) growth triangle already has become an important instrument for ensuring

Singapore's national security, particularly as a means of managing the interplay with its powerful Indonesian neighbor.

Yet the industrial park in Batam would prove to be a prototype not merely for economic growth in the metropolitan region of Singapore, but also for a project located very far away from the city-state. In this chapter, the establishment of the township project in Suzhou, China, is compared with this prototype.

The Batamindo Industrial Park (BIP)

The Batam project is an essential part of the Growth Triangle concept, and occupies a special position by being Singapore's first industrial park ever to be established on foreign territory. The construction of the park began in February, 1990 and, already in August of that year, the first factory was ready for production. At the official inauguration in April 1992, 29 MNCs had set up manufacturing plants in the BIP. Four years later, the number had increased to almost 70 MNCs. The annual growth rate was about 9 per cent during the initial years, and the value of exports for 1996 was estimated to equal US$1 billion. The park mostly consists of light high-tech production facilities with low levels of pollution; for instance in electronics, mechanics, metal, and optics. Almost all of the MNCs have their regional headquarters in Singapore.

Below, the BIP will be analyzed by focusing on the seven Singaporean factors mentioned above, in order to determine whether this industrial park can be seen as an instance of exporting Singapore's development model.

It could be argued that the individual workers, or at least their families, exercise a free choice when they sign their contracts. Once inside the BIP, however, the workers are not expected to participate in any decision-making process. In addition, housing in the BIP is organized in such a way that it is difficult for the employees to fail to appear at work without a valid excuse. The mostly female workers live in blocks made up of eight-person lodgings with each block under the control of a block leader. These block leaders exercise a high degree of social control. In addition, the entire industrial park and the blocks are fenced in, with guarded entrances. An interview with the management of the BIP revealed that the declared purpose of the fences was to prevent 'illegal sex': the Muslim parents of the young women who predominate the workforce (85 per cent) are very careful about ensuring that the stay at the BIP will not ruin the young women's chances on the 'marriage market' at home. More importantly, this structure gives the BIP leadership almost total control of its work-force. The MNCs also seem content to accept the workers' lack of personal freedom and democratic rights.

Regarding the factor 'one-stop and non-corrupt management', it is well known that Indonesia faces major institutional problems in regard to both corruption and a labyrinthine bureaucracy. By creating an autonomous unit placed under a Singaporean institutional umbrella, the investors have the opportunity to increase production in a competitive environment with Singaporean guarantees and seemingly low political risks. The BIP has a fairly unique institutional structure, which in some ways resembles the early technological new town of Milton Keynes in Britain.

The BIP is run by an intergovernmental committee, appointed by the Indonesian president in Jakarta, the Singaporean government and the Economic Development Board in Singapore. At the time of the establishment of the industrial park, there were only 7000 inhabitants on the island but, by the spring of 1996, the population had increased to approximately 130 000. Thus, at the starting-point, Batam was economically a rather uninteresting part of populous Indonesia, and the establishment of the BIP was considered a green-field project. However, when the BIP was developed beyond its traditional regional control, it became a source of irritation for the regional government of the Province of Riau.

The managers of the BIP are largely recruited from Singapore. The BIP is already perceived as an example of efficient management, and apparently succeeds in attracting an increasing number of MNCs, thereby functioning as a prototype for investments in other Asian environments. In the BIP's latest promotional video, a society as efficient as a circuit card is portrayed, where even the physical lay-out of the park resembles a printed circuit card. The BIP can be seen as an expression of state-led growth and, in this context, the illiberal democracy of Singapore probably implies that it has a political advantage in its relations with the Indonesian government.

Concerning the factor 'a developed physical infrastructure', it is obvious that the BIP largely has succeeded with its implementation of an industrial policy which is similar to that which is employed in Singapore itself. Originally, the BIP was 'set to become a prosperous self-contained industrial area.' The industrial park is therefore located at the center of the island in order to have access to a satisfactory water supply. Also, it has developed its own power supply, sewage treatment and international telecommunication facilities. The park has most of the facilities essential for a functioning society. Apart from the many esthetically designed industrial buildings, there are dormitories for workers located close to the factories, housing for executives, as well as social and recreational facilities. Moreover, Batam has been provided with a relatively large airport, and has had its harbor and ferry services improved. A possible bone of contention between Indonesia and Singapore is the further development of the airport. The Indonesian government plans to expand the airport's role to include international flights, a hub role surely not desired by Singapore.

The fourth factor, 'an industrious, disciplined and well-trained work-force,' is only partially valid. In fact, Singapore is very careful about not relocating production that requires a high standard of attainment from the work-force. Instead, it relocates production that has a subcontracting and supporting function for the production in Singapore. Yet the productivity of the work-force is above the average for Indonesia, and the employees are given opportunities for further education at the BIP. On the other hand, the nature of the work-force is perfectly captured by the criterion 'industrious and disciplined.'

Regarding the factor 'well established global trading and financial links,' Singapore has developed a very adaptable strategy. Typical GLCs such as the Singapore Technologies Industrial Corporation, Jurong Environmental Engineering, and the Indonesian Salim Group, took up the cudgels for their investments. A significant number of MNCs in Singapore were informed about the BIP, and were offered key-ready facilities. In other words, Batam became an integrated part of the 'Singapore Metropolitan Region' as far as the MNCs and GLCs were concerned, which was also facilitated by the geographical proximity of Batam. For the citizens, obviously, the region did not work that way.

Turning to the sixth factor, 'relatively cheap labor,' it is obvious that the BIP lives up to this to a great extent. The 70 000 employees do not primarily come from the Province of Riau, but are mainly drawn from Java through an advanced recruitment system. Each year approximately 10 000 new workers are employed in this way. The young women are offered a two-year contract, which can be extended by one or more additional periods, with a salary considerably above the minimum wage in Indonesia. However, in comparison with Singapore, the wage level is of course very competitive.

Finally, regarding the factor 'excellent geo-economic position,' the proximity to Singapore ensures that the BIP shares the central location of Singapore.

Suzhou township

Eighty kilometers west of Shanghai, at Suzhou in the province of Jiangsu, we find Singapore's most ambitious venture in China, which was initiated in February 1994. Singapore-Suzhou township (ST) is often called 'Singapore II'. When ST has been fully developed in 20 to 30 years, it is planned to house 600 000 people and offer employment to 360 000 people, with total investments amounting to around US$20 billion.

The official history of its establishment goes back to the mid-1970s, when China's senior leader, Deng Xiaoping, made a historic state visit to Singapore. He was deeply impressed by Singapore's success, and inquired about the possibility of exploiting Singapore's experience in managing industrial estates. The then prime minister of Singapore, Lee Kuan Yew, responded by offering China an opportunity to learn about the 'software' behind Singapore's economic management. This visit was the precursor of deepened contacts and many meetings at different levels between representatives of the two states. Drawing on experiences from the Batam project, Singapore decided to commit itself to a number of cooperative ventures, including an attempt to create a large-scale Batam-inspired project. In October 1992, Singapore's deputy prime minister, Ong Teng Cheong, offered the following proposal to China: 'Give us a piece of Suzhou or Wuxi, and let us have a free hand to develop it fully for you. And if we do a good job of it, then other Chinese cities can emulate us.' (*Straits Times*, 10 October 1992). These townships were chosen because they were imbued with beautiful scenery to charm tourists yet, at the same time, had the robust modern character to attract foreign investors. The proximity to the metropolitan city of Shanghai was an additional reason for the choice of location. Another reason was the judgement that, as Shanghai takes off, this will spill over to Suzhou and Wuxi, whose relationships to Shanghai were considered to be analogous to Johor's and Batam's relationships with Singapore in the Growth Triangle. Six months later, the Chinese responded at Ong Teng Cheong's meeting with the Chinese deputy prime minister, Li Lanqing: 'Pick a site for any city it (Singapore) can help develop, and China will give the Republic favorable terms and conditions.' However, Mr Ong knew that Suzhou was classified as a 'coastal economic open area' (with a corporate tax rate of 24 per cent), while townships such as Nigbo and Pudong belonged to the category of 'coastal open cities,' which are more profitable from an investment point of view (i.e., a tax rate of 15 per cent). Also, the Chinese leaders were asked to submit proposals on townships with more significant comparative advantages than Suzhou.

Li Lanqing subsequently promised to afford Suzhou the same advantages as the 'coastal open cities,' and to investigate possible alternatives to Suzhou. This became the starting-point for stiff competitive bidding between Chinese provinces and townships for a 'mini-

Singapore.' The main adversaries in this bidding came to be Suzhou and townships in Shandong province. Eventually, Singapore decided to locate the new township at Suzhou. The question then arose as to what extent Suzhou would be able to emulate Singapore's features.

Regarding illiberal democracy, it seems likely that the authoritarian Chinese government does not expect any subversive political activity on Chinese soil as a part of the Suzhou concept. As far as we have been able to register, democracy was never an issue in this project. Nevertheless, the existing Chinese township, autonomous or not, was not a partner in this deal. Singapore has developed a number of institutional arrangements in order to strengthen the legitimacy of Singapore II. Thus, in February 1994, a joint body was created: The People's Republic of China (PRC) – Singapore Joint Steering Committee. The official task of this intergovernmental committee is to promote the smooth development of the township as well as to monitor and advise on the progress of the Singapore-Suzhou 'software transfer' project, whereby Singapore's economic and public administration will be made compatible with Suzhou's municipal political structure.

Such was the Chinese enthusiasm that the local government ceded majority control to the Singaporean side. This is the only place in China where a foreign government body has been given such a free hand. At the time, Zhang Xinsheng, the mayor of Suzhou, explained that Beijing's support reflected its preference for the example of Singapore's disciplined development to the *laissez-faire* Hong Kong model. The Chinese government would hence monitor the success of the industrial township, with a view to replicating the formula elsewhere in China.

In order to develop an efficient management structure, a precondition seemed to be that the township is being run separately from the surrounding context, thereby enjoying considerable institutional autonomy. In May 1994, 19 Singapore-based corporations created a company called Singapore-Suzhou Township Development Company (SSTD) for the purpose of developing Singapore II as a joint venture with the Suzhou United Development Company (SUD), which acts as the representative body of Suzhou's local government. Singaporean interests exert a great deal of influence in the joint venture China – Singapore Suzhou Industrial Park Development Co. Ltd (CSSD), since 65 per cent of the shares are controlled by the SSTD and 35 per cent by the SUD. In September of the same year, the Chinese government and the provincial authorities promised to grant autonomy to the township and to ensure the reliability and adequacy of its power supply. In principle, the township should have as much autonomy as possible in order to solve most problems internally

(*Straits Times*, 12 September 1994). The position of the CSSD was tested in October of the same year, when the industrial park decided to ban an unauthorized Chinese construction project, Zhong Fu Garden, from the area, even though that company had leased the land for fifty years and had undertaken major investments in water supply, bridges, telephone communications, roads, and electricity. The message was unambiguous: the local government of Suzhou no longer controlled the territory of the CSSD.[3]

Despite the intergovernmental concensus and the top-down model, a conflict arose between SIP and a rival industrial park, the Suzhou New District (SND), which was under the control of the Suzhou authorities. A regional conflict thus emerged between the top-down SIP and the bottom-up SND in spite of the centralized political structure of China. Being a city-state, Singapore had had no experience of dealing with local governments. The conflict became public when Suzhou's vice-mayor, Wang Jonhua, told a group of German investors in Hamburg in November 1997, that he disagreed that the SIP had the support of Chinese President Jiang Zemin, and further advised them to invest in China directly without consulting Singapore. In Cologne a few days later, he mentioned that all of Jiangsu's resources would go to the SND and not to the SIP: 'To restore confidence, we must resolve the problem openly... If we gloss over the issues, SIP will become another run-of-the-mill park, creating no special value for its shareholders, its tenants, or China.' In Singapore's parliament, senior minister Lee Kuan Yew said: 'We are in contact with them [the municipal government of Suzhou]. We are now studying the problem in order to have a considered, mature response which we will convey to the Chinese side as our view of how to deal with this problem. We expect the Chinese side to study that and give us their response in due course... President Jiang Zemin has given his full support to resolving the problem. Singapore too is fully committed to the success of SIP' (*Straits Times*, 15 January 1998).

However, it remains to be seen if governmental understanding is enough to solve the problem of the local competition between the parks. In any case, the situation illustrates the institutional weakness of SIP/BIP-solutions to regional growth which exists even in authoritarian states.

The second factor, 'one-stop and non-corrupt management', is certainly essential for the future of Suzhou. If the SIP has difficulties in the competition for international capital with the SND, it might demonstrate that investors are not impressed by the SSTD management and are willing to deal with Chinese bureaucracy.

The third factor, 'a developed physical infrastructure,' is a cornerstone of the entire project. The SSTD has had a significant influence in the decision-making about infrastructural investments in the township (Murray and Perera 1995, p. 70). The investments are divided into three phases, each of which runs over a period of 5 to 10 years. The area east of Suzhou City is located at the intersection of China's two main economic development belts: the Coastal and the Yangtze River economic belts. In addition, Suzhou township is linked by rail, expressways and waterways to major international airports and ports in Shanghai.

In the first phase, an 8 sq. km business center was planned and constructed, with office buildings, hotels and shopping complexes, and lakeside commercial and recreational facilities. Ready-built two-, four-, and six-story factories are to be constructed for lease or purchase by manufacturers. Investors may also choose to build their own factories. The range of industrial activities planned for the start-up area includes the production of everything from semiconductors to canned drinks. Residential developments and transportation infrastructure are also planned for the area (Murray and Perera 1995).

In the second phase, a technology hub will be constructed comprising high-tech industries and tertiary institutions and, in the third phase, an industrial town with factories requiring larger parcels of land will be established. In order to make the township self-sufficient from the problematic energy perspective in China, US$3 billion will be invested in a power plant with a generating capacity almost equal to all the electricity consumed in Singapore in 1993 (Tan 1995).

The fourth factor, 'an industrious, disciplined and well trained work-force,' is partly realized since the region historically belongs to the same cultural domain as Singapore. Yet it is obvious that the workforce in Suzhou will have a much lower productivity than in Singapore. Efficient management is also about knowledge, and therefore Singapore has involved itself in education programs for officials from Suzhou. It remains to be seen whether they will recruit prominent and relatively well educated officials. China has the largest labor market in the world, and Shanghai alone has a population of 14 million. In this perspective, the prospects are good for recruiting a mobile and highly skilled work-force. The predicament is how to organize the recruitment of 360 000 employees in 20 years, and to decide what kind of employees to recruit.

The fifth factor, 'well established global trading and financial links,' demands that Singapore can actually establish a nexus in the global networks far away from its own territory. In this connection, by introducing the notion of Singapore Inc., Singapore has produced a political innovation. The innovation is not the terminology itself, for this has been developed in other places, for instance in Hong Kong, but rather the method of providing substance to the concept. In the words of the official program, 'Singapore 2000':

> 'Singapore Inc.' describes Singapore's approach to economic development which involves the cooperation and support of all parties in Singapore – political leaders and government, institutions and academia, chambers of commerce and trade associations, industrialists and labor, foreign investors and local companies, and all who have identified themselves to be the nation's stakeholders. These stakeholders form Singapore Inc., working together like entities in a large corporation, each responsible for a specific aspect of Singapore's economic value chain.

Singapore Inc. is nothing less than an ambition to mobilize Singapore's total resources for transboundary regionalization, by using Singapore's own experiences of state-led growth. And, in this connection, no distinction is made between Singaporean companies and MNC's; they are all welcome to share this partnership. Perhaps the Suzhou township could be seen as the first real test of the Singapore Inc. vision.

The composition of the original fourteen investors in Suzhou (SSTD) in 1994, shows that seven came from Singapore. It is noteworthy that the initial investor was the Keppel Corporation, which is a typical Singaporean GLC. In January 1998, Singapore's government disclosed information concerning the invested capital in Suzhou for the first time. Total invested capital amounted to US$155.22m (of which Statutory Boards US$19.65, GLCs US$45.85, Singaporean companies US$65.50 and non-Singaporean MNCs US$24.22, which implies that nearly half the investments are politically motivated) (*Straits Times*, 15 January 1998).

The sixth factor, 'relatively cheap labor,' is definitely applicable to the SIP. The possibility of recruiting cheap labor appears to be almost inexhaustible, though recruiting skilled labor is much more difficult, since stiff competition exists from the rapidly expanding Shanghai region, potentially leading to higher labor costs for the skilled segment of the work-force.

Finally, the seventh factor, 'excellent geo-economic location,' is of course difficult to reproduce outside of Singapore. Even though the location is hardly as strategic as that of Singapore, the proximity to Shanghai implies major advantages. A favorable development of tourism in the old city of Suzhou may also induce investments in efficient transport systems and increase the attractiveness of the location.

Regional transplants: a key to success?

The analysis of the role model (Batam) and the blueprint (Suzhou) projects shows that in the 1990s, Singapore is trying to develop modernized Singapore-style enclaves in traditional East Asian environments. The starting point is always 'green field planning'; it is considered necessary to start from square one, and to build a brand new community based upon principles and institutions quite different from those of the surrounding context. Existing villages and infrastructure in the 'green fields' are swept away, as happened to around 7000 farmers in the case of Suzhou. So far, the venture has been successful in the sense that investments are implemented and that there is economic growth. A more narrow focus on the benefits conferred on Singapore and individual MNCs is, of course, interesting, yet a more crucial question is whether these enclaves may generate growth beyond their local boundaries, that is to say within the wider regional economy.

With the incorporation of Hong Kong in the summer of 1997, yet another modernized enclave is to be found within China's borders. It is most likely that Hong Kong, with its larger scale and tradition of independence, will inspire more significant waves of regional development than Suzhou, but perhaps it will also lead to a delicate political situation for investors. There is no counterpart to Suzhou's Singaporean institutional umbrella in Hong Kong, aside from official declarations of 'one country, two systems.' Still, the official guarantees for the autonomy of the SIP are probably of less significance than the informal pressure of the international community on China to fulfill its Hong Kong commitment. China has more to lose in Hong Kong than in Suzhou in terms of face and international credibility. In the long run, the success of the Suzhou township depends on the MNC's evaluation of its comparative advantages and the political risks in China.

The unresolved question is whether Suzhou township is compatible with the present political and economic system in China. An additional question is whether in the future Suzhou township will be associated with the *ancien regime*, or if it will be considered an early spearhead of later developments. It also remains to be seen how regional development in China will be affected by the Singaporean presence.

It is of course still too early to evaluate the Singaporean model of regional development. Today we know more about the volume of infrastructure investments, the size of the work-force, and the organization of the parks than about productivity and profits. Some signs of weakness have however already appeared, which are predominantly related to the top-down blue-print approach to growth. In small one-level city-states it is perhaps possible to combine centralized decision-making with flexibility and openness. If the same model is transplanted into huge multi-level political systems, the rigidity of plans and bureaucratic organizations become real problems. In China, as well as in Indonesia, the new parks have generated conflicts with established regional and local governments. In spite of the authoritarian character of both China and Indonesia, those countries cannot, in practice, implement regional growth plans if they disregard local actors and enterprises. The confrontation between bottom-up-oriented SND and top-down-constructed SIP illustrates this institutional dilemma. Given the fact that global production increasingly is organized in production networks, which are difficult to control politically and demand a high level of flexibility, this dilemma is profound. The Singapore model is also challenged by alternative spontaneous strategies of market-led regional development. But that is a topic for another paper.

Notes

1. The Economic Committees' Report. ECR: Singapore, pp. 76–7.
2. For a general analysis of the Growth Triangles in East Asia, see Toh and Low (1993).
3. The developer CFC Suzhou Development Corporation received a letter from its firm of lawyers, Lee and Lee, advising it not to proceed with the launch that day: 'It would appear that the approvals and permits obtained earlier by CFC Suzhou Development Corporation for the proposed development are no longer valid. As such, CFC may not be able to claim ownership to the land which CFC intends to develop and any construction proceeded with on the land would be demolished' (*Straits Times*, 10 October 1994).

References

Murray, G. and A. Perera, *Singapore: The Global St*ate (Folkestone, Kent: China Library, 1995).

Somjee, A.H. and G. Somjee, *Development Success in Asia Pacific* (New York: St. Martin's Press, 1995).

Tan, C.H., *Venturing Overseas: Singapore's External Wing* (Singapore: McGraw-Hill, 1995).

Toh, M.H. and L. Low, *Regional Cooperation and Growth Triangles in ASEAN* (Singapore: Academic Times, 1993).

18

Japanese Transition to Knowledge Arenas: an Infrastructural Perspective

Kiyoshi Kobayashi

Macroeconomic and regional corridors are developing in Europe, North America, and South-East Asia. In the Pacific Rim, the rudiments of an East Asian development corridor have become identifiable, incorporating the Japan Corridor and cutting across China, Korea, Taiwan and Hong Kong. A Southeast Asian corridor can also be recognized and a merger between the two is possible in the future. The key to understanding contemporary regional integration occurring in Asia Pacific lies in transnational interactions among individuals, firms, and organizations. The independent policy options of states have been limited by structural change in international political economies.

Since the 1980s, structural change in finance, technology, knowledge and politics has led to growing interdependence and increased rivalries both among states and among firms. The end of the Cold War era has lowered the political barriers to transnational trade in goods and services, and encouraged flows of capital, labor, technology and information. The integration of these new areas into the world economic system have been matched by a new regionalism. The intensification of rivalries between states and regions in the world economy is leading to the creation of transnational economic corridors, brought about to combat uncertainties and unpredictability stemming from the transition of an industrial age into a knowledge-based one. Already, many integrated regional economies have been recognized in Asia Pacific as part of a new economic and world alignment. Although it lacks the cohesion of regions like the EU and NAFTA right now, it is exemplified on a macro-scale by the Asian-Pacific Economic Cooperation (APEC) forum.

After the explosion of the economic bubble in the early 1990s, the Japanese economy has struggled for structural transition from being an industrial economy to becoming a knowledge-based one. This transition may be observed when we consider the fact that the Japanese working population reached its peak at the end of 1994. It is forecast that after the year 2007, the nation's population will decrease dramatically at a rate that no other country has ever experienced. The Japanese economy has enjoyed increasing returns brought about by an increased population. Population increase enlarges the size of a market, allowing for greater specialization in resource utilization, which in turn increases the productivity of all inputs. However, the Japanese economy can no longer enjoy economic fruits brought about by population increase today. Newer sources of increasing returns should be sought.

Knowledge as a source of increasing returns

In the *Wealth of Nations*, Adam Smith identified the primary source of economic development to be the division or specialization of labor, whose effectiveness depends on the size of the market (Smith, 1776). Much more value can be generated in an economy where different persons, or groups of persons, produce different goods and then exchange these goods among themselves. In the past, families moved closer to the inherited previous locators and towns took shape, specialization increased. Innovation in transportation and communication both preceded and followed increases in specialization. Individuals and families came to accept the complex interlinkage of a wide market nexus as a natural phenomenon. Put differently, Smith's ideas can be elaborated in terms of increasing returns to the size of the whole network of exchange, and to the size of the economy as measured by quantities of inputs supplied to the nexus.

The rediscovery of Allyn Young's economic ideas brought an advance in understanding widely observed increases in returns in many different economies throughout the world (Young, 1928). Young's approach to the origins of increasing returns entailed a detailed analysis of Smith's division of labor. As part of their modernization journey, higher income countries are argued to have achieved greater increasing returns owing to: 1) division of labor, 2) specialization, 3) advances in technology, 4) augmentation of human capital, 5) ideas and knowledge as economic entities, 6) institution as an economic entity, 7) economic organization, and 8) restoration of economic equilibrium.

More recently, economists and engineers have acknowledged the importance of knowledge as a major source of increasing returns (Romer,

1986; Lucas, 1988), in particular, the public-goods-like property of knowledge (Kobayashi *et al.,* 1991). If knowledge can be shared by individuals, firms, and organizations, it becomes a non-rival but partially excludable good. The common usage of knowledge can help to increase the productivity of knowledge production and consumption. The possibility might even exist that average production costs would decrease with higher outputs of industries, even though individual firms may have adopted decreasing-returns-to-scale technology. Knowledge can be invested in production without being used up. This idea is akin to the concept of externality by Marshall (Marshall, 1876). The external effects of knowledge in the form of human capital spill over from one person to another. At each skill level people are more productive in high human-capital environments, and human capital enhances the productivity of both labor and physical capital. Arthur (1994) extended Marshall's insight by observing that, although the parts of the economy that are resource-based are still for the most part subject to diminishing returns, the important parts of the economy that are knowledge-based are largely subject to increasing returns. Increasing returns makes for many possible equilibrium points. Once accidental events select a particular path, the choice may become locked-in regardless of the advantages of the alternatives. Steering an economy with increasing returns into the best of its many possible equilibrium states requires good timing. Theory can help to identify these states, and guide policy-makers in applying the right amount of efforts to dislodge locked-in structures (Arthur, 1994).

The productivity of knowledge

Developed countries spend roughly one-fifth of their GNP on the production and dissemination of knowledge. Formal schooling costs about one-tenth of GNP. However, very few countries set aside a similar portion of their GNP to accumulate traditional capital. Yet the productivity of knowledge has become more decisive in a country's economic and social success today. Knowledge is effectively transnational and perfectly mobile. It cannot be controlled any longer by states, and not even by states acting together. In this respect, no country has any natural advantage or disadvantage. The only advantage that a country has is how it makes knowledge universally available. The one thing that will increasingly matter in national as well as in international economies, is a country's geographical and psychological ability in making knowledge more accessible.

The economic aspect of knowledge exchangeability can be illustrated in a simple way in the context of bilateral face-to-face contacts. The benefits of meetings are attributed to all the agents concerned. The agreement to the meeting by the concerned agents is the premise for the realization of this type of contact. The meeting fails if either of the two does not agree to it. The extent of this failure is likely to rise with increasing scarcity of time, which makes it more pressing to decline a meeting.

As the market becomes more extensive, covering a wider spectrum of life, more incentives to meet others are needed. Similarly, with subjective cost of time rising, the pressure to balance the advantage of face-to-face contacts will increase. As long as the time cost is relatively low, and because of fewer opportunities for additional work, the net cost of each specific time-absorbing activity connected with face-to-face contacts will also be relatively low. The effect is to whittle down the number of face-to-face contacts to a level that leaves everyone wishing they had more at the expense of fewer material goods.

The large increase in personal mobility in knowledge economies adds to the problem by making interactability more of a public and less of a private good. The more people move, the lower will be the chances of face-to-face contacts being reciprocated directly on a bilateral basis. As Tibor Scitovsky asserted, since interactability is not bought and sold, an external economy is involved and individual decisions will lead to suboptimal interactability (Scitovsky, 1976). The optimum requires socially rational behavior where individual rationality is modified by adherence to moral rules, and activated incentives for more contacts, or something similar.

The increased pressure on time helps to explain why these interactions are now under strain. If interactability develops progressively, public benefits are more evenly distributed and interactability will become less responsive to individual demand. We may want interactability more than ever to increase knowledge productivity, yet we cannot, individually and separately, express that want in a way that secures it. This analysis helps to explain a frequent casual observation, which otherwise appears economically puzzling, that human contact in knowledge economies is increasingly sought but decreasingly attained.

In this chapter, we contend that the view that the advent of advanced telecommunications technology will substitute part of face-to-face communications is rather misleading. There are irreconcilable dilemmas between the increase of knowledge productivity and that of time value. This leads us to ask the following question: how can we improve knowledge exchangeability under the pressure of increasing time value by use of more advanced infrastructural arrangements? In what follows, the basic suggestions pertaining to improvements in exchangeability are discussed from two different points of view on infrastructural arrangements: the work ethic as moral (non-physical) infrastructure, and communication networks as knowledge (physical) infrastructure.

Work ethic as moral infrastructure

Long-term tendencies towards a shorter working-time society can be observed in every advanced country. However, the benefits arising from less working-time need further scrutiny. Leisure is different from other valued end uses of resources because it is a non-market good. It is also beyond the set of goods that are produced within the network of economic interdependence that determines the range of specialization (Buchanan, 1994). Each person produces his or her own leisure; specialization in production of this good is logically impossible. The increase of leisure time inevitably diminishes the externality in the public domain.

In individual work and leisure choices, one takes into account a significant but less known externality. The individual's choice to work more generates external benefits to others. The efficiency of knowledge exchange also largely relies upon this type of externality. This externality can be typically illustrated by shops' opening hours. If shops open weekends, everyone (except workers in shops) is made better off thanks to the additional availability of shop services. An economy in which all persons simply allow their naked preferences to mandate their choices between work and leisure will not be efficient. All persons can be made better off, by their own reckoning, by a scheme that gives incentives to everyone to increase the supply of work on the part of everyone else.

There should be a socially optimal allocation of one's time resources between work and leisure. The optimal level of leisure time is, of course, conditional to the level of communication technology and on the level of infrastructural services available. But we lack devices and mechanisms that can achieve the social optimal allocation of time resources. The contractual processes of political and economic exchange preclude the optimal allocation of time resources and more incentives for mutual interactability. The natural outlet for such incentives is investment in those institutions that embody attempts to modify behavior non-contractually (Buchanan, 1994). Each participant has an incentive to invest more resources in enhancing interactions, even though free-ridership may emerge here as with all public relationships. We should acknowledge that preferences may themselves be modified in

Table 18.1 The comparison of working-time composition

Working time by category	*Japan*	*Germany*	*France*
Total working time	10.29 hrs./day	9.46 hrs./day	9.07 hrs./day
Working time in office	8.51	7.57	8.02
Real working	7.34	7.39	7.32
Lunch	0.25	0.55	0.34
Taking rest in office	0.31	0.00	0.07
Idling time before jobs	0.37	0.18	0.11
Other	0.11	0.00	0.09
Commuting	1.38	1.22	1.05
Part-time jobs	0.00	0.27	0.00
Working for family	0.07	0.21	1.18

Note: This working-time composition is calculated only for the men working at the headquarters of the major private companies.
Source: Yuzawa 1995.

the process of socialization and acculturation in such a way that describes the operation of the whole social environment in which a person exchanges their ideas and knowledge.

For the Japanese, there have been no clear distinctions between public and private domains in daily lives, and between leisure and work. As shown in Table 18.1, although there are no substantial differences in real working time among the Japanese, Germans and French, most Japanese tend to consume more time resources for informal activities in offices than the Germans and French. The Japanese sense of leisure can be interpreted as the means through which they internalize the work choice externality. The Confucian sense of guilt in loafing – a work ethic – exerts, to some extent, beneficial effects. This work ethic becomes a major source of comparative advantage for this country. It is clearly possible that under some circumstances, the ethical constraints can become overly severe, and thereby act to reduce rather than increase the individual's well-being.

Knowledge, under Confucianism, is knowing what to say and how to say it, all of which contribute to advancement and earthly success. Formal knowledge is seen as both a key personal resource and a key economic resource. The traditional factors of production, like physical capital, labor and land become increasingly secondary. They can be easily obtained if there is knowledge. Knowledge in this new context is knowledge as a utility, and the means to obtain social and economic results.

We do not require that a person exhibits a preference for his or her own preferences with some view towards reforms aimed at becoming a more developed person as defined by preferences (Sen, 1982; Becker, 1996). Each of us is concerned with the knowledge of tastes and preferences of others than ourselves. Whereas it seems quite straightforward to postulate that a person's preference is exogenously determined and not subjected to his/her own meta preferences, we cannot extend the exogeneity to imply that my preferences are totally immune to influence by others' preferences. There are hidden linkages among people's preferences. In this circulation, a person's preferences are endogenous. Knowledge for a better life and being a better human being is a prime input for preference change. Work ethics need no longer be applied to work itself, but to knowledge work. No distinctions between work and leisure are necessary in knowledge work as seen in the Japanese sense of work. Knowledge work should be made over the full spectrum of ones' activities. Thus, quite naturally, we can conclude that the knowledge orientation of preference networks is a central policy issue for the transformation of Japanese society into a knowledge-based one. This task is common to all Confucian-based societies in East Asia.

Communication networks as knowledge infrastructure

Palander has pointed out the importance of communication costs in location decisions of the city. This moves beyond the scope of the pioneering works by Thünen and other earlier works in location theory (Palander, 1935). According to Palander, one of the most conspicuous characteristics of modern city activities is the frequent and wide range of communications activities with other cities. The amount of knowledge produced and concentrated in the big cities is increasing remarkably.

Human beings exchange their scientific ideas (such as knowledge and information), psychological services (such as friendship and affection), and goods through meetings. If the thing to be exchanged differs, the frequency and characteristics also differ. The one-to-one communication is the elemental form of meeting and the most common way to exchange ideas in the most condensed manner. This form of communication is most frequently conducted in exchanges related to psychological services such as friendship and affection. Similarly, in the case of scientific ideas, one-to-one communication allows people to exchange ideas with high concentration. The one-to-one meeting is, however, not always the most effective way of knowledge exchange. The progress of a society as it becomes a knowledge-based one, based on high levels of

Table 18.2 The comparison of network characteristics

	Transportation Network	*Human Network*
Node	Origin; Destination	Individual
Link	Roads; Railways	Meeting; Communication
Input	Trip demand	Idea; Friendship, etc.
Output	Realized trips	Evolution of ideas; Deepening of friendships, etc.
Observable variable	Transportation trip	Number of meetings
State variable(s)	Transportation conditions	Functions of ideas, friendship etc.
Objective variable(s)	Travel time; Costs	Exchange of knowledge and ideas
Medium	Transportation methods	Discussion
Activity reachability	Long distance	Short distance

research and development, leads to an increase in the variety of scientific ideas and also in the frequency of knowledge exchange. If all the knowledge exchanges are done by one-to-one contacts, then the total number of exchanges should increase exponentially. If a large number of people gather in the same places such as conferences and conventions, the efficiency of knowledge exchange would be improved extensively.

Traffic and communication behaviors expand on two kinds of networks: the 'human network' and the 'physical network'. Except for traffic behaviors conducted independently from other decision makers, these two networks play important roles in the realization of traffic and communications systems. Table 18.2 clarifies the characteristic differences of the transportation network and the human network, both of which play substantial roles in the face-to-face communication aspect (Beckmann 1994).

The human network is the network from which scientific ideas, psychological services and other ideas flow. One remarkable characteristic of the human network is that the individual human functions as a node which accumulates ideas, and the meeting is a link where ideas are exchanged. In the human network, 'whether to meet or not', 'where to meet and when', and others are determined. Here, the 'agreement by all participants' is a fundamental principle, and the decision-making by several people is part of the formation of a meeting. On the other hand, the physical network basically consists of the 'telecommunications network' and the 'transportation network'. In the telecommunications network, the network itself functions as the medium from which meetings may be realized; for example, facsimiles. In this case, the monetary and temporal resources to be consumed by the communicating agents are relatively low. Although the parties concerned communicate with one another while implicitly taking for granted the formation of communication, no mutual agreements by parties is required. This form of network, with fewer requirements and conditions for pre-agreement on communication and meeting, constitutes an efficient method of organizing meetings.

A node and a link in the communication network do not always correspond to a node and a link in the human network. Individuals who are nodes in the human network, move along the links in the transportation network. Many meetings use meeting facilities (nodes) such as hotels, convention halls, and cafés in town. The household, an important link in the human network, is also a node in the transportation network. The consultations made in transit and the unexpected chat with strangers represent the cases where the link in the transportation network is utilized as a link in the human network.

One remarkable characteristic of the transportation network is that decision-making on usage of the network is entrusted to the discretion of the persons who make trips in the network. The transportation network is a place which many trip-makers use simultaneously, and each individual decision is affected by the 'results' from the decisions made by others. Therefore, the concern here is the 'result' of decisions made by many and unspecified persons, and no agreement among the participating individuals is formed. In the transportation network, without any agreement, individuals have to make decisions under uncertain conditions. The decisions under uncertainty may not lead to a socially preferable, efficient and effective state. The transportation and traffic information provided by public sectors may induce individual behaviors, resulting in more desirable decisions as a whole.

As societies become more knowledge-based, many social and economic fundamental structures will be reorganized. For example, the standardization of the five-day-week system, or, progress in research and development, would change the structure of, and decisions in, the human network. This may lead to a change in individual traffic behaviors. Micro surveys on individual traffic behaviors based on the fundamental paradigm of methodological individualism has contributed to the clarification of individual traffic behaviors. Such surveys, however, investigate the traffic behaviors in the transportation network, and therefore bring about highly limited and fragmented information on the meeting behaviors in the human network. There is still a long way to go before one can fully grasp the whole picture of meeting, which is one of the most fundamental communication forms in the modern knowledge society.

The future of communication networks in a knowledge society

Traditionally, the consolidation of the network infrastructure has concentrated on the refinement of its function of linkage. In the knowledge society, however, the function of the nodes will play an increasingly important role. It is especially noteworthy that in the human network the meeting functions as the fundamental linkage. The spatially fixed meeting facilities are important network factors constituting the nodes of the physical network. The human network, however, is not spatially fixed in its location. A meeting can be held when the persons are in a transport network. Conferences utilizing virtual reality reflect technology that links spatially distant locations as if they were on the same node.

The nodes connect different links systematically. In order to fulfill complicating meeting demands on the human network, it is necessary to construct and reinforce a complex network with various nodes. Also, marketing strategies to provide new types of traffic services made up of the combination of information services and the various conventional traffic services are necessary. The city is the accumulated place of nodes constituting various physical networks, such as nodes connecting the city to other outside regions. The density and efficiency of the nodes are primary conditions for expansion of the networks in the knowledge society.

The future of the cities in the knowledge arenas depends on the realization of the mutual effects of human and physical networks. In the short run, the human network determines the city potential. The structure of this human network is, however, very vulnerable and unstable. It is possible that one decision made in the human network changes the fundamental structure of the network in a moment. Examples are the founding, separation and discontinuance of scientific societies and associations. The hub structure of the network may also change drastically. The human network, however, is dependent on the structure of the physical network in the long run. The physical networks evolve slowly; thus, the physical networks can be regarded as being constant or stable in the short run. On this physical network, the human networks self-organize. While the physical network gradually evolves, approaches, and eventually exceeds a certain threshold, the human networks in the short term can still possibly make catastrophic changes. A node at a comparatively disadvantageous position has the chance to recover its potential in the long run, if it holds a highly advanced accessibility position in the physical network.

Asia Pacific's economic landscape is in the process of being re-made. Increasing interdependence is clearly observed in the change of point-to-point interactions between spatially dispersed locations. The global communications networks in the Pacific Rim have a discrete structure and will have a hub and spoke character. Figure 18.1 shows the major non-stop flight routes in the Pacific Rim as at August 1989. The most impressive feature is the major corridor between Jakarta and Taipei, in which Hong Kong plays an important and pivotal role, stemming from its connections with China. The key feature, however, is Tokyo's role as the dominant gateway to Asia Pacific arising from its strong local markets within Japan, and its being a fuel stop on trans-Pacific flights. Within these corridors, network hubs are benefiting from being national and international finance centers and headquarters of global network corporations. They are trying to capture potential synergies and collective knowledge inherent in the dominant communications and transport networks (Rimmer, 1991).

The development of the Japan Corridor is being contrasted with an emerging East Asian development corridor. The Japan Corridor has only been designed to accommodate Japanese corporations rather than to attract overseas investors. It does not open to neighboring countries. Tokyo has been a major network hub in international air transport and telecommunications. This has resulted in the relative neglect of its regional role in East Asia. Reference to the Japan Corridor is too narrow because of the rapid economic growth brought about by the transnationalization of Japanese capital and post-Cold War changes occurring in Asia Pacific. After the collapse of Japan's bubble economy, there has been some restructuring through investments by corporations with headquarters in Hong Kong, South Korea and Taiwan. Against an ever-increasing demand for contacts, dynamic coordination of logistical networks in the Pacific Rim can only be sustained by the creation of well coordinated, multi-layered, multi-modal transport and communications infrastructure in these areas. The implication for each nation's policies is that the past preoccupation with short-term futures, based on classical principles of planning and systems science, may need to be abandoned in favor of long-term strategic planning, the focus of which is on qualitative features of a dynamic integration process. The new planning approach may be identified more with abilities to understand

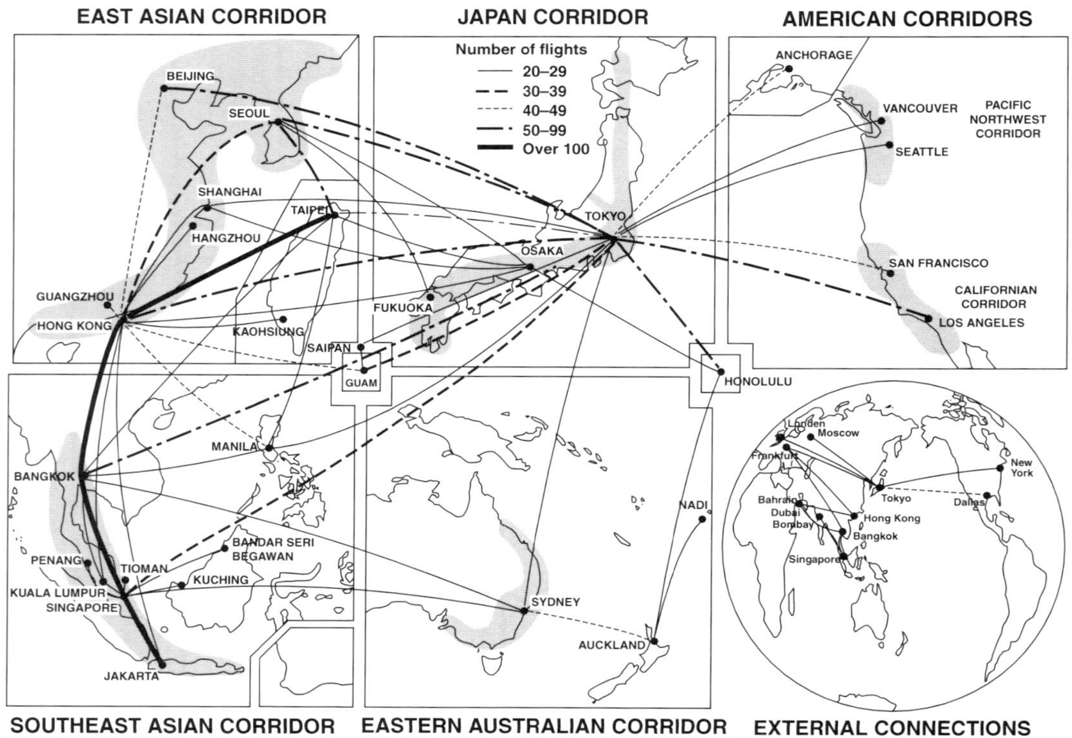

Figure 18.1 Twenty or more non-stop flights in the Pacific Rim
Source: Rimmer, P.J., 1991 'The emerging infrastructural arena in Pacific Asia since the early 1970s', *Proc. of Japan Society of Civil Engineers*, Vol. 431)

the complexity of societies and economies. Instead of ensuring that decision makers' choices lead to their desired ends, the emphasis will be on whether their decisions lead to ends which are ethically desirable for present and future generations.

Conclusion

The knowledge orientation of various networks is the new engine for economic development in a knowledge-based society. This is especially true for Japan. Traditional sources of increasing returns will no longer function sufficiently, once Japan shifts into a new era of declining population. For further progress in society, the togetherness of various sources of increasing returns has to work as Allyn Young postulated. The major focuses for increasing returns are upon knowledge, not upon market sizes. As a society matures with shorter working weeks, the work–leisure choices become more crucial in determining the productivity of knowledge. Human interactability becomes a major factor in explaining a nation's comparative advantage. Society is required to increase human interactability under the pressure of the increasing value of time. The exploitation of an economy of scope in preferences and knowledge networks will become a central policy issue for Japan in the twenty-first century.

References

Arthur, W.B., *Increasing Returns and Path Dependence in the Economy* (Ann Arbor: University of Michigan Press, 1994).

Becker, G.S., *Accounting for Tastes* (Cambridge, Mass.: Harvard University Press, 1996).

Beckmann, M.J., 'Knowledge Networks, The Case of Scientific Interaction at a Distance', *Annals of Regional Science*, 28 (1994) 233–42.

Buchanan, J.M., *Ethics and Economic Progress* (Norman: University of Oklahoma Press, 1994).

Kobayashi, K., D.F. Batten, and Å.E. Andersson, 'The Sequential Location of Knowledge-oriented Firms over Time and Space', *Papers of Regional Science Association*, 70 (1991) 381–97.

Lucas, R.E., 'On the Mechanics of Economic Development', *Journal of Monetary Economics*, 22 (1988) 3–22.

Marshall, A., *Principles of Economics* (London: Macmillan, 1876).

Palander, T., *Beitrage zur Standortstheorie* (Uppsala, 1935).

Rimmer, P.J., 'The Emerging Infrastructural Arena in Pacific Asia since the Early 1970s', *Proc. of Japan Society of Civil Engineers*, 431 (1991) 1–17.

Romer, P.M., 'Increasing Returns and Long-Run Growth', *Journal of Political Economy*, 94 (1986) 1002–37.

Scitovsky, T., *The Joyless Economy* (New York: Oxford University Press, 1976).
Sen, A., *Choice, Welfare and Measurement* (London: Basil Blackwell, 1982).
Smith, A., *An Inquiry into the Nature and Causes of the Wealth of Nations*, in E. Cannan (ed.), Vol. 2 (New York: Methuen, 1976).
Young, A.A., 'Increasing Returns and Economic Progress', *Economic Journal*, 38 (1928) 527–40.
Yuzawa, Y., *Kazokumondai no Genzai (The Contemporary Issues around the Households)* (NHK Books, 1995).

19
Emerging Knowledge Networks in Eastern Asia

David E. Andersson

There are many different kinds of international networks. The import and export of goods and services are perhaps the most dissected network phenomenon. It is much less common to analyze scientific papers from a network perspective. Such an analysis can, however, provide information about much more than the location of important linkages. Geographically discrete agglomerations of specialized knowledge are only a partial cause of cross-border cooperation. Cultural, historical, and political affinities are other important factors.

When politicians or journalists describe trade between countries, they often convey the impression that countries are like gigantic, horizontally and vertically integrated, corporations. Japan exports cars to the United States while the United States exports word-processing programs to Japan. Such an interpretation is almost entirely specious. The overwhelming majority of all international networks come into existence because actors in the market make decentralized decisions with the objective of maximizing utilities or profits. When Acer exports a personal computer from a plant in Taiwan to a consumer in the United States, it is because the firm attempts to increase its profits while the buyer wants to increase her utility.

The same process (mostly) explains scientific cooperation. Although it sometimes happens that governments dispatch scientific delegations to shore up political alliances, it is much more common that cooperation results from individual decisions. Such cooperation could, for example, be triggered by a Korean graduate deciding to pursue graduate studies at Stanford, or by a chance meeting between participants at some international conference.

There are many conceivable measures of scientific cooperation. I have chosen to measure it by looking at co-authored articles in recognized

Table 19.1 Scientific nodes in East Asia: total number of published co-authored articles in three urban regions, science, medicine, and engineering, 1990–94

Urban region	*Number of articles*	*Population (1990)*
Taipei–Taoyuan–Hsinchu	14 696	8 200 000
Hong Kong	7 299	6 300 000
Singapore	6 031	3 100 000

Source: Science Citation Index

journals in the natural sciences, medicine, and engineering.[1] Most earlier studies have focused on Western Europe or North America (Andersson and Persson, 1993; Wichmann-Matthiessen and Andersson, 1993). By contrast, the area of interest in this study is East and Southeast Asia. The countries included are the six so-called 'Dynamic Asian Economies' (DAEs) of Hong Kong, Malaysia, Singapore, South Korea, Taiwan, and Thailand. I shall look at which countries within, and without, the region the DAEs cooperate with, as well as test various hypotheses regarding the causes of scientific cooperation.

The total number of co-authored articles is not evenly distributed within the region. The urban region centered on Taipei generated the greatest number of co-authored papers between 1990 and 1994, followed by Hong Kong and Singapore (Table 19.1). The scientific cooperation profiles also differ markedly between the DAEs. Quantitatively, the most important links are between Taiwan and the United States and between South Korea and the United States (Table 19.2). Interactions within the region are much less common. The most important link, between Taiwan

Table 19.2 Extra-DAE cross-border co-authorships in science, medicine, and engineering, Dynamic Asian Economies, 1990–94

Authors' countries of residence	*Number of published co-authored articles*
Taiwan – United States	3099
South Korea – United States	2836
South Korea – Japan	893
Hong Kong – United States	721
Thailand – United States	586
Hong Kong – Britain	566
Singapore – United States	467
Hong Kong – China	446
Taiwan – Japan	382
Singapore – Britain	374

Source: Science Citation Index.

Table 19.3 Intra-DAE cross-border co-authorships in science, medicine, and engineering, Dynamic Asian Economies, 1990–94

Authors' countries of residence	*Number of published co-authored articles*
Hong Kong – Taiwan	98
Hong Kong – Singapore	55
Singapore – Taiwan	44
Malaysia – Singapore	39
South Korea – Taiwan	36
Hong Kong – Malaysia	27

Source: Science Citation Index.

and Hong Kong, comprises fewer than a hundred co-authorships (Table 19.3).

Another interesting aspect is to look at which countries outside the region are over-represented in cooperating with the six countries. Since we can expect countries with large economies to contain relatively more scientific activities than small countries, we first adjust for differences in Gross Domestic Product when describing the level of interactivity. Such a comparison reveals that scientists in English-speaking countries are most likely to collaborate with Asian scientists. Except for Switzerland, the only countries that surpass the United States in their interactivity levels with the DAEs are Australia, Britain, Canada, and New Zealand (Table 19.4). Not even Japan reaches America's level of interactivity, and scientists in continental Europe do very little scientific research together with DAE scientists. Moreover, it seems as if different countries differ in their relative

Table 19.4 GDP-adjusted co-authorships with DAEs, selected OECD countries, US = 100, 1990–94

Country	*PPP$ Index*	*MER$ Index*
Australia	192	240
New Zealand	154	208
Britain	143	158
Switzerland	109	66
Canada	107	119
United States	100	100
Japan	60	33
France	31	26
Germany	30	25
Italy	18	19

Source: Science Citation Index.

interactivity within the region. While American scientists cooperate extensively with South Korea and Taiwan, the cooperation partners of Britons and Australians are mostly in Hong Kong and Singapore. French and German scientists, on the other hand, almost exclusively cooperate with South Korea.

Explaining cooperation patterns

Andersson and Persson (1993) have shown how some very realistic assumptions lead to a gravity-type reduced form. The assumptions build on Narin and Whitlow's (1990) observation that international co-authored papers are cited more than twice as frequently as other papers. Assuming that an individual scientist has a quantitative production expressed as the number of published papers (q_i), the (expected) quality (v_i) then depends on the frequency of co-authorships with scientists (j) in other countries for L_{ij} $(j = 1,...,m)$. Additional assumptions are diminishing marginal quality of scientific contacts between two scientists, and increasing marginal quality of contacts as a function of the production volume of the other scientist. Finally, we assume the price of contacts to be an increasing function of distance. The distance measure may include travel time and so called affinity factors, for example language commonalities. On the macro-level, we can formalize this as

$$(\delta v_i/\delta L_{ij}) = L_{ij}^{-\beta} q_j^{a}; \qquad 0 < \alpha, \beta < 1$$

Then

$$L_{ij} = q_i^{\lambda_1} q_j^{\lambda_2} c_{ij}^{-\mu}$$

where L_{ij} = frequency of contacts from region i to region j, q_i = article production in region i, q_j = article production in region j, c_{ij} is unit cost of contacts between i and j, $\lambda_1 = 1/\beta$; $\lambda_2 = \alpha/\beta$; $\mu = 1/\beta$. This implies that the advantage of visiting a (foreign) region is proportional to a weighted product of the time spent interacting and the scientific production of j.

A common assumption in applications of the gravity model is that the number of interactions between two nodes is a decreasing function of geographical distance, other things being equal. When the time cost of the geographical distance is subject to long-haul economies, the geographical distance becomes a non-linear effect. This is even true of the in-flight time in air transportation, because of the magnitudes and variations in the collection and distribution portions of the trip. Apart from the distance effect, gravity models offer a favorable framework for testing hypotheses on affinity and barrier effects. For example, one recurrent hypothesis is that two regions with the same language will have more interactions than two regions with different languages.

The specification of a gravity model for scientific interactions requires consideration of several questions. After formulating reasonable hypotheses, we also must specify the functional relationship (for example, are we dealing with a continuous effect or a 'threshold effect'?). As mentioned above, we may expect a region to cooperate more with a neighboring than with a distant region. Since most international meetings involve air transportation, the travel time by air seems a pertinent measure. Apart from the distance effect, we may also expect large countries to engender more interactions than small ones. Most earlier studies have used the number of published articles as the measure of the size of a country or region. This study departs from that tradition by looking at the hypothesized underlying causes of scientific production: the size of the economy and the level of economic development. Apart from that, we may expect two countries of comparable size to interact more than a large and a small country with a comparable combined economic output. Hence, we define the size effect as the product of the GDPs of country i and country j, not the sum of the two amounts.

Underdeveloped economies tend to specialize in agricultural production, whereas developing countries tend to be at various stages of industrialization. The most advanced economies, on the other hand, increasingly specialize in the production of knowledge. A high volume of scientific research should thus reflect a high level of economic development. My gravity model uses *per capita* GDP as the measure of economic development. By analogy with the size effect, I use products rather than sums.

An accurate conversion of currencies into a numeraire currency is a somewhat elusive problem. The traditional method is to use market exchange rates (MER), which would be the preferred method if the currency market were in equilibrium. Such an equilibrium also would imply stable exchange rates and uniform prices (if we disregard transport costs and the price of immobile assets such as land). The historical evidence, however, shows that strong disequilibrating forces are intrinsic to the currency market, not least in Asia. An alternative exchange rate is the purchasing-power parity (PPP) exchange rate, which has been constructed to account for international differences in the price of goods and services. This rate is often regarded as an approximate equilibrium rate. A problem with purchasing-power parities is that the relative weighting of goods and services is far from obvious and should,

Table 19.5 Nominal US dollar GDP model. Dependent variable: ln(x) of co-authored articles involving country i^a and j^b, 1990–94

Variable	*Coefficient (b)*	*t-value*
Constant	–6.25	
ln of time distance	–0.44	–3.7
ln (GDP_i) * ln (GDP_j)	0.81	11.9
ln (*per capita* GDP_i) * ln (*per capita* GDP_j)	0.07	1.1
Ethnic Chinese majority[c]	1.33	2.9
English official language[c]	0.83	2.7
US + (Korea, Thailand, Taiwan)[c]	1.94	2.9
Two commonwealth nations or Hong Kong[c,d]	1.70	4.5

$R^2 = 0.684$, N = 165.
[a]i = 1, ... , 6 (six DAEs).
[b]j = 1, ... , 31 (six DAEs and 25 major OECD and developing countries).
[c]Dummy variable.
[d]Pair-wise combinations of Australia, Canada, New Zealand, Hong Kong, India, Malaysia, Singapore, UK.

additionally, vary between countries (e.g., beer is a more important good in Belgium than in Malaysia). I therefore estimate two gravity models using, respectively, the market exchange rate (Table 19.5), and the purchasing-power parity rate (Table 19.6). Both models test the existence of four types of affinity effects: language, historical relationship, religion, and membership of a supranational institution.

Table 19.6 PPP dollar GDP model. Dependent variable: ln(x) of co-authored articles involving country i^a and j^b, 1990–94

Variable	*Coefficient (b)*	*t-value*
Constant	–19.92	
ln of time distance	–0.45	–3.8
ln (GDP_i) * ln (GDP_j)	0.84	12.4
ln (*per capita* GDP_i) * ln (*per capita* GDP_j)	0.84	8.4
Ethnic Chinese majority[c]	1.12	2.5
English official language[c]	1.00	3.3
US + (Korea, Thailand, Taiwan)[c]	1.64	2.5
Two commonwealth nations including Hong Kong[c,d]	1.37	3.7

$R^2 = 0.695$, N = 165
[a]i = 1, ... , 6 (Six DAEs).
[b]j = 1, ... , 31 (Six DAEs and 25 major OECD and developing countries)
[c]Dummy variable.
[d]Pair-wise combinations of Australia, Canada, New Zealand, Hong Kong, India, Malaysia, Singapore, UK.

The empirical models estimate the effects of the independent variables by means of pair-wise combinations of the six Asian countries, as well as pair-wise combinations between each of the six Asian countries and 25 countries in the rest of the world. The time distance proves to be one important explanation for the number of co-authored articles. According to both estimated models we may expect a one per cent increase in the distance to lead to slightly less than a half per cent decrease in the number of co-authored articles.

The economic effects also take the expected signs. While it is relatively unimportant if the size of an economy is measured using market exchange rates or purchasing-power parity rates, the estimated effects of economic development deviate substantially from each other. The estimated effect using MERs amounts to a 0.07 per cent increase in co-authorships for every one per cent increase in the product of MER *per capita* income. The corresponding effect using the PPP measure is 0.84 per cent.

The greater magnitude of the PPP-measured effect does not necessarily imply that it is a better measure of general economic development. However, it is a more significant determinant of interaction frequencies. But with the additional assumption that international scientific cooperation is an indicator of general economic development, the PPP measure of *per capita* income also becomes a more accurate measure of development. (In other economic contexts, the PPP rate is the most common measure of living standards, while the MER is used for measuring labor costs.)

Several analyses of Asia-Pacific trade have shown that the linkages between these countries and the rest of the world are stronger than the linkages within the region (see Chapter 14). Consequently, East Asia is a much less integrated region than Western Europe or North America. This analysis reinforces that conclusion. Membership of regional organizations such as ASEAN or APEC is not in any way associated with scientific interactions. Perhaps even more interestingly, there is neither a Confucian nor a Muslim community of scientists. Fukuyama (1995) has argued that Chinese Confucianism and Japanese Confucianism are more different from each other than either is from Judeo–Christian Western traditions. He describes Chinese Confucianism as emphasizing filial relationships at the expense of perceived duties within the larger community. Japanese Confucianism, on the other hand, gives priority to obligations within large-scale hierarchies. (It is also noteworthy that Hong Kong and Taiwan have modeled their universities on Western institutions, with an emphasis on producing published articles, whereas Japanese universities place a greater emphasis on hierarchical duties and seniority-based chains of command.) If this argument is true, it should come as no surprise that a historical institutional association with Japan (in South Korea and Taiwan) has no reinforcing effect on current interactions. A special historical relationship with the United States,[2] on the other hand, is the strongest estimated cultural affinity factor for the region, closely followed by a British colonial legacy. The use of English as an official language also has a reinforcing effect. The British effect is especially remarkable, since it seems to be the most important factor leading to more interactions within the region (between Hong Kong, Malaysia, and Singapore).

The conclusion of the analysis is that East Asia is not an integrated region regarding scientific cooperation. Some of the countries in the region are, however, important nodes in the global scientific network. A cultural link between ethnic Chinese is the only cultural affinity factor that seems to exist within the region. But although there are some integrating tendencies between ethnic Chinese scientists in the region, Taiwanese scientists are culturally in closer proximity to the United States than to China or Hong Kong. Scientists in Hong Kong and Singapore, meanwhile, primarily interact with English-speaking countries generally and, in particular, with Commonwealth countries.

Notes

1. The information was retrieved by Olle Persson, Inforsk, University of Umeå.
2. I define a country with a special historical relationship with the United States as a current or earlier host nation for US military bases.

References

Andersson, Å.E. and O. Persson, 'Networking Scientists', *Annals of Regional Science*, 27 (1993) 11–21.

Fukuyama, F., *Trust: The Social Virtues and the Creation of Prosperity* (New York: Free Press, 1995).

Narin, F. and E.S. Whitlow, 'Measurement of Scientific Cooperation and Coauthorship in CEC-related Areas of Science', *Commission of the European Communities Vol. 1 (EUR 12900 EN)* (Brussels, 1990).

Wichmann-Matthiessen, C. and Å.E. Andersson, *Øresundsregionen: Kreativitet, Integration, Voekst* (Copenhagen: Munksgaard, 1993).

Index